Conference of the North American Chapter of the Association for Computational Linguistics: Human Language Technologies (NAACL HLT 2018)

Demonstrations

New Orleans, Louisiana, USA
1 – 6 June 2018

ISBN: 978-1-5108-6350-7

NAACL HLT 2018

**The 2018 Conference of the
North American Chapter of the
Association for Computational Linguistics:
Human Language Technologies**

Proceedings of the Demonstrations Session

June 2-June 4, 2018
New Orleans, Louisiana

Introduction

Welcome to the Demonstrations Session of NAACL HLT 2018 in New Orleans, Louisiana, USA.

The demonstrations session is an opportunity for researchers and developers to present their systems and programs related to natural language processing. We received 39 outstanding papers, of which we accepted 20.
These systems will be displayed during the conference.

Organizers:

Yang Liu, Liulishuo Silicon Valley AI Lab (USA)
Tim Paek, Apple (USA)
Manasi Patwardhan, Tata Consultancy Services Research (India)

Program Committee:

Anuj Kumar, Facebook (USA)
Arzucan Özgür, Bogazici University (Turkey)
Ashish Garg, Apple Inc (USA)
Bin Liu, carnegie Mellon University (USA)
Boyang Li, Liulishuo Silicon Valley AI Lab (USA)
Brigitte Krenn, Austrian Research Institute for Artificial Intelligence (OFAI)
Catherine Havasi, Luminoso
Changsong Liu, Michigan State University (USA)
Chen chen, Google Inc. (USA)
Chen Li, Microsoft (USA)
Duc Le, Facebook (USA)
Francisco Guzmán, Facebook (USA)
Girish Palshikar, Tata Consultancy Services Research (India)
Guodong Zhou, Soochow University (China)
Huy Nguyen, University of Pittsburgh (USA)
Indrajit Bhattacharya, Tata Consultancy Services Research (India)
Irene Russo, Italian National Research Council (Italy)
Ivan Vladimir Meza Ruiz,Insituto de Investigaciones en Matemáticas Aplicadas y en Sistemas
(IIMAS-UNAM) (Mexico)
Junyi Jessy Li, University of Texas at Austin (USA)
Keith Carlson, Dartmouth College (USA)
Kirk Roberts, University of Texas Health Science Center at Houston (USA) Le Sun, Chinese
Academy of Sciences (China)
Liang-Chih Yu, Yuan Ze University (Taiwan)
Lipika Dey, Tata Consultancy Services Research (India)
Maarten van Gompel, Radboud University Nijmegen (Netherlands)
Marc Vilain, MITRE Cooperation (USA)
Margaret Mitchell, Google Research and Machine Intelligence (USA)
Marie-Jean Meurs, University of Quebec in Montreal (Canada)
Mark Finlayson, Florida International University (USA)
Masoud Rouhizadeh, Johns Hopkins University (USA)
Minwoo Jeong, Apple (USA)
Montse Cuadros Oller, Vicomtech-IK4 (spain)
Ni Lao, SayMosaic (USA)
Omar Alonso, Microsoft Research (USA)
Patrick Nguyen, Google (USA)
Petya Osenova, Sofia University and IICT-BAS (Bulgaria)
Robby Walker, Apple (USA)
Sebastian Sulger, University of Konstanz (Gernamy)
Sravana Reddy, Spotify (USA)

Stelios Piperidis, Athena RC/ILSP (Greece)
Stephanie Lukin, US Army Research Laboratory (USA)
Sunil Kumar Kopparapu, Tata Consultancy Services Research (India)
Thierry Declerck, DFKI GmbH (Germany)
Tsuyoshi Okita, Kyushuu Institute of Technology University (Japan)
Xian Li, Facebook (USA)
Xian Qian, Facebook (USA)
Yi Sun, Liulishuo (USA)
Željko Agić, IT University of Copenhagen (Denmark)
Zhuoran Yu, Google (USA)

Table of Contents

vii

Conference Program

Saturday June 2, 2018

10:30–12:00   **Posters and Demos**

NLP Lean Programming Framework: Developing NLP Applications More Effectively
Marc Schreiber, Bodo Kraft and Albert Zündorf

Pay-Per-Request Deployment of Neural Network Models Using Serverless Architectures
Zhucheng Tu, Mengping Li and Jimmy Lin

An automated medical scribe for documenting clinical encounters
Gregory Finley, Erik Edwards, Amanda Robinson, Michael Brenndoerfer, Najmeh Sadoughi, James Fone, Nico Axtmann, Mark Miller and David Suendermann-Oeft

CL Scholar: The ACL Anthology Knowledge Graph Miner
Mayank Singh, Pradeep Dogga, Sohan Patro, Dhiraj Barnwal, Ritam Dutt, Rajarshi Haldar, Pawan Goyal and Animesh Mukherjee

Saturday June 2, 2018

15:30–17:00   **Posters and Demos**

ArgumenText: Searching for Arguments in Heterogeneous Sources
Christian Stab, Johannes Daxenberger, Chris Stahlhut, Tristan Miller, Benjamin Schiller, Christopher Tauchmann, Steffen Eger and Iryna Gurevych

ClaimRank: Detecting Check-Worthy Claims in Arabic and English
Israa Jaradat, Pepa Gencheva, Alberto Barrón-Cedeño, Lluís Màrquez and Preslav Nakov

360° Stance Detection
Sebastian Ruder, John Glover, Afshin Mehrabani and Parsa Ghaffari

DebugSL: An Interactive Tool for Debugging Sentiment Lexicons
Andrew Schneider, John Male, Saroja Bhogadhi and Eduard Dragut

Sunday June 3, 2018

10:30–12:00   **Posters and Demos**

ELISA-EDL: A Cross-lingual Entity Extraction, Linking and Localization System
Boliang Zhang, Ying Lin, Xiaoman Pan, Di Lu, Jonathan May, Kevin Knight and
Heng Ji

Entity Resolution and Location Disambiguation in the Ancient Hindu Temples Domain using Web Data
Ayush Maheshwari, vishwajeet kumar, Ganesh Ramakrishnan and J. Saketha Nath

Madly Ambiguous: A Game for Learning about Structural Ambiguity and Why It's Hard for Computers
Ajda Gokcen, Ethan Hill and Michael White

VnCoreNLP: A Vietnamese Natural Language Processing Toolkit
Thanh Vu, Dat Quoc Nguyen, Dai Quoc Nguyen, Mark Dras and Mark Johnson

Sunday June 3, 2018

15:30–17:00   **Posters and Demos**

CNNs for NLP in the Browser: Client-Side Deployment and Visualization Opportunities
Yiyun Liang, Zhucheng Tu, Laetitia Huang and Jimmy Lin

Generating Continuous Representations of Medical Texts
graham spinks and Marie-Francine Moens

Vis-Eval Metric Viewer: A Visualisation Tool for Inspecting and Evaluating Metric Scores of Machine Translation Output
David Steele and Lucia Specia

Monday June 4, 2018

10:30–12:00   Posters and Demos

Know Who Your Friends Are: Understanding Social Connections from Unstructured Text
Lea Deleris, Francesca Bonin, Elizabeth Daly, Stephane Deparis, Yufang Hou, Charles Jochim, Yassine Lassoued and Killian Levacher

RiskFinder: A Sentence-level Risk Detector for Financial Reports
Yu-Wen Liu, Liang-Chih Liu, Chuan-Ju Wang and Ming-Feng Tsai

Monday June 4, 2018

14:00–15:30   Posters and Demos

SMILEE: Symmetric Multi-modal Interactions with Language-gesture Enabled (AI) Embodiment
Sujeong Kim, David Salter, Luke DeLuccia, Kilho Son, Mohamed R. Amer and Amir Tamrakar

Decision Conversations Decoded
Lea Deleris, Debasis Ganguly, killian Levacher, Martin Stephenson and Francesca Bonin

Sounding Board: A User-Centric and Content-Driven Social Chatbot
Hao Fang, Hao Cheng, Maarten Sap, Elizabeth Clark, Ari Holtzman, Yejin Choi, Noah A. Smith and Mari Ostendorf

NLP Lean Programming Framework: Developing NLP Applications More Effectively

Marc Schreiber
FH Aachen
Jülich, Germany
marc.schreiber@fh-aachen.de

Bodo Kraft
FH Aachen
Jülich, Germany
kraft@fh-aachen.de

Albert Zündorf
University of Kassel
Kassel, Germany
zuendorf@uni-kassel.de

Abstract

This paper presents NLP Lean Programming framework (NLPf), a new framework for creating custom natural language processing (NLP) models and pipelines by utilizing common software development build systems. This approach allows developers to train and integrate domain-specific NLP pipelines into their applications seamlessly. Additionally, NLPf provides an annotation tool which improves the annotation process significantly by providing a well-designed GUI and sophisticated way of using input devices. Due to NLPf's properties developers and domain experts are able to build domain-specific NLP applications more efficiently. NLPf is Opensource software and available at https://gitlab.com/schrieveslaach/NLPf.

1 Introduction

Nowadays more and more business models rely on the processing of natural language data, e. g. companies extract relevant eCommerce data from domain-specific documents. The required eCommerce data could be related to various domains, e. g. life-science, public utilities, or social media, depending on the companies' business models.

Furthermore, the World Wide Web (WWW) provides a huge amount of natural language data that provides a wide variety of knowledge to human readers. This amount of knowledge is unmanageable for humans and applications try to make this knowledge more accessible to humans, e. g. Treude and Robillard (2016) make natural language text about software programming more accessible through a natural language processing (NLP) application.

All these approaches have in common that they require domain-specific NLP models that have been trained on a domain-specific and annotated corpus. These models will be trained by using dif-ferent NLP frameworks and these models have to be evaluated for every annotation layer. For example, named entity recognition (NER) of Stanford CoreNLP (Manning et al., 2014) might work better than NER of OpenNLP (Reese, 2015, Chapter 1); the chosen segmentation tool, e. g. UD-Pipe (Straka and Straková, 2017), might work better than Stanford CoreNLP's segmentation tool, and so on. Existing studies show that domain specific training and evaluation is a common approach in the NLP community to determine the best-performing NLP pipeline (Buyko et al., 2006; Giesbrecht and Evert, 2009; Neunerdt et al., 2013; Omran and Treude, 2017).

Developers of NLP applications are forced to create domain-specific corpora to determine the best-performing NLP pipeline among many NLP frameworks. During this process they face various obstacles:

- The training and evaluation of different NLP frameworks requires a lot of effort of scripting or programming because of incompatible APIs.

- Domain experts who annotate domain-specific documents with a GUI tool struggle with an insufficient user experience.

- There are too many combinations how developers can combine these NLP tools into NLP pipelines.

- The generated NLP models as a build artifact have to be integrated manually into the application code.

NLP Lean Programming framework (NLPf) addresses these issues. NLPf provides a standardized project structure for domain-specific corpora (see Section 2), an improved user experience for annotators (see Section 3), a common build process to train and evaluate NLP models in conjunc-

Proceedings of NAACL-HLT 2018: Demonstrations, pages 1–5
New Orleans, Louisiana, June 2 - 4, 2018. ©2018 Association for Computational Linguistics

tion with the determination of the best-performing NLP pipeline (see Section 4), and a convenient API to integrate the best-performing NLP pipeline into the application code (see Section 5).

2 Annotated Corpus Project Structure

Maven as a build management tool has standardized the development process of Java applications by standardizing the build life-cycle, standardizing the project layout, and standardizing the dependency management. These standardization are evolved by utilizing convention over configuration (CoC) as much as possible and developers have to make less decisions while developing software.

Such conventions are missing for the development of domain-specific NLP applications and developers have to make many decisions and have to write many scripts to build their applications. NLPf provides conventions by utilizing Maven and its project object model (POM). Listing 1 shows the basic project configuration to train and evaluate domain-specific NLP models with NLPf.

```
<project>
  <modelVersion>4.0.0</modelVersion>

  <groupId>your.company</groupId>
  <artifactId>domain-specific-corpus</artifactId>
  <version>1.0-SNAPSHOT</version>
  <packaging>nlp-models</packaging>

  <build>
    <plugins>
      <plugin>
        <groupId>de.schrieveslaach.nlpf</groupId>
        <artifactId>nlp-maven-plugin</artifactId>
        <version>1.0.0</version>
        <extensions>true</extensions>
      </plugin>
    </plugins>
  </build>
</project>
```

Listing 1: POM of Annotated Corpus

Unlike standard Java projects this project uses the custom packaging method `nlp-models` which configures Maven to use NLPf's plugin (see `nlp-maven-plugin`) which trains and evaluates the domain-specific models. By convention, each document stored in `src/main/corpus` will be used as an input document for the training process and each document stored in `src/test/corpus` will used to evaluate the derived NLP models.

NLPf supports multiple document formats which need to be configured as Maven dependency (see `io-odt` in Listing 2). Most formats supported by DKPro Core[1] (de Castilho and Gurevych, 2014) are supported by NLPf but we recommend to use ODT documents because developers can just paste natural language text into the ODT documents and then annotate them without preparing specific document formats.

```
<dependency>
  <groupId>de.schrieveslaach.nlpf</groupId>
  <artifactId>io-odt</artifactId>
  <version>1.0.0</version>
</dependency>

<dependency>
  <groupId>de.tudarmstadt.ukp.dkpro.core</groupId>
  <artifactId>
    de.tudarmstadt.ukp.dkpro.core.opennlp-asl
  </artifactId>
  <version>1.9.0</version>
</dependency>
```

Listing 2: Dependencies of Annotated Corpus

Additionally, NLPf supports different NLP frameworks which are also provided as Maven dependency (see `de.tudarmstadt.ukp.dkpro.core.opennlp-asl` in Listing 2). NLPf supports all NLP frameworks which provide trainer capabilities of DKPro Core[2]: Stanford CoreNLP, OpenNLP, and LingPipe. When the project has been configured, the annotators can start to annotate the documents.

3 Quick Pad Tagger: Annotate Documents

NLPf provides the annotation tool Quick Pad Tagger (QPT) which provides a well-designed GUI, drawing the attention to the essential GUI elements of the annotation task. Figure 1 provides a screenshot of the QPT, showing how the user annotates named entities (NEs) in a document. At the bottom of the GUI the part of the document will be displayed and at the top of the screen the QPT shows a stream of tokens while the user can select multiple tokens (see blue boxes) to assign a NE type. Through the spinner on top of the stream of tokens the user chooses a type for each of the NEs.

This design has been implemented consequently for each annotation layer and the design draws the attention to the actual important annotation task, e.g. assign NE types or part-of-speech (POS) tags to tokens. Figure 2 compares for the POS tag annotation layers of the state-of-the-art tool Webanno (Eckart de Castilho et al., 2016) and the QPT, showing that the QPT draws the attention

---

[1] https://dkpro.github.io/dkpro-core/

[2] More information is provided here: https://github.com/dkpro/dkpro-core/pull/1114

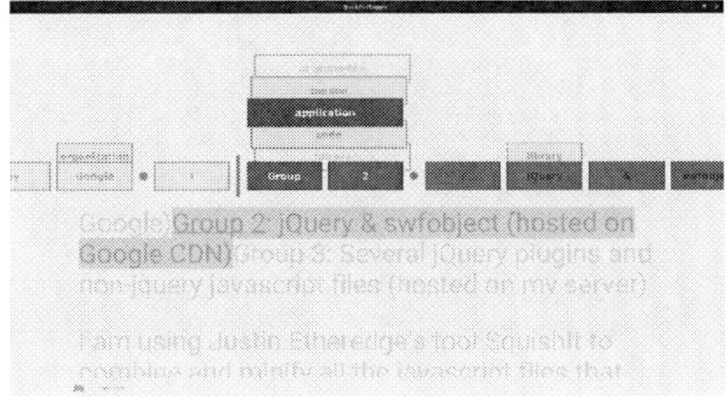

Figure 1: QPT Screenshot: NE Tagging

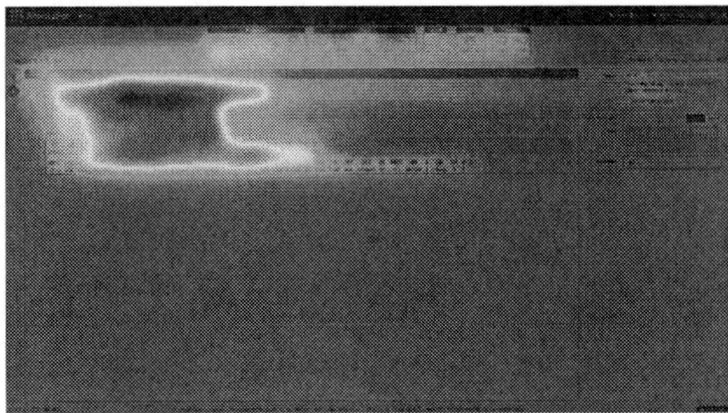

(a) Webanno Screenshot

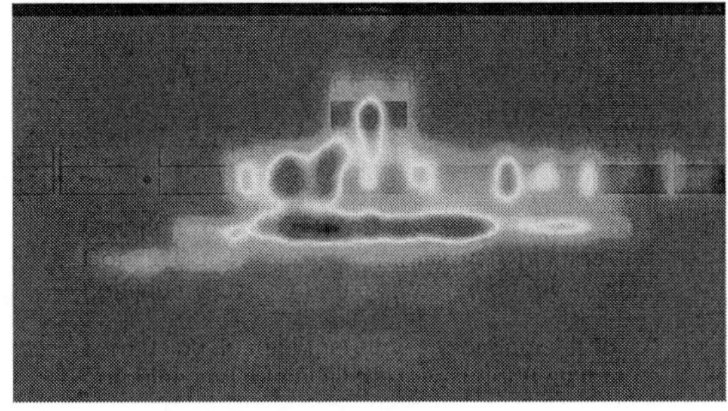

(b) QPT Screenshot

Figure 2: Attention Map of POS Tagging Annotation Tools, Obtained Using the EyeQuant Attention Analytics Software (www.eyequant.com)

to the annotation task and the document text (the relevant parts) whereas Webanno draws the attention to all annotations at once.

The user can use a Xbox 360 controller to annotate the structure of natural language. This type of input device provides a more comfortable and playful user experience and in conjunction with the GUI design the annotation process is less painful and less exhausting. Additionally, the QPT provides a semi-automatic annotation process (Schreiber et al., 2015) which speeds up the annotation process further. In summary, the QPT reduces the required annotation time by half.

4 Install Best-performing NLP Pipeline Artifact

When documents of the corpus project have been annotated by annotators, developers can use a single command to train all available NLP tools, determine the best-performing NLP pipeline, and create an artifact which will be used in an NLP application (see Section 5). These steps will be performed by `mvn install` and the custom Maven plugin (see `nlp-maven-plugin` in Listing 1) passes following customized life-cycle:

- At first, the Maven plugin validates the annotated documents, for example, it ensures that every or no token of a document have been annotated with a corresponding POS tag.

- After that, the Maven plugin looks up all available NLP trainer classes which are available on the classpath (c. f. `de.tudarmstadt.ukp.dkpro.core.opennlp-asl` in Listing 2). Each discovered trainer class will be used to create a domain-specific NLP model if the required annotations are available and the configuration will be stored in the `target` directory. The configurations are stored in a format compatible to the Unstructured Information Management Architecture (UIMA) framework (Ferrucci and Lally, 2004).

- If NLP tools do not provide any training, e. g. the segmentation tool of Stanford CoreNLP, developers can provide engine factories which create configurations for these tools (see Listing 3) which will be stored in the `target` directory.

- All available configurations will be used to create all possible domain-specific NLP pipeline configurations and each NLP pipeline will be evaluated with F_1 score by running the pipelines on the test documents and by comparing the results on the provided test annotations. The configuration of the best-performing NLP pipeline will be stored into the target directory.

- Based on the previous steps the Maven plugin creates a Java archive (JAR) which contains the NLP models and configuration of the best-performing NLP pipeline.

- Finally, the created JAR artifact can be installed or deployed into any Maven repository.

```java
public class StanfordCoreNlpEngineFactory {

  public AnalysisEngineDescription
    ↪ createStanfordSegmenter() throws Exception {
    return createEngineDescription(
        StanfordSegmenter.class,
        StanfordSegmenter.PARAM_LANGUAGE_FALLBACK,
        ↪ "en");
  }
}
```

Listing 3: Engine Factory for NLP Tools Without Training Support

5 API Running the Best-performing NLP Pipeline

When the best-performing NLP pipeline is available as JAR artifact in a Maven repository, developers can integrate this artifact as Maven dependency into the NLP application. Therefore, developers insert the project coordinates of the domain specific corpus into the application's POM, illustrated by Listing 4. Additionally, developers need to add the `plumbing` library which provides an API to execute the best-performing NLP pipeline.

```xml
<dependency>
  <groupId>your.company</groupId>
  <artifactId>domain-specific-corpus</artifactId>
  <version>1.0-SNAPSHOT</version>
</dependency>

<dependency>
  <groupId>de.schrieveslaach.nlpf</groupId>
  <artifactId>plumbing</artifactId>
  <version>1.0.0</version>
</dependency>
```

Listing 4: Dependencies of NLP Application

The provided API integrates seamlessly into the API of the UIMA framework which provides an interface to run NLP components on unstructured data such as natural language text, c. f. method `runPipeline` in Listing 5. However, the best-performing NLP has to be configured manually. NLPf's `plumbing` JAR artifact provides the method `createBestPerformingPipelineEngineDescription()` which reads the configuration of the JAR that contains the configuration and models of the best-performing NLP pipeline.

```java
CollectionReaderDescription readerDescription =
  ↪ createReaderDescription(
    OdtReader.class,
    OdtReader.PARAM_SOURCE_LOCATION, new
    ↪ File("plain.odt"));
```

```java
AnalysisEngineDescription writerDescription =
  ↪ createEngineDescription(
    OdtWriter.class,
    OdtWriter.PARAM_TARGET_LOCATION, new File("."),
    OdtWriter.PARAM_OVERWRITE, true);

runPipeline(readerDescription,
    createBestPerformingPipelineEngineDescription(),
    // integrate custom engine descriptions here
    writerDescription);
```

Listing 5: Example Application Java Code

The example code provided in Listing 5 performs following steps, executed by `runPipeline`:

- It reads an ODT file with the name `plain.odt`, c. f. `readerDescription`.

- Then, it runs the best-performing NLP pipeline which annotates the whole document with the natural language structure.

- Finally, it stores the annotations into an ODT file into the current directory, c. f. `writerDescription`.

Developers can integrate custom analyses as they require them (see `// integrate custom...` in Listing 5). Therefore, they need to implement UIMA annotators which use the typesystem of DKPro Core. The conjunction of UIMA, DKPro Core, and NLPf allows developers to implement NLP applications effectively.

6 Summary

This paper provides a demonstration of NLP Lean Programming framework (NLPf) which enables developers to create domain-specific NLP pipelines more effectively, making less decisions through CoC. NLPf provides a standardized environment and the well-designed annotation tool Quick Pad Tagger (QPT) with an improved input mechanism to improve the annotation process. Additionally, the best-performing NLP pipeline will be determine through the convenient build tool Maven and the resulting artifact can be integrated as Maven dependency into any application conveniently.

NLPf is Open-source software, released under the LGPL version 3, and available at https://gitlab.com/schrieveslaach/NLPf. All artifacts are available on Maven central and they can also be used with Jython in Python programs.

References

Ekaterina Buyko, Joachim Wermter, Michael Poprat, and Udo Hahn. 2006. Automatically adapting an nlp core engine to the biology domain. In *Proceedings of the Joint BioLINK-Bio-Ontologies Meeting. A Joint Meeting of the ISMB Special Interest Group on Bio-Ontologies and the BioLINK Special Interest Group on Text Data M ining in Association with ISMB.* pages 65–68.

Richard Eckart de Castilho and Iryna Gurevych. 2014. A broad-coverage collection of portable NLP components for building shareable analysis pipelines. In Nancy Ide and Jens Grivolla, editors, *Proceedings of the Workshop on Open Infrastructures and Analysis Frameworks for HLT at COLING 2014.* Association for Computational Linguistics and Dublin City University, Dublin, Ireland, pages 1–11.

Richard Eckart de Castilho, Éva Mújdricza-Maydt, Seid Muhie Yimam, Silvana Hartmann, Iryna Gurevych, Anette Frank, and Chris Biemann. 2016. A web-based tool for the integrated annotation of semantic and syntactic structures. In *Proceedings of the workshop on Language Technology Resources and Tools for Digital Humanities (LT4DH) at COLING 2016.* pages 76–84.

David Ferrucci and Adam Lally. 2004. Uima: An architectural approach to unstructured information processing in the corporate research environment. *Natural Language Engineering* 10(3–4):327–348. https://doi.org/10.1017/S1351324904003523.

Eugenie Giesbrecht and Stefan Evert. 2009. Is part-of-speech tagging a solved task? an evaluation of pos taggers for the german web as corpus. In *Proceedings of the 5th Web as Corpus Workshop.* WAC5, pages 27–35.

Christopher D. Manning, Mihai Surdeanu, John Bauer, Jenny Finkel, Steven J. Bethard, and David McClosky. 2014. The Stanford CoreNLP natural language processing toolkit. In *Association for Computational Linguistics (ACL) System Demonstrations.* pages 55–60.

Melanie Neunerdt, Bianka Trevisan, Michael Reyer, and Rudolf Mathar. 2013. Part-of-speech tagging for social media texts. pages 139–150. https://doi.org/10.1007/978-3-642-40722-2_15.

Fouad Nasser A Al Omran and Christoph Treude. 2017. Choosing an nlp library for analyzing software documentation: A systematic literature review and a series of experiments. In *Proceedings of the 14th International Conference on Mining Software Repositories.* IEEE Press, Piscataway, NJ, USA, MSR '17, pages 187–197. https://doi.org/10.1109/MSR.2017.42.

Richard M. Reese. 2015. *Natural Language Processing with Java.* Packt Publishing Ltd.

Marc Schreiber, Kai Barkschat, Bodo Kraft, and Albert Zündorf. 2015. Quick Pad Tagger: An Efficient Graphical User Interface for Building Annotated Corpora with Multiple Annotation Layers. *Computer Science & Information Technology* 4:131–143. https://doi.org/10.5121/csit.2015.50413.

Milan Straka and Jana Straková. 2017. Tokenizing, pos tagging, lemmatizing and parsing ud 2.0 with udpipe. Association for Computational Linguistics, Vancouver, Canada, pages 88–99.

Christoph Treude and Martin P. Robillard. 2016. Augmenting api documentation with insights from stack overflow. In *Proceedings of the 38th International Conference on Software Engineering.* ACM, New York, NY, USA, pages 392–403. https://doi.org/10.1145/2884781.2884800.

Pay-Per-Request Deployment of Neural Network Models Using Serverless Architectures

Zhucheng Tu, Mengping Li, and Jimmy Lin
David R. Cheriton School of Computer Science
University of Waterloo
{michael.tu, m282li, jimmylin}@uwaterloo.ca

Abstract

We demonstrate the serverless deployment of neural networks for model inferencing in NLP applications using Amazon's Lambda service for feedforward evaluation and DynamoDB for storing word embeddings. Our architecture realizes a pay-per-request pricing model, requiring zero ongoing costs for maintaining server instances. All virtual machine management is handled behind the scenes by the cloud provider without any direct developer intervention. We describe a number of techniques that allow efficient use of serverless resources, and evaluations confirm that our design is both scalable and inexpensive.

1 Introduction

Client–server architectures are currently the dominant approach to deploying neural network models for inferencing, both in industry and for academic research. Once a model has been trained, deployment generally involves "wrapping" the model in an RPC mechanism (such as Thrift) or a REST interface (e.g., Flask in Python), or alternatively using a dedicated framework such as TensorFlow-Serving (Olston et al., 2017). This approach necessitates provisioning machines (whether physical or virtual) to serve the model.

Load management is an important aspect of running an inference service. As query load increases, new server instances must be brought online, typically behind a load-balancing frontend. While these issues are generally well understood and industry has evolved best practices and standard toolsets, the developer still shoulders the burden of managing these tasks. A server-based architecture, moreover, involves a minimum commitment of resources, since *some* server must be running all the time, even if it is the smallest and cheapest virtual instance provided by a cloud service. Particularly relevant for academic researchers, this means that a service costs money to run even if no one is actually using it.

As an alternative, we demonstrate a pay-per-request serverless architecture for deploying neural network models for NLP applications. We applied our approach to two real-world CNNs: the model of Kim (2014) for sentence classification and the CNN of Severyn and Moschitti (2015) for answer selection in question answering (SM CNN for short). On Amazon Web Services, the models cost less than a thousandth of a cent per invocation. Model inference does not require the developer to explicitly manage machines, and there are zero ongoing costs for service deployment. We show that our design can transparently scale to moderate query loads without requiring any systems engineering expertise.

2 Serverless Architectures

A serverless architecture does not literally mean that we can magically perform model inference without requiring servers; the computation must happen somewhere! A serverless design simply means that the developer does not need to explicitly manage servers—the cloud provider shoulders this burden behind the scenes.

Serverless architectures make use of what is known as function as a service (FaaS), where developers specify blocks of code with well-defined entry and exit points and the cloud provider handles the invocation. Typically, function invocation involves spinning up virtual machine instances and bootstrapping the execution environment, but all of these tasks are handled by the cloud provider. The developer pays per function invocation no matter the query load; scalability and elasticity are the responsibility of the cloud provider. In most cases, these invoked functions are stateless, with state usually offloaded to another cloud ser-

Proceedings of NAACL-HLT 2018: Demonstrations, pages 6–10
New Orleans, Louisiana, June 2 - 4, 2018. ©2018 Association for Computational Linguistics

vice. The standard design pattern begins with the invoked function reading from a persistent store and writing results back to the same or a different store. The serverless paradigm meshes well with microservice architectures that are in fashion today, and multiple cloud providers (Amazon, Google, Microsoft) have FaaS offerings.

Recently, Crane and Lin (2017) proposed a novel search engine built using a serverless architecture on Amazon Web Services whereby postings lists are stored in DynamoDB and query execution is encapsulated in Lambda functions. We explore how similar techniques can be applied to neural network models for NLP applications. We are aware of a recent blog post describing the deployment of NN models using Lambda (Dietz, 2017). However, that work focuses on vision applications; the additional technical challenge we overcome is the need to access word embeddings for NLP applications, which requires more than just Lambda deployment.

3 Serverless Neural Network Inference

In this work, we selected Amazon Web Services (AWS) as our deployment platform due to its market-dominant position, although other cloud providers have similar offerings.

To enable serverless neural network inference for NLP, the trained models are packaged together with the function to be invoked and dependent software libraries. The cloud provider is responsible for creating the environment for execution. During inference, the Lambda function takes input text, which is supplied externally via an API gateway. Sentences need to be first transformed into an embedding matrix constructed using word vectors, in our case from word2vec (Mikolov et al., 2013). These are fetched from DynamoDB. Finally, the Lambda function applies feedforward evaluation on the embedding matrix according to the supplied model, yielding a final prediction. Figure 1 illustrates this architecture, described in detail below.

3.1 Lambda Deployment Package

A complete Lambda deployment package comprises the code of the function as well as its dependencies. In this work, we use PyTorch v0.3.1 for inference. Thus, our deployment package requires PyTorch as well as its dependencies, the model definition, the model weights, and a handler that specifies how the function should be ex-

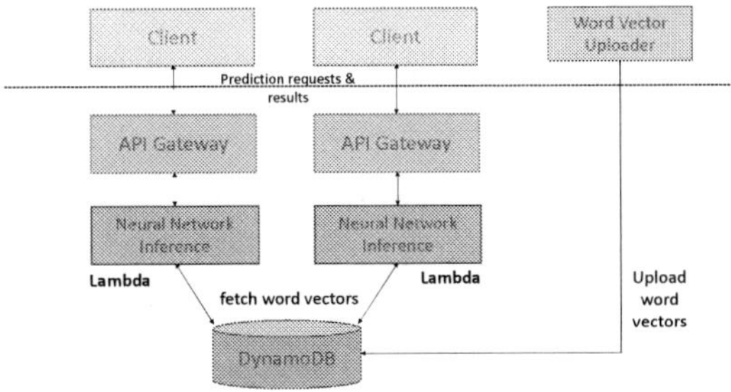

Figure 1: Serverless architecture for deploying NNs.

ecuted. Note that although an emerging deployment pattern is to use PyTorch for training models and Caffe2 for running inference in a production environment through the use of ONNX,[1] support for this approach remains immature and thus we rely on PyTorch for inference as well.

There is a 250 MB limit on the size of the Lambda deployment package. To stay within this limit, we had to build PyTorch from source on an AWS EC2 machine to exclude CUDA and other unnecessary dependencies. The machines that execute Lambda functions do not have GPU capabilities, so this does not incur any performance penalties. The deployment package is compressed and uploaded to S3, Amazon's object storage service. In the Lambda execution model, an Execution Context is initialized upon invocation of the Lambda function, which is a runtime environment that bootstraps the dependencies in the deployment package. The Execution Context may be costly to set up (as in our case) and therefore the Lambda API provides hooks that facilitate reuse for subsequent invocations.

3.2 DynamoDB Storage of Word Vectors

Most neural networks for NLP use pre-trained word vectors to build an input representation as the first step in inference. In a serverless architecture, these word vectors need to be stored somewhere. Due to the size restrictions described above, the word vectors cannot be stored in the deployment package itself.

To overcome this issue, we adopt the solution of storing the word embedding vectors in DynamoDB, much like how Crane and Lin (2017) store postings lists. DynamoDB (DeCandia et al., 2007) is a hosted "NoSQL" database service that offers low latency access to arbitrary amounts of data, as Amazon scales up and down capacity au-

---

[1]https://onnx.ai/

tomatically. We use DynamoDB as a key–value store for holding the word vectors, where each word is the key and its word vector is the value stored as a List type. Kim CNN uses 300 dimensional word vectors from word2vec trained on the Google News corpus and SM CNN uses 50 dimensional word vectors from word2vec trained on English Wikipedia. Thus, we created separate DynamoDB tables for these 50 and 300 dimensional word vectors. For expediency in running experiments, we only load the word vectors for words in the vocabulary of the datasets we use.

3.3 Neural Network Inference

Our API for invoking the NN models comprises a JSON request sent to the AWS API Gateway via HTTP, which is a proxy that then forwards the request to Lambda. A request for feedforward inference using Kim CNN consists of a single sentence in the request body, whereas for SM CNN, the request body holds a pair of sentences.

Upon receiving a request, the Lambda handler first tokenizes and downcases the input. It then issues `BatchGetItem` requests to DynamoDB to fetch the word vectors for unique words in the input. These queries retrieve the word vectors in parallel to reduce latency. The function then blocks until all word vectors are retrieved, after which they are concatenated together to construct a sentence embedding matrix.

In our implementation, the model is initialized outside of the Lambda handler function scope so that if an existing Event Context is available, a previously-loaded model can be reused. If the model has not been initialized, it will be loaded from the deployment package. Note that context reuse is completely opaque: unbeknownst to us, AWS performs caching to support efficient invocations as query load ramps up, but we have no explicit control over the exact mechanisms for eviction, warmup, etc. The sentence embeddings are fed into the model for feedforward evaluation (handled by PyTorch) and the result is returned as JSON from the handler.

4   Experiments

We first provide some implementation details: Kim CNN is a sentence classification model that consists of convolutions over a single sentence input matrix and pooling followed by a fully-connected layer with dropout and softmax out-

put. We used the variant where the word embeddings are not fine-tuned via backpropagation during training (called the "static" variant). SM CNN is a model for ranking short text pairs that consists of convolutions using shared filters over both inputs, pooling, and a fully-connected layer with one hidden layer in between. We used the variant described by Rao et al. (2017), which excludes the similarity matrix (found to increase accuracy) as well as the additional features that involve inverse document frequency. In our experiments, we are focused only on execution performance, which is not affected by these minor tweaks, primarily for expediency. All of our code and experiment utilities are open-sourced on GitHub.[2]

Before detailing our experimental procedure and results, we need to explain Amazon's cost model. Lambda costs are very straightforward, billed simply by how long each function executes in increments of 100ms, for a particular amount of allocated memory that the developer specifies. DynamoDB's cost model is more complex: it supports two modes of operation, termed manual provisioning and auto scaling. In the first mode, the developer must explicitly allocate read and write capacity. Amazon provides the capacity, but the downside is a fixed cost, even if the capacity is not fully utilized (and over-utilization will result in timeouts). Thus, this mode is not truly "pay as you go". The alternative is what Amazon calls auto scaling, where the service continuously monitors and adjusts capacity on the fly.

For our experiments, we opted to manually provision 500 Read Capacity Units (RCUs), which translates into supporting a DynamoDB query load of 1000 queries per second (fetching the word vector for each word constitutes a query). This choice makes our experimental results easier to interpret, since we have little insight into how Amazon handles auto scaling behind the scenes. Note however, that we adopted this configuration for experimental clarity, because otherwise we would be conflating unknown "backend knobs" in our performance measurements. In production, auto scaling would be the preferred solution.

To evaluate performance, we built a test harness that dispatches requests in parallel, with a single parameter to control the number of outstanding requests allowed when issuing queries. We call this

---

[2]https://github.com/castorini/
serverless-inference

C	tput (QPS)	Latency (ms)			Cost ($/10^6$ Q)
		mean	p50	p99	
5	7.0	700	678	1285	$1.46
10	13.0	740	722	1283	$1.66
20	23.7	802	779	1357	$1.87
30	32.3	845	817	1447	$1.87

Table 1: Latency, throughput, and cost of serverless Kim CNN under different loads (C).

C	tput (QPS)	Latency (ms)			Cost ($/10^6$ Q)
		mean	p50	p99	
5	12.1	410	381	657	$1.04
10	21.1	468	443	780	$1.04
15	30.8	467	439	827	$1.04
20	38.5	496	486	785	$1.04
25	44.4	530	519	814	$1.25

Table 2: Latency, throughput, and cost of serverless SM CNN under different loads (C).

the concurrency parameter, which we vary to simulate different amounts of query load. With different concurrency settings (ramping down from maximum load), we measured latency (mean, 50th and 99th percentile) and throughput. For Kim CNN, we used input sentences from the validation set of the Stanford Sentiment Treebank (1101 sentences). For SM CNN, we used input sentence pairs from the validation set of the TrecQA dataset (1148 sentences). We conducted each experimental trial multiple times before taking measurements to "warm up" the backend.

Results are shown in Table 1 for Kim CNN and Table 2 for SM CNN. Our deployment package is bundled with OpenBLAS to take advantage of optimized linear algebra routines. In both cases, we see that latency increases slightly as throughput ramps up. This suggests that we are not achieving perfect scale up. In theory, AWS should be proportionally increasing backend resources to maintain constant latency. It is not clear if this behavior is due to some nuance in Lambda usage that we are not aware of, or if there are actual bottlenecks in our design. Note that Kim CNN is slower because it is manipulating much larger word vectors (300 vs. 50 dimensions).

The final column in Tables 1 and 2 report Lambda charges in US dollars per million queries based on the mean latency. As of February 2018,

for functions allocated 128 MB of memory, the cost is $0.000000208 for every 100ms of running time (rounded up). Note that these costs do not include provisioning DynamoDB, which costs 0.013 cents per Read Capacity Unit per hour. We have not probed the scalability limits of our current architecture, but it is likely that our design can handle even larger query loads without additional modification.

We performed additional analyses to understand the latency breakdown: logs show that approximately 60–70% of time inside each function invocation is spent building the embedding matrix, which requires fetching word vectors from DynamoDB. In other words, inference latency is dominated by data fetching. This is no surprise since these queries involve cross-machine requests. The rest of the time is spent primarily on feedforward evaluation. The amortized cost of loading the model is negligible since it can be reused in subsequent invocations.

5 Future Work and Conclusions

We describe a novel serverless architecture for the deployment of neural networks for NLP tasks. Our design appears to be feasible, and experiments show that it scales up to moderate query loads inexpensively. For reference, a sustained query throughput of 20 queries per second translates into 1.7 million queries per day. While there are certainly many web-scale services that handle larger query loads, our serverless design is able to achieve this scale with *zero* engineering effort, since the cloud provider handles all aspect of load management without any developer intervention.

In terms of design improvements within our control, tackling the latency of DynamoDB queries would yield the biggest impact, since fetching the word vectors accounts for most of the request latency. One simple idea would be to retain a cache of the most frequent words in the Lambda itself. This would not improve "cold" startup latency, but would speed up requests once the cache has been populated. Beyond elements in our control, further advances in cloud infrastructure "behind the scenes" will improve usability, performance, and cost, making serverless architectures increasingly attractive.

Acknowledgments. This research was supported by the Natural Sciences and Engineering Research Council (NSERC) of Canada.

References

Matt Crane and Jimmy Lin. 2017. An exploration of serverless architectures for information retrieval. In *Proceedings of the 3rd ACM International Conference on the Theory of Information Retrieval (ICTIR 2017)*, pages 241–244, Amsterdam, The Netherlands.

Giuseppe DeCandia, Deniz Hastorun, Madan Jampani, Gunavardhan Kakulapati, Avinash Lakshman, Alex Pilchin, Swami Sivasubramanian, Peter Vosshall, and Werner Vogels. 2007. Dynamo: Amazon's highly available key-value store. In *Proceedings of the 21st ACM Symposium on Operating Systems Principles (SOSP 2007)*, pages 205–220, Stevenson, Washington.

Michael Dietz. 2017. Serverless deep/machine learning in production—the pythonic way. https://blog.waya.ai/deploy-deep-machine-learning-in-production-the-pythonic-way-a17105f1540e.

Yoon Kim. 2014. Convolutional neural networks for sentence classification. In *Proceedings of the 2014 Conference on Empirical Methods in Natural Language Processing (EMNLP 2014)*, pages 1746–1751, Doha, Qatar.

Tomas Mikolov, Kai Chen, Greg Corrado, and Jeffrey Dean. 2013. Efficient estimation of word representations in vector space. *arXiv:1301.3781*.

Christopher Olston, Noah Fiedel, Kiril Gorovoy, Jeremiah Harmsen, Li Lao, Fangwei Li, Vinu Rajashekhar, Sukriti Ramesh, and Jordan Soyke. 2017. TensorFlow-Serving: Flexible, high-performance ML serving. In *Workshop on ML Systems at NIPS 2017*.

Jinfeng Rao, Hua He, and Jimmy Lin. 2017. Experiments with convolutional neural network models for answer selection. In *Proceedings of the 40th International ACM SIGIR Conference on Research and Development in Information Retrieval*, pages 1217–1220. ACM.

Aliaksei Severyn and Alessandro Moschitti. 2015. Learning to rank short text pairs with convolutional deep neural networks. In *Proceedings of the 38th Annual International ACM SIGIR Conference on Research and Development in Information Retrieval (SIGIR 2015)*, pages 373–382, Santiago, Chile.

An automated medical scribe for documenting clinical encounters[*]

Greg P. Finley, Erik Edwards, Amanda Robinson, Najmeh Sadoughi, James Fone, Mark Miller, David Suendermann-Oeft
EMR.AI Inc.
San Francisco, CA, USA
`greg.finley@emr.ai`

Michael Brenndoerfer
University of California
Berkeley, CA, USA

Nico Axtmann
DHBW, Karlsruhe, Germany

Abstract

A medical scribe is a clinical professional who charts patient–physician encounters in real time, relieving physicians of most of their administrative burden and substantially increasing productivity and job satisfaction. We present a complete implementation of an *automated* medical scribe. Our system can serve either as a scalable, standardized, and economical alternative to human scribes; or as an assistive tool for them, providing a first draft of a report along with a convenient means to modify it. This solution is, to our knowledge, the first automated scribe ever presented and relies upon multiple speech and language technologies, including speaker diarization, medical speech recognition, knowledge extraction, and natural language generation.

1 Introduction

A recent study from the University of Wisconsin concluded that primary care physicians spend almost two hours on tasks related to electronic medical record (EMR) systems for every one hour of direct patient care (Arndt et al., 2017). This result illustrates the omnipresent complaint that medical practitioners are overly burdened by the administrative overhead of their work.

One solution to this issue is to have someone other than the physician take care of most of the EMR-related work associated with patient care. In particular, a *medical scribe* assumes the role of a clinical paraprofessional entering information into and, in some cases, extracting required information from EMR systems during patient–physician encounters (Earls et al., 2017). Scribes produce data entries in real time, entering narrative and discrete data points into templates of the EMR system. They can be either physically present in the physician's office or connected through phone or internet, interacting with the EMR system offline or by way of remote desktop connections. The latter are referred to as "virtual scribes."

Several studies show that the use of human scribes saves physicians substantial time on documentation, improves their work-life balance, and enhances clinicians' productivity. The resulting revenue increase has the potential to be multiple times higher than the cost of the scribe (Koshy et al., 2010; Bastani et al., 2014; Earls et al., 2017).

Despite these considerable advantages, there are some drawbacks to using medical scribes:

- scribes require extended training time and cost before developing their full potential—e.g., Walker et al. (2016) found the average training cost to be $6,317;

- scribes are often medical or premedical students (Walker et al., 2016) who, after being sufficiently exposed to the training experience the position of a scribe offers, tend to move on to attend medical school full time[1]; this fast-paced turnover in conjunction with the aforementioned training time and cost greatly reduces their effectiveness;

- scribes are costly: Earls et al. (2017) states that their scribes are paid $39,750 p.a.; Walker et al. (2016) quotes an average salary of $15.91 per hour for their virtual scribes which equals approximately $29,000 p.a.; Brady and Shariff (2013) estimates the annual cost of an on-site scribe to be $49,000 and for a virtual scribe $23,000.

In order to mitigate these disadvantages while preserving the strengths of employing scribes in the

---

[*]Patent pending.

[1]E.g., Stanford University's scribe program is purposefully limited to 12 months and is designed to prepare future medical students (Lin et al., 2017).

Proceedings of NAACL-HLT 2018: Demonstrations, pages 11–15
New Orleans, Louisiana, June 2 - 4, 2018. ©2018 Association for Computational Linguistics

first place, we have developed a fully automated scribe, a prototype of which is presented here. It makes use of a full stack of state-of-the-art speech and natural language processing (NLP) components which are concisely described in this paper. To the best of the authors' knowledge, this is the very first automated scribe implementation ever presented to the scientific community.

We see at least two main avenues for deploying this technology. The first is to serve as a direct stand-in for human scribes—useful in cases where hiring scribes is either economically or logistically infeasible. In this case, the output of our system would be subject to review and correction by the physician. The second is as an assistive tool to (human) virtual scribes: our system displays an inital draft of the report and a summary of the information present in the conversation. The virtual scribe will be able to make any necessary corrections either to this information, in which case the report can be re-generated, or directly to the text. Either way, the availability of our automated system promises to streamline the human scribe's work and increase their throughput dramatically. Note that a similar workflow is commonplace for transcribing dictated clinical reports: the dictation is passed through an automatic speech recognition (ASR) and formatting system, then manually corrected by professional transcriptionists off-site.

2 Design

The automated scribe features a linear processing pipeline of speech-processing modules followed by NLP modules. We briefly introduce and motivate all modules in this section, then describe each individually in the following sections.

The initial stages transform the recorded conversation into a text format: first, a speaker diarization module determines who is speaking when and uses this information to break the audio recording into segments coded for speaker, which are then passed through a medical ASR stage. These steps are described in Sections 3 and 4.

Following ASR, the scribe must convert a transcribed spontaneous conversation into a concise and fully formatted report. This goal is exemplified in Figure 1, which shows an excerpt of a conversation and its realization in the report. The system does not perform this translation directly— this would require enormous amounts of parallel data to solve, end to end, with any single tech-

nique. Instead, we employ a two-stage approach in which the scribe mines the conversation for information and saves it in a structured format, then exports this structured data to the final report. In this way, the bulk of the NLP work is divided into two well-studied problems: knowledge extraction (KE; Section 5) and natural language generation (NLG; Section 7). (Between these two stages, structured data is processed directly to prepare it for export [Section 6].) Generating structured data as an intermediate step has numerous other advantages: it can be kept in the patient's history for reference to improve results on future episodes; it can be used by other systems that process structured data (e.g. billing, decision support); and it can be corrected manually if needed, which can be less error-prone than correcting final text directly.

3 Speaker diarization

Speaker diarization is the "who spoke when" problem, also called speaker indexing (Wellekens, 2001; Miró et al., 2012; Moattar and Homayounpour, 2012). The input is audio features sampled at 100 Hz frame rate, and the output is framelabels indicating speaker identify for each frame. Four labels are possible: speaker 1 (e.g. the doctor), speaker 2 (e.g. the patient), overlap (both speakers), and silence (within-speaker pauses and between-speaker gaps). Note that the great majority of doctor-patient encounters involve exactly two speakers. Although our method is easily generalizable to more speakers, we currently report on the two-speaker problem.

The diarization literature broadly distinguishes "bottom-up" vs. "top-down" approaches. The former (Gish et al., 1991) operate by merging neighboring frames by similarity (clustering); we found initial results unsatisfactory. The later operate with a prior model such as HMM–GMM (Hidden Markov, Gaussian mixture model) to represent the likely audio features and timing (transition) characteristics of dialogs. We have introduced our own top-down approach that utilizes a modified expectation maximization (EM) algorithm at decoding time to learn the current speaker and background silence characteristics in real time. It is coded in plain C for maximum efficiency and currently operates at $\sim 50 \times$ real-time factor.

Diarization requires an expanded set of audio features compared to ASR. In ASR, only phoneme identity is of final interest, and so audio features

Conversation	Report
Dr: "okay great and in terms of your past medical history do you have any other medical conditions you have"	FAMILY MEDICAL HISTORY The patient's aunt had lung cancer.
Pt: "no i have not had any medical conditions but my auntie actually she had lung cancer so that's why i kind of…"	

Figure 1: An excerpt from a typical input and output for the NLP segment of the scribe. Note that the ASR output has no punctuation or case; the doctor ('Dr.') and patient ('Pt.') identifiers illustrate the contribution of the diarizer.

are generally insensitive to speaker characteristics. By contrast, in diarization, only speaker identity is of final interest. Also note that diarization performs a *de facto* speech activity detection (SAD), since states 1–3 vs. state 4 are speech vs. silence. Therefore features successful for SAD (Sadjadi and Hansen, 2013) are helpful to diarization as well. Accordingly, we use an expanded set of gammatone-based audio features for the total SAD + diarization + ASR problem (details to be reported elsewhere).

4 Speech recognition

ASR operates on the audio segments produced by the diarization stage, where each segment contains one conversational turn (1 speaker + possibly a few frames of overlap). Currently, the diarization and ASR stages are strictly separated and the ASR decoding operates by the same neural network (NN) methodology that we recently reported for general medical ASR (Edwards et al., 2017). In brief, the acoustic model (AM) consists of a NN trained to predict context-sensitive phones from the audio features; and the language model (LM) is a 3- or 4-gram statistical LM prepared with methods of interpolation and pruning that we developed to address the massive medical-vocabulary challenge. Decoding operates in real time by use of weighted finite-state transducer (WFST) methodology (Mohri et al., 2002; Allauzen et al., 2007; Povey et al., 2011) coded in C++. Our current challenge is to adapt the AM and LM to medical conversations, which have somewhat different statistics compared to dictations.

5 Knowledge extraction

Extracting information from spontaneous conversational speech is a notoriously difficult problem. There has been some recent work on extracting keywords (Habibi and Popescu-Belis, 2013) or facts such as biographical details (Jing et al., 2007), but it is unclear whether known methods are effective for clinical conversation specifically.

We apply a novel strategy to simplify the KE problem by tagging sentences and turns in the conversation based upon the information they are likely to contain. These classes overlap largely with sections in the final report—chief complaint, medical history, etc. Then, we apply a variety of strategies, depending on the type of information being extracted, on filtered sections of text.

We use hierarchical recurrent neural networks (RNNs) to tag turns and sentences with their predicted class; each sentence is represented by a single vector encoded by a word-level RNN with an attention mechanism. (Our approach is similar to the influential document classification strategy of Yang et al. (2016), although we classify the sentences individually rather than the entire document.) In most cases, we can generate a sentence vector from an entire speech turn; for longer turns, however, we have to detect sentence boundaries. This is essentially a punctuation restoration task, which we have successfully undertaken previously using RNNs with attention (Salloum et al., 2017).

To extract information from tagged sentences, we apply one or more of several strategies:

- Complete or partial string match to identify terms from ontologies. This is effective for concepts which do not vary much in representation, such as certain medications.

- Extractive rules using regular expressions, which are well suited to predictable elements such as medication dosages, or certain temporal expressions (e.g. dates and durations).

- Other unsupervised or knowledge-based strategies, such as Lesk-style approaches (Lesk, 1986) in which semantic overlap with dictionary definitions of terms is used to normalize semantically equivalent phrases, as has been done successfully for medical concepts (Melton et al., 2010). This might be suitable for concepts that usually vary in expression, such as descriptions of symptoms.

- Fully supervised machine learning approaches, which we employ for difficult or highly specialized tasks—for example, identifying when a patient complains of symptoms generally worsening.

The KE stage also relies on extractive summary techniques where necessary, in which entire sentences may be copied directly if they refer to information that is relevant but difficult to represent in our structured type system—for example, a description of how a patient sustained a workplace injury. (To handle such cases using natural language understanding is a highly complex problem requiring a domain-general solution, which is beyond the scope of the medical scribe.) At a later stage, extracted text is processed to fit seamlessly into the final report (e.g. changing pronouns).

6 Processing structured data

Following the information extraction stage is a module which performs several functions to validate the structured knowledge and prepare it for NLG. This often entails correcting for any gaps or inconsistencies in the extracted knowledge, as may occur when there is critical information that is not explicitly mentioned during the encounter (as is frequently the case), or if there are errors in diarization, ASR, or KE. Typically, problems can be resolved through a series of logical checks or by relying on other structured data in the patient's history (when available). If not, conflicts or grave omissions can be flagged for the user.

Wherever appropriate, data is also encoded in structures compatible with the HL7 FHIR v3 standard (Bender and Sartipi, 2013) to facilitate interoperability with other systems. As a concrete example, if the physician states an intent to prescribe a medication, a FHIR MedicationRequest resource is generated. The output of this stage can be made available to the user if he or she wishes to amend the structured information, and any changes can be propagated instantly to NLG.

7 Natural language generation

The NLG module produces and formats the final report. Medical reports follow a loosely standardized format, with sections appearing in a generally predictable order and with well-defined content within each section. Our strategy is a data-driven templatic approach supported by a finite-state "grammar" of report structure.

The template bank consists of sentence templates annotated for the structured data types necessary to complete them. We fill this bank by clustering sentences from a large corpus of medical reports according to semantic and syntactic similarity. The results of this stage are manually curated to ensure that strange or imprecise sentences cannot be generated by the system, and to ensure parsimony in the resulting type system. Kondadadi et al. (2013) employ a similar method of clustering and manual review to quickly and effectively generate a full template bank from data.

Using the same reports, we induce the grammar using a probabilistic finite-state graph, where each arc outputs a sentence and a single path through the graph represents one actual or possible report. Decoding optimizes the maximal use of structured data and the likelihood of the path chosen. The grammar helps to improve upon one common criticism of templatic NLG approaches, which is the lack of variation in sentences (van Deemter et al., 2005), in a way that does not require any "inflation" of the template bank with synonyms or paraphrases: during decoding, different semantically equivalent templates may be selected based on context and the set of available facts, thus replicating the flow of natural language in existing notes.

Note that, as format can vary considerably by note type, specialty, and healthcare provider, we build separate NLG models to handle each type of output.

Finally, all notes pass through a processor that handles reference and anaphora (e.g. replacing some references to the patient with gender pronouns), truecasing, formatting, etc.

8 Conclusion

The presented automated scribe can take over or supplement the role of human scribes documenting encounters between patients and physicians. At the current stage, the system is still limited in its functionality and scope, and major enhancements are being made to improve performance and content coverage of several of the involved components. In particular, we plan to expand the use of machine learning techniques as soon as enough data has been accumulated in various pilot studies currently underway. Additionally, we are working to compile a large set of parallel inputs and outputs to allow for a true end-to-end evaluation of the system.

References

C Allauzen, M Riley, J Schalkwyk, and M Mohri. 2007. OpenFst: a general and efficient weighted finite-state transducer library. In *Proc CIAA*, volume LNCS 4783, pages 11–23. Springer.

BG Arndt, JW Beasley, MD Watkinson, JL Temte, W-J Tuan, CA Sinsky, and VJ Gilchrist. 2017. Tethered to the EHR: primary care physician workload assessment using EHR event log data and time-motion observations. *Ann Fam Med*, 15(5):419–426.

A Bastani, B Shaqiri, K Palomba, D Bananno, and W Anderson. 2014. An ED scribe program is able to improve throughput time and patient satisfaction. *Am J Emerg Med*, 32(5):399–402.

D Bender and K Sartipi. 2013. HL7 FHIR: an Agile and RESTful approach to healthcare information exchange. In *Proc Int Symp CBMS*, pages 326–331. IEEE.

K Brady and A Shariff. 2013. Virtual medical scribes: making electronic medical records work for you. *J Med Pract Manage*, 29(2):133–136.

K van Deemter, M Theune, and E Krahmer. 2005. Real versus template-based natural language generation: a false opposition? *Comput Linguist*, 31(1):15–24.

ST Earls, JA Savageau, S Begley, BG Saver, K Sullivan, and A Chuman. 2017. Can scribes boost FPs' efficiency and job satisfaction? *J Fam Pract*, 66(4):206–214.

E Edwards, W Salloum, GP Finley, J Fone, G Cardiff, M Miller, and D Suendermann-Oeft. 2017. Medical speech recognition: reaching parity with humans. In *Proc SPECOM*, volume LNCS 10458, pages 512–524. Springer.

H Gish, M-H Siu, and JR Rohlicek. 1991. Segregation of speakers for speech recognition and speaker identification. In *Proc ICASSP*, volume 2, pages 873–876. IEEE.

M Habibi and A Popescu-Belis. 2013. Diverse keyword extraction from conversations. In *Proc ACL*, volume 2, pages 651–657. ACL.

H Jing, N Kambhatla, and S Roukos. 2007. Extracting social networks and biographical facts from conversational speech transcripts. In *Proc ACL*, pages 1040–1047. ACL.

R Kondadadi, B Howald, and F Schilder. 2013. A statistical NLG framework for aggregated planning and realization. In *Proc ACL*, pages 1406–1415. ACL.

S Koshy, PJ Feustel, M Hong, and BA Kogan. 2010. Scribes in an ambulatory urology practice: patient and physician satisfaction. *J Urol*, 184(1):258–262.

ME Lesk. 1986. Automatic sense disambiguation using machine readable dictionaries: how to tell a pine cone from an ice cream cone. In *Proc SIGDOC*, pages 24–26. ACM.

S Lin, K Osborn, A Sattler, I Nelligan, D Svec, A Aaronson, and E Schillinger. 2017. Creating the medical school of the future through incremental curricular transformation: the Stanford Healthcare Innovations and Experiential Learning Directive (SHIELD). *Educ Prim Care*, 28(3):180–184.

GB Melton, S Moon, M Bridget, and S Pakhomov. 2010. Automated identification of synonyms in biomedical acronym sense inventories. In *Proc Louhi Workshop*, pages 46–52. ACL.

XA Miró, S Bozonnet, N Evans, C Fredouille, G Friedland, and O Vinyals. 2012. Speaker diarization: a review of recent research. *IEEE Trans Audio Speech Lang Process*, 20(2):356–370.

MH Moattar and MM Homayounpour. 2012. A review on speaker diarization systems and approaches. *Speech Commun*, 54(10):1065–1103.

M Mohri, FCN Pereira, and M Riley. 2002. Weighted finite-state transducers in speech recognition. *Comput Speech Lang*, 16(1):69–88.

D Povey, G Boulianne, L Burget, O Glembek, NK Goel, M Hannemann, P Motlícek, Y Qian, P Schwarz, and J Silovsky. 2011. The Kaldi speech recognition toolkit. In *Proc ASRU*, pages 1–4. IEEE.

SO Sadjadi and JHL Hansen. 2013. Unsupervised speech activity detection using voicing measures and perceptual spectral flux. *IEEE Signal Process Lett*, 20(3):197–200.

W Salloum, GP Finley, E Edwards, M Miller, and D Suendermann-Oeft. 2017. Deep learning for punctuation restoration in medical reports. In *Proc Workshop BioNLP*, pages 159–164. ACL.

KJ Walker, W Dunlop, D Liew, MP Staples, M Johnson, M Ben-Meir, HG Rodda, I Turner, and D Phillips. 2016. An economic evaluation of the costs of training a medical scribe to work in emergency medicine. *Emerg Med J*, 33(12):865–869.

CJ Wellekens. 2001. Seamless navigation in audio files. In *Proc Odyssey*, pages 9–12. ISCA.

Z Yang, D Yang, C Dyer, X He, A Smola, and E Hovy. 2016. Hierarchical attention networks for document classification. In *Proc NAACL-HLT*, pages 1480–1490. ACL.

CL Scholar: The ACL Anthology Knowledge Graph Miner

Mayank Singh, Pradeep Dogga,* Sohan Patro,* Dhiraj Barnwal,* Ritam Dutt,*
Rajarshi Haldar, Pawan Goyal and Animesh Mukherjee
Department of Computer Science and Engineering
Indian Institute of Technology, Kharagpur, WB, India
mayank.singh@cse.iitkgp.ernet.in

Abstract

We present *CL Scholar*, the ACL Anthology knowledge graph miner to facilitate high-quality search and exploration of current research progress in the computational linguistics community. In contrast to previous works, periodically crawling, indexing and processing of new incoming articles is completely automated in the current system. *CL Scholar* utilizes both textual and network information for knowledge graph construction. As an additional novel initiative, *CL Scholar* supports more than 1200 scholarly natural language queries along with standard keyword-based search on constructed knowledge graph. It answers *binary*, *statistical* and *list* based natural language queries. The current system is deployed at `http://cnerg.iitkgp.ac.in/aclakg`. We also provide REST API support along with bulk download facility. Our code and data are available at `https://github.com/CLScholar`.

1 Introduction

ACL Anthology[1] is one of the popular initiatives of the Association for Computational Linguistics (ACL) to curate all publications related to computational linguistics and natural language processing at one common place. At present, it hosts more than 44,000 papers and is actively updated and maintained by Min Yen Kan. Since its inception, ACL Anthology functions as a repository with the collection of papers from ACL and related organizations in computational linguistics. However, it does not provide any additional statistics about authors, papers, venues, and topics. Also, it lacks advance search features such as article ranking by factoring in popularity or relevance, natural language query support, author profiles, topical search etc.

1.1 Previous systems built on ACL anthology

Owing to above limitations, ACL anthology remained an archival repository for quite a long time. Bird et al. (2008) developed the *ACL Anthology Reference Corpus (ACL ARC)* as a collaborative attempt to provide a standardized testbed reference corpus based on the ACL Anthology. Later, Radev et al. (2009) have invested humongous manual efforts to construct *The ACL Anthology Network Corpus (AAN)*. AAN consists of a manually curated database of citations, collaborations, and summaries and statistics about the network. They have utilized two OCR processing tools PDFBox[2] and ParsCit (Councill et al., 2008) for curation. AAN was continuously updated till 2013 (Radev et al., 2013). Recently, this project has been moved to Yale University as part of the new LILY group[3].

1.2 The computational linguistic knowledge graph

As a similar initiative, in this paper, we demonstrate the development of *CL Scholar* which automatically mines ACL anthology and constructs computational linguistic knowledge graph (hereafter 'CLKG'). The current framework automatically crawls new articles, processes, indexes, constructs knowledge graph and generates searchable statistics without involving tedious manual annotations. We leverage state-of-the-art scientific article processing tool OCR++ (Singh et al., 2016) for robust and automatic information extraction from scientific articles. OCR++ is an open-source framework that can extract from scholarly articles the metadata, the structure and the bibliography.

The constructed $CLKG$ is modeled as a heterogeneous graph (Sun et al., 2009) consisting of four

---

*These authors contributed equally to the study.
[1]https://aclweb.org/anthology/

[2]https://pdfbox.apache.org/
[3]http://tangra.cs.yale.edu/newaan/

Proceedings of NAACL-HLT 2018: Demonstrations, pages 16–20
New Orleans, Louisiana, June 2 - 4, 2018. ©2018 Association for Computational Linguistics

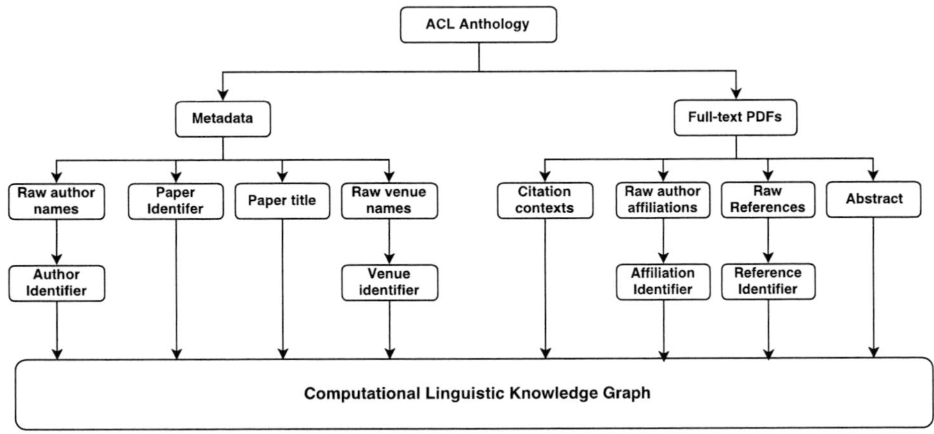

Figure 1: Data processing flow diagram.

entities: author, paper, venue, and field. We utilize metapaths (Sun and Han, 2012) to implement the query retrieval framework.

1.3 Natural language queries

In the first-of-its-kind initiative, we extend the functionalities of *CL Scholar* to answer natural language queries (hereafter '*NLQ*') along with standard keyword-based queries. Currently, it answers *binary*, *statistical* and *list* based NLQ. Overall, we handle more than 1200 variations of NLQ.

Outline: The rest of the paper is organized as follows. Section 2 describes the ACL Anthology dataset. Section 3 details step by step extraction procedure for $CLKG$ construction. In section 4, we describe $CLKG$. We describe our framework in section 5. We conclude in section 6 and identify future work.

Table 2: General statistics about the ACL Anthology dataset.

Number of papers	42,069
Year range	1965–2017
Total authors	37,752
Total unique authors	33,372
Total unified venues	33

2 Dataset

CL Scholar uses metadata and full-text PDF research articles crawled from ACL Anthology. ACL Anthology consists of more than 40,000 research articles published in more than 33 computational linguistic events (venues) including conferences, workshops, and journals. Table 2 presents general statistics of the crawled dataset.

We crawl both metadata information (unique article identifier, article title, authors' names, and venue) as well as full-text PDF articles. Next, we describe in detail several pre-processing steps and knowledge graph construction methodology.

3 Pre-processing and knowledge graph construction

We process full-text PDFs using state-of-the-art extraction tool $OCR++$ (Singh et al., 2016). We extract references, citation contexts, author affiliations and URLs from full-text. $OCR++$ also provides reference to citation contexts mapping. Raw information with several variations like author names, venue names and affiliations are assigned unique identifiers using standard indexing approaches. We only consider those reference papers that are present in ACL anthology. This rich textual, as well as citation relationship information, is utilized in the construction of $CLKG$. Figure 1 presents the $CLKG$ construction from metadata and full-text PDF files crawled from ACL anthology.

4 Computational linguistic knowledge graph

Computational linguistic knowledge graph ($CLKG$) is a *heterogeneous graph* (Sun et al., 2009) consisting of four entities: author (A), paper (P), venue (V) and field (F) as nodes. Each entity is associated with few properties, for example, properties of P are publication year, title, abstract, etc. Similarly, properties of A are name, publication trend, affiliation etc. We utilize *metapaths* (Sun and Han, 2012) between entities to express semantic relations. For example, simple metapaths like $A{\rightarrow}P$ and $V{\rightarrow}P$ represent "author of" and "published at" relations respectively, whereas complex metapaths like $V{\rightarrow}A{\rightarrow}P$ and $F{\rightarrow}A{\rightarrow}P$ represent "authors of papers published at" and "authors of papers in" relations respectively. We leverage metapaths to develop *CL Scholar* (described in the next section).

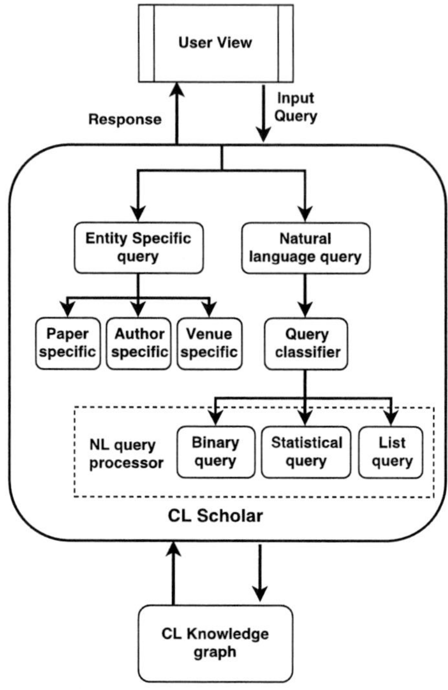

Figure 3: CL Scholar framework.

5 CL Scholar

CL scholar fetches information from $CLKG$ as per the input query from the user. The current framework is divided into two modules – 1) natural language based query retrieval, and 2) entity specific query retrieval. Figure 3 shows *CL Scholar* framework.

5.1 Natural language query retrieval

The first module answers natural language queries (NLQ). It consists of two sub-modules, 1) the query classifier, and 2) the NL query processor. *Query classifier* classifies user input into one of the three basic types of NLQ using regular expression patterns. *NL query processor* processes query based on its type determined by query classifier. Given an input natural language query, we utilize longest subsequence match to identify entity instances. The three types of NLQ are:

1. **Binary queries:** These represent a set of queries for which user demands a 'yes' or 'no' type answer. Table 4 lists few interesting binary queries.

2. **Statistical queries:** These represent set of queries which the knowledge base returns with some statistics. Currently, we support three types of statistics – 1) temporal, 2) cumulative, and 3) comparison. Temporal represents year-wise statistics, cumulative represents overall statistics and comparison represents comparative statistics between two or more instances of the same entity type. Table 4 lists few representative statistical queries.

3. **List queries:** These represent set of queries for which the knowledge base returns a list of papers, authors or venues. Table 4 also enumerates few representative list queries.

5.2 Entity specific query retrieval

CL scholar also supports entity specific retrieval. As described in section 4, $CLKG$ consists of four entities: paper, author, venue, and field. Currently, our system supports three[4] entity specific retrieval schemes handled by three sub-modules:

1. **Paper specific:** This sub-module returns paper specific information. Currently, we retrieve and display author names and affiliations, abstract, publication year and venue, cumulative and year-wise citations, list of references, citer papers, co-cited papers present in ACL anthology and list of URLs present in the paper text. We also show average sentiment score received by the queried paper by utilizing incoming citation contexts. Table 5 shows three representative paper specific queries.

2. **Author specific:** This sub-module handles author specific queries. Given an author name, the system shows its cumulative and year-wise publication and citation count, collaborator list with an average number of collaborations, current and temporal H-index and temporal topic distribution. We also list author's publications in ACL anthology. Table 5 lists three author specific queries with first name, last name and full name respectively.

3. **Venue specific:** We also answer venue specific queries. For each venue specific query, the system shows cumulative and year-wise

---

[4]The fourth sub-module is still under development.

Table 4: Representative queries from three natural language query classes. A represents author, P represents paper, V represents venue and F represents field. The list of supported queries is available online at *CL Scholar* portal.

	Binary queries	**Statistical queries**	**List queries**
1.	Is V accepting papers from F	How many F papers are published in V over the years	List the papers from F accepted in V
2.	Has A published any paper	How many papers are published by A	List the papers published by A
3.	Does A publish papers on F	How many papers are published by A in F	List the papers published by A on F
4.	Are there any papers published by A_1 and A_2 together	How many papers are published by A_1 and A_2 together	List the papers published by $A1$ and $A2$ together
5.	Are there any papers of A with positive sentiment	How many papers are there of A with positive sentiment	List of papers with positive sentiment of A

publication and citation count, 2-year impact factor, recently held year and list of collaborating venues. Table 5 shows three representative venue specific queries.

Table 5: Representative entity specific queries.

Paper specific	**Author specific**	**Venue specific**
OCR	Chris	NAACL
Deep learning	Singh	SIGDAT
Word embeddings	Aravind Joshi	ACL

5.3 Additional insights

We provide two additional insights by analyzing incoming citation contexts. First, we present a summary generated from incoming the citation contexts (Qazvinian and Radev, 2008). Currently, we show five summary sentences against each paper. Second, we also compute sentiment score of each citation context by leveraging a standard sentiment analyzer (Athar and Teufel, 2012). We aggregate by averaging over the sentiment score of all the incoming citation contexts.

5.4 Ranking

Currently, we employ popularity based ranking of retrieved results. We utilize current citation count as a measure of popularity. In future, we plan to deploy other ranking schemes like recency, impact, sentiment, relevance, etc.

5.5 Deployment

CL Scholar is developed using ReactJS framework. The system also supports REST API requests which are powered by a NodeJS server with data being served using MongoDB. It is currently accessible at our research group page[5]. More information about API usage is available at API support page[6]. In addition, the entire knowledge graph can also be easily downloaded in a plain text format. Figure 6 shows a snapshot of the *CL Scholar* landing page.

Figure 6: Snapshot of CL Scholar landing page.

The current system is still under development. Currently, we assume that spellings are correct for NLQ. We do not support instant query search. We also do not support query recommendations.

6 Conclusion

In this paper, we propose a fully automatic approach for the development of computational linguistic knowledge graph from full-text PDF articles available in ACL Anthology. We also develop first-of-its-kind academic natural language query retrieval system. Currently, our system can answer three different types of natural language queries. In future, we plan to extend the query set. We also plan to append structural information within knowledge graphs such as section labeling of citations, figure and table captions etc. We also plan to conduct extensive evaluation to compare *CL Scholar* with state-of-the-art systems.

[5]http://cnerg.iitkgp.ac.in/aclakg
[6]http://cnerg.iitkgp.ac.in/aclakg/api

References

Awais Athar and Simone Teufel. 2012. Context-enhanced citation sentiment detection. In *Proceedings of the 2012 Conference of the North American Chapter of the Association for Computational Linguistics: Human Language Technologies*, NAACL HLT '12, pages 597–601, Stroudsburg, PA, USA. Association for Computational Linguistics.

Steven Bird, Robert Dale, Bonnie J Dorr, Bryan Gibson, Mark Thomas Joseph, Min-Yen Kan, Dongwon Lee, Brett Powley, Dragomir R Radev, and Yee Fan Tan. 2008. The acl anthology reference corpus: A reference dataset for bibliographic research in computational linguistics.

Isaac G Councill, C Lee Giles, and Min-Yen Kan. 2008. Parscit: an open-source crf reference string parsing package. In *LREC*, volume 8, pages 661–667.

Vahed Qazvinian and Dragomir R. Radev. 2008. Scientific paper summarization using citation summary networks. In *Proceedings of the 22Nd International Conference on Computational Linguistics - Volume 1*, COLING '08, pages 689–696, Stroudsburg, PA, USA. Association for Computational Linguistics.

Dragomir R Radev, Pradeep Muthukrishnan, and Vahed Qazvinian. 2009. The acl anthology network corpus. In *Proceedings of the 2009 Workshop on Text and Citation Analysis for Scholarly Digital Libraries*, pages 54–61. Association for Computational Linguistics.

DragomirR. Radev, Pradeep Muthukrishnan, Vahed Qazvinian, and Amjad Abu-Jbara. 2013. The acl anthology network corpus. *Language Resources and Evaluation*, pages 1–26.

Mayank Singh, Barnopriyo Barua, Priyank Palod, Manvi Garg, Sidhartha Satapathy, Samuel Bushi, Kumar Ayush, Krishna Sai Rohith, Tulasi Gamidi, Pawan Goyal, and Animesh Mukherjee. 2016. Ocr++: A robust framework for information extraction from scholarly articles. In *Proceedings of COLING 2016, the 26th International Conference on Computational Linguistics: Technical Papers*, pages 3390–3400, Osaka, Japan. The COLING 2016 Organizing Committee.

Yizhou Sun and Jiawei Han. 2012. Mining heterogeneous information networks: principles and methodologies. *Synthesis Lectures on Data Mining and Knowledge Discovery*, 3(2):1–159.

Yizhou Sun, Yintao Yu, and Jiawei Han. 2009. Ranking-based clustering of heterogeneous information networks with star network schema. In *Proceedings of the 15th ACM SIGKDD international conference on Knowledge discovery and data mining*, pages 797–806. ACM.

ArgumenText: Searching for Arguments in Heterogeneous Sources

Christian Stab and **Johannes Daxenberger** and **Chris Stahlhut** and **Tristan Miller**
Benjamin Schiller and **Christopher Tauchmann** and **Steffen Eger** and **Iryna Gurevych**
Ubiquitous Knowledge Processing Lab (UKP-TUDA)
Department of Computer Science, Technische Universität Darmstadt
`https://www.ukp.tu-darmstadt.de/`

Abstract

Argument mining is a core technology for enabling argument search in large corpora. However, most current approaches fall short when applied to heterogeneous texts. In this paper, we present an argument retrieval system capable of retrieving sentential arguments for any given controversial topic. By analyzing the highest-ranked results extracted from Web sources, we found that our system covers 89% of arguments found in expert-curated lists of arguments from an online debate portal, and also identifies additional valid arguments.

1 Introduction

Information retrieval (IR) and question answering (QA) are mature NLP technologies that excel at finding factual information relevant to a given query. But not all information needs can be satisfied with factual information. In many search scenarios, users are not seeking a universally accepted ground truth, but rather an overview of viewpoints and arguments surrounding a controversial topic. For example, in a legal dispute, an attorney might have to search for precedents and multifaceted legal opinions supporting the case at hand, and anticipate counterarguments that opposing counsel will make. Similarly, a policymaker will survey pros and cons of prospective legislation before she proposes or votes on it. While IR and QA can help with such *argument search* tasks, they provide no specialized support for them.

Despite its obvious applications, argument search has attracted relatively little attention in the argument mining community. In this paper, we present ArgumenText, which we believe is the first system for topic-relevant argument search in heterogeneous texts. It takes a large collection of arbitrary Web texts, automatically identifies arguments relevant to a given topic, classifies them as "pro" or "con", and

presents them ranked by relevance in an intuitive interface. The system thereby eases much of the manual effort involved in argument search.

We present an evaluation of our system in which its top-ranked search results are compared with arguments aggregated and curated by experts on a popular online debate portal. The results show that our system has high coverage (89%) with respect to the expert-curated lists. Moreover, it identifies many additional valid arguments omitted or overlooked by the human curators, affording users a more complete overview of the controversy surrounding a given topic. Nonetheless, precision remains an issue, with slightly less than half (47%) the results being irrelevant to the topic or misclassified with respect to argument stance.

2 Related Work

Most existing approaches consider argument mining at the discourse level and address tasks like argument unit identification (Ajjour et al., 2017), component classification (Mochales-Palau and Moens, 2009), or argument structure identification (Eger et al., 2017). These approaches focus on recognizing arguments within a single text but do not consider relevance to user-defined topics.

Until now, there has been little work on identifying topic-relevant arguments. Wachsmuth et al. (2017) present a generic framework for argument search that relies on pre-structured arguments from debate portals. Levy et al. (2014) present a system designed specifically for detecting topic-relevant claims from Wikipedia, which was later extended to mine supporting statements for claims (Rinott et al., 2015). The MARGOT system (Lippi and Torroni, 2015) is trained on Wikipedia data and extracts claims and evidence from user-provided texts. However, all these systems focus on specific text types and are not yet able to extract arguments

21

Proceedings of NAACL-HLT 2018: Demonstrations, pages 21–25
New Orleans, Louisiana, June 2 - 4, 2018. ©2018 Association for Computational Linguistics

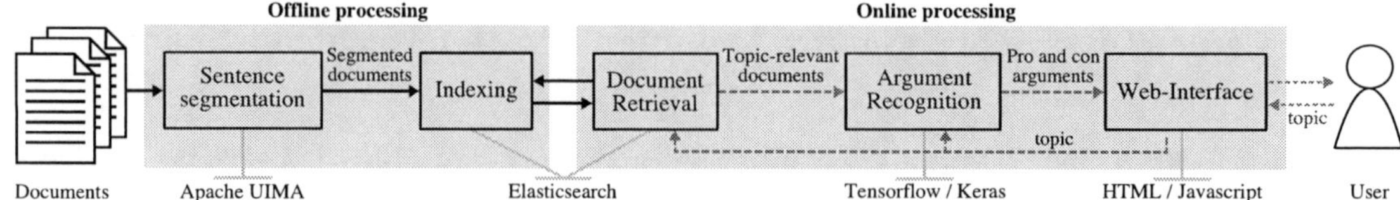

Figure 1: System architecture.

from a large collection of arbitrary texts. The approach most similar to ours, introduced by Hua and Wang (2017), extracts claim-relevant arguments from different text types, but is limited to sentential "pro" arguments.

3 System Description

Our system allows searching for arguments relevant to a user-defined topic. A *topic* is some matter of controversy that can be concisely expressed through keywords. We define an *argument* as a sentence expressing evidence or reasoning that can be used to either *support* or *oppose* a given topic. For example, "It carries a risk of genetic defects." is a "con" argument for the topic "cloning" while "Cloning should be permitted." is not an argument at all since it lacks a relevant reason.

Retrieving arguments from a large document collection is computationally expensive. In particular, argument mining methods that consider the relevance to a specific topic need to be applied for each query individually, resulting in poor response times if the collection is too big. To address this challenge, our system first retrieves a list of documents relevant to a given topic and then applies an argument mining model to the top-ranked documents. The system's architecture (Fig. 1) is split into offline and online processing parts. The *offline processing* consists of components not depending on the user's query such as boilerplate removal, sentence segmentation, and document indexing. The *online processing* covers all components that depend on the user-defined topic and thus need to be applied for each query. The following subsections describe each of these components in detail.

3.1 Data

As our objective is to search for arguments in any text domain, we build upon the English part of CommonCrawl,[1] the largest Web corpus available to date. Before further processing, we followed

Habernal et al. (2016) for de-duplication, boilerplate removal using jusText (Pomikálek, 2011), and language detection.[2] This left us with 400 million heterogeneous plain-text documents in English, with an overall size of 683 GiB.

3.2 Tokenization and Sentence Segmentation

Each document is segmented into sentences with an Apache UIMA pipeline using components from DKPro Core (Eckart de Castilho and Gurevych, 2014). To facilitate processing of other languages in future work, we chose Apache OpenNLP which currently supports six languages. The modular nature of our setup allows us to easily integrate other sentence segmentation methods for currently unsupported languages. Finally, the document text, the tokenized sentences, and the metadata (e.g., document titles and timestamps) are converted into a JSON format for indexing.

3.3 Indexing and Retrieval

To retrieve documents relevant to a given topic, we index the data using Elasticsearch.[3] The entire offline processing of our data, using 40 parallel processes on a server equipped with two Intel Xeon E5-2699 v4 CPUs (22 cores each) and 512 GiB of memory, required 19 days in total.

For each request, Elasticsearch scores all documents containing the keywords of the topic according to BM25 (Robertson et al., 1994). It then returns the top-ranked documents, including the segmented sentences and metadata, in the aforementioned JSON format. We can optionally restrict the search to specific fields in the metadata, such as the publication date or source domain.

3.4 Argument Identification and Stance Recognition

For extracting topic-relevant arguments from the list of retrieved documents, we build on the corpus of Stab et al. (2018), which includes annotated

---

[1]http://commoncrawl.org/

[2]We use the Language Detection Library available at https://github.com/shuyo/language-detection.
[3]https://www.elastic.co/

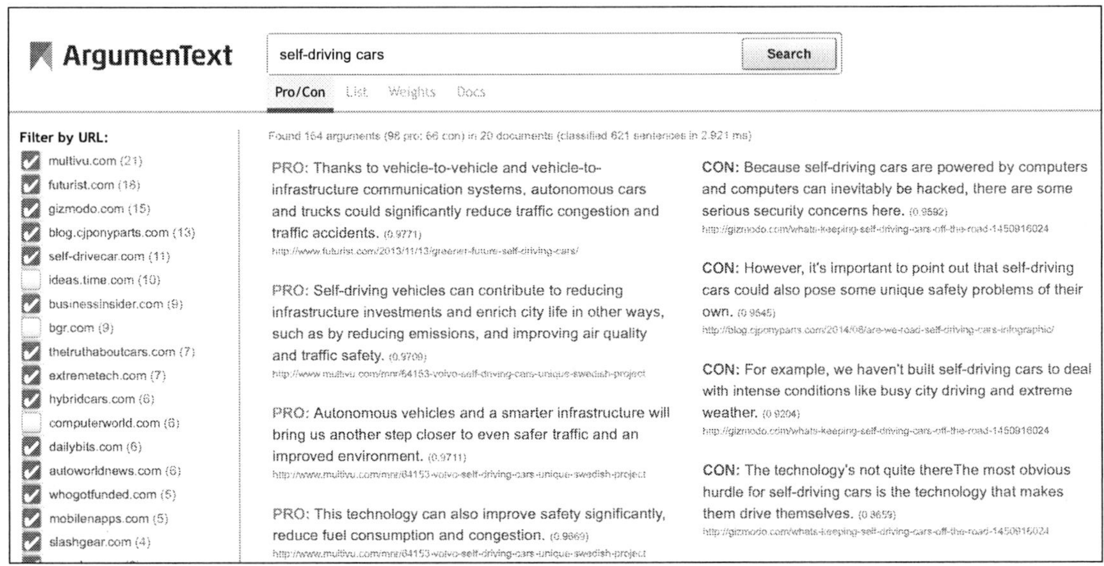

Figure 2: The UI's Pro/Con view, showing "pro" and "con" arguments for the query "self-driving cars".

sentences for eight topics. To cover a wider range of topics, we extended the corpus with 41 additional topics, such as "self-driving cars" and "basic income", using the same procedure: we queried Google for each topic, extracted 600 sentences for each topic from the search results, and had seven crowd workers annotate each sentence as either a "pro" argument, a "con" argument, or not an argument. As in Stab et al. (2018), we used MACE (Hovy et al., 2013) with a threshold of 0.9 to merge the annotations. This process provided us with an additional 22,691 annotated sentences, of which 27% are annotated as "pro" arguments, 18% as "con" arguments, and 55% as not an argument.

Using this extended corpus, we first trained the attention-based neural network presented by Stab et al. (2018) which classifies each sentence as *argument* or *no argument* with respect to the user-defined topic. Second, we apply a BiLSTM model to determine the stance (*pro* or *con*) of each topic-relevant argument.[4] To evaluate these models, we conduct a leave-one-topic-out evaluation—i.e., we trained the models on $n - 1$ topics and evaluated their performance on the left-out topic. The results show that the models benefit from the broader range of topics in our extended corpus. In particular, the performance of argument identification improves to 73.84 macro F score as compared to 65.8 macro F-score when trained on the initial corpus with eight topics.

The stance model is trained on the "pro" and "con" arguments and achieves an average macro F-score of 76.61 across all topics. It outperforms by a large margin a logistic regression baseline with unigram features achieving 67.92 macro F-score.

3.5 User Interface

The user interface resembles a typical search engine and allows queries for any controversial topic. To provide the user with arguments of the highest confidence, the retrieved arguments are sorted by the average confidence score of the argument extraction and stance recognition model. The user can choose between three argument-based views (1–3) and a document-based view (4):

(1) *Pro/Con view.* This view (Fig. 2) presents the user with a ranked list of "pro" and "con" arguments next to each other. To provide access to the origin and context of arguments, the document URL is displayed for each argument as well as the average confidence score.

(2) *List view.* This view provides the same information as the Pro/Con view, but shows all arguments interleaved in a single list instead of as two separate lists.

(3) *Attention Weights view.* To show which words most influence the classifier in its decision, we visualize attention weights for each word of an argumentative sentence. Important words are underlined in the view; the more intense the colour of the underlining, the more important

---

[4]Using two different models gave us slightly better results than using a single three-label model.

Topic	# pro	# con
cellphones	75	102
social networking	224	64
animal testing	455	609

Table 1: Arguments considered in the evaluation study.

the word is to the topic. The view is otherwise structured like the Pro/Con view.

(4) *Documents view.* This view ranks documents by the number of arguments they contain. It shows the number of "pro" and "con" arguments in bar charts next to the document titles, which can be expanded to list their arguments.

Each view features a filtering function for excluding arguments from specific sources (e.g., websites the user considers unreliable—see left side of Fig. 2). By default, arguments from all sources are shown.

4 Evaluation

As we believe that our system will be beneficial for a broad range of applications, we decided not to focus on a particular use case for the evaluation. Rather, we compared the output of the system against expert-created argument summaries from the online debate platform ProCon.org. For three randomly selected topics excluded from our training data, we extracted 1529 arguments from our system output (see Table 1). For the same topics, we then collected all expert-created "pro" and "con" arguments from ProCon.org.

In a manual evaluation study with three undergraduate and graduate students of computer science, we assessed the perceived quality of the system-discovered arguments and their overlap with expert-created arguments from ProCon.org.[5] Each student went through the entire list of system-discovered arguments and decided whether each one (i) could be mapped to one or more of the expert-created "pro" arguments; (ii) could be mapped to one or more of the expert-created "con" arguments; (iii) was not an argument, was nonsensical, or had the wrong stance; or (iv) was a completely new argument. Since our interest is in the perceived usefulness of the system rather than its ability to precisely match a carefully crafted gold standard, we simply aggregated votes for each of the above categories and averaged them for the three participants of the study.

The results provided some high-level insights about the potential and limitations of the system.

First, we discovered that our system's coverage (i.e., the percentage of expert-created arguments mapped to one or more arguments from our system) is very high—89% across the three topics. "Social networking", with 46 unique expert-curated arguments, was the only topic with less than perfect argument coverage (78%). Second, 12% of the aggregated votes indicated that a sentence is a completely new argument (i.e., a valid argument, not necessarily unique, with no expert-created counterpart)—a strong indicator that our system is not just usable to detect arguments for a broader range of topics as compared to expert-curated platforms, but also to get a more complete picture about individual topics. Third, we also discovered that on average 47% of arguments fell into category (iii), meaning that while the coverage of our system is high, precision is still a problem.

We also assessed the ranking by repeating the evaluation for only the top 10, 50, and 100 arguments. The percentage of system-discovered new arguments is identical across ranks. As for coverage, a bit more than 40% of expert-curated arguments can be found among the first ten results on average, while 71% can be found among the first 50 and 79% among the first 100. While nonsensical sentences were more common at lower ranks, the percentage of both non-arguments and arguments with incorrect stance remains stable across ranks at about 30% and 12%, respectively.

5 Conclusion and Future Work

We have presented ArgumenText,[6] an argument search system capable of retrieving "pro" and "con" arguments relevant to a given topic from heterogeneous sources.[7] By comparing the top-ranked results to arguments from debate portals, we have shown that our system achieves a high coverage compared to expert-created lists of arguments, and that it is even capable of finding additional valid arguments. In future work, we aim to improve the precision of the system by employing more sophisticated deep learning architectures like adversarial neural networks, to experiment with other argument ranking methods, and to adapt the approach to other languages such as German.

---

[5]For the sake of comparison, we considered only the ProCon.org summary sentence of each argument—e.g., "Animal testing is cruel and inhumane."

[6]Available at http://www.argumentsearch.com

[7]This work has been supported by the German Federal Ministry of Education and Research (BMBF) under the promotional reference 03VP02540 (ArgumenText).

References

Yamen Ajjour, Wei-Fan Chen, Johannes Kiesel, Henning Wachsmuth, and Benno Stein. 2017. Unit segmentation of argumentative texts. In *Proceedings of the 4th Workshop on Argument Mining*. Association for Computational Linguistics, pages 118–128. http://www.aclweb.org/anthology/W17-5115.

Richard Eckart de Castilho and Iryna Gurevych. 2014. A broad-coverage collection of portable NLP components for building shareable analysis pipelines. In *Proceedings of the Workshop on Open Infrastructures and Analysis Frameworks for HLT*. Association for Computational Linguistics and Dublin City University, pages 1–11. http://www.aclweb.org/anthology/W14-5201.

Steffen Eger, Johannes Daxenberger, and Iryna Gurevych. 2017. Neural end-to-end learning for computational argumentation mining. In *Proceedings of the 55th Annual Meeting of the Association for Computational Linguistics (Volume 1: Long Papers)*. Association for Computational Linguistics, pages 11–22. http://aclweb.org/anthology/P17-1002.

Ivan Habernal, Omnia Zayed, and Iryna Gurevych. 2016. C4Corpus: Multilingual Web-size corpus with free license. In *Proceedings of the 10th International Conference on Language Resources and Evaluation*. European Language Resources Association (ELRA), pages 914–922. http://www.lrec-conf.org/proceedings/lrec2016/pdf/388_Paper.pdf.

Dirk Hovy, Taylor Berg-Kirkpatrick, Ashish Vaswani, and Eduard Hovy. 2013. Learning whom to trust with MACE. In *Proceedings of the 2013 Conference of the North American Chapter of the Association for Computational Linguistics: Human Language Technologies*. Association for Computational Linguistics, pages 1120–1130. http://www.aclweb.org/anthology/N13-1132.

Xinyu Hua and Lu Wang. 2017. Understanding and detecting supporting arguments of diverse types. In *Proceedings of the 55th Annual Meeting of the Association for Computational Linguistics (Volume 2: Short Papers)*. Association for Computational Linguistics, pages 203–208. http://aclweb.org/anthology/P17-2032.

Ran Levy, Yonatan Bilu, Daniel Hershcovich, Ehud Aharoni, and Noam Slonim. 2014. Context dependent claim detection. In *Proceedings of COLING 2014, the 25th International Conference on Computational Linguistics: Technical Papers*. Dublin City University and Association for Computational Linguistics, pages 1489–1500. http://www.aclweb.org/anthology/C14-1141.

Marco Lippi and Paolo Torroni. 2015. MARGOT: A web server for argumentation mining. *Expert Systems with Applications* 65:292–303. https://doi.org/10.1016/j.eswa.2016.08.050.

Raquel Mochales-Palau and Marie-Francine Moens. 2009. Argumentation mining: The detection, classification and structure of arguments in text. In *Proceedings of the 12th International Conference on Artificial Intelligence and Law*. Association for Computing Machinery, pages 98–107. https://doi.org/10.1145/1568234.1568246.

Jan Pomikálek. 2011. *Removing Boilerplate and Duplicate Content from Web Corpora*. Doctoral thesis, Masaryk University, Faculty of Informatics, Brno, Czech Republic. https://is.muni.cz/th/45523/fi_d/phdthesis.pdf.

Ruty Rinott, Lena Dankin, Carlos Alzate Perez, Mitesh M. Khapra, Ehud Aharoni, and Noam Slonim. 2015. Show me your evidence – An automatic method for context dependent evidence detection. In *Proceedings of the 2015 Conference on Empirical Methods in Natural Language Processing*. Association for Computational Linguistics, pages 440–450. http://aclweb.org/anthology/D15-1050.

Stephen E. Robertson, Steve Walker, Susan Jones, Micheline M. Hancock-Beaulieu, and Mike Gatford. 1994. Okapi at TREC-3. In *Proceedings of the Third Text REtrieval Conference*. NIST, pages 109–126. http://trec.nist.gov/pubs/trec3/papers/city.ps.gz.

Christian Stab, Tristan Miller, and Iryna Gurevych. 2018. Cross-topic argument mining from heterogeneous sources using attention-based neural networks. *arXiv preprint* 1802.05758. https://arxiv.org/abs/1802.05758.

Henning Wachsmuth, Martin Potthast, Khalid Al Khatib, Yamen Ajjour, Jana Puschmann, Jiani Qu, Jonas Dorsch, Viorel Morari, Janek Bevendorff, and Benno Stein. 2017. Building an argument search engine for the Web. In *Proceedings of the 4th Workshop on Argument Mining*. Association for Computational Linguistics, pages 49–59. http://www.aclweb.org/anthology/W17-5106.

ClaimRank: Detecting Check-Worthy Claims in Arabic and English

Israa Jaradat[1], Pepa Gencheva[2]
Alberto Barrón-Cedeño[1], Lluís Màrquez[3]* and Preslav Nakov[1]
[1] Qatar Computing Research Institute, HBKU, Qatar
[2] Sofia University "St. Kliment Ohridski", Bulgaria
[3] Amazon, Barcelona, Spain
{ijaradat, albarron, pnakov}@hbku.edu.qa   pepa.k.gencheva@gmail.com   lluismv@amazon.com

Abstract

We present ClaimRank, an online system for detecting check-worthy claims. While originally trained on political debates, the system can work for any kind of text, e.g., interviews or regular news articles. Its aim is to facilitate manual fact-checking efforts by prioritizing the claims that fact-checkers should consider first. ClaimRank supports both Arabic and English, it is trained on actual annotations from nine reputable fact-checking organizations (PolitiFact, FactCheck, ABC, CNN, NPR, NYT, Chicago Tribune, The Guardian, and Washington Post), and thus it can mimic the claim selection strategies for each and any of them, as well as for the union of them all.

1 Introduction

The proliferation of fake news demands the attention of both investigative journalists and scientists. The need for automated fact-checking systems rises from the fact that manual fact-checking is both effort- and time-consuming. The first step towards building an automated fact-checking system is to identify the claims that are worth fact-checking.

We introduce ClaimRank, an automatic system to detect check-worthy claims in a given text. ClaimRank is multilingual and at the moment it is available for both English and Arabic. To the best of our knowledge, it is the only such system available for Arabic. ClaimRank is trained on actual annotations from nine reputable fact-checking organizations (PolitiFact, FactCheck, ABC, CNN, NPR, NYT, Chicago Tribune, The Guardian, and Washington Post), and thus it can be used to predict the claims by each of the individual sources, as well as their union. This is the only system we are aware of that offers such a capability.

2 Related Work

ClaimBuster is the first work to target check-worthiness (Hassan et al., 2015). It is trained on data annotated by students, professors, and journalists, and uses features such as sentiment, TF.IDF-weighted words, part-of-speech tags, and named entities. In contrast, (*i*) we have much richer features, (*ii*) we support English and Arabic, (*iii*) we learn from choices made by nine reputable fact-checking organizations, and (*iv*) we can mimic the selection strategy of each of them.

In our previous work, we focused on debates from the US 2016 Presidential Campaign and we used pre-existing annotations from online fact-checking reports by professional journalists (Gencheva et al., 2017). Here we use roughly the same features, with some differences (see below). However, (*i*) we train on more debates (seven instead of four for English, and also Arabic translations for two debates), (*ii*) we add support for Arabic, and (*iii*) we deploy a working system.

Patwari et al. (2017) focused on the 2016 US Election campaign as well and independently obtained their data in a similar way. However, they used less features, they did not mimic any specific website, nor did they deploy a working system.

3 System Overview

The run-time model is trained on seven English political debates and on the Arabic translations of two of the English debates. For evaluation purposes, we need to reserve some data for testing, and thus the model is trained on five English debates, and tested on the other two (either original English or their Arabic translations). In both cases, the data is first preprocessed and passed to the feature extraction module. The feature vectors are then fed to the model to generate predictions.

---

*Work conducted while this author was at QCRI.

Proceedings of NAACL-HLT 2018: Demonstrations, pages 26–30
New Orleans, Louisiana, June 2 - 4, 2018. ©2018 Association for Computational Linguistics

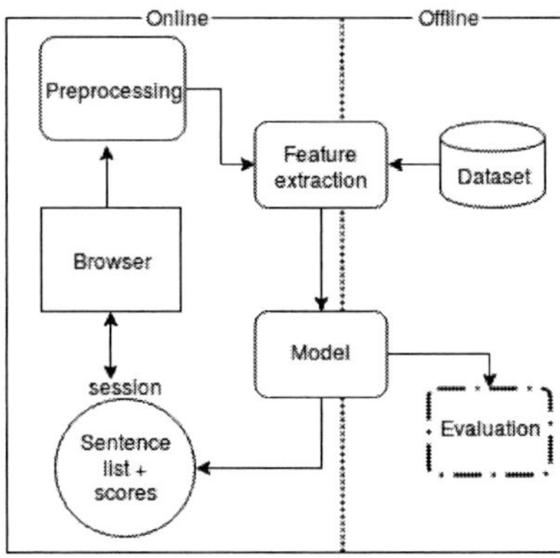

Figure 1: System architecture.

3.1 General Architecture

Figure 1 illustrates our general architecture. ClaimRank is accessible via a Web browser. When a user submits a text, the server handles the request by first detecting the language of the text using Python's `langdetect`. Then, the text is split into sentences using NLTK for English and a custom splitter for Arabic. An instance of the sentence list is stored in a session after being JSON-fied. After that, features are extracted for each sentence and fed into the model, which in turn generates the check-worthiness score for each sentence. Scores are displayed in the client next to each sentence, along with their corresponding color codes. Scores are also stored in the session object along with the sentence list as parallel arrays. In case the user wants the sentences sorted by their scores, or wants to mimic one of the annotation sources strategy in sentence selection, the server gets the text from the session, and re-scores/orders it and sends it back to the client.

3.2 Features

Here we do not propose new features, but rather reuse features that have been previously shown to work well for check-worthiness (Hassan et al., 2015; Gencheva et al., 2017).

From (Hassan et al., 2015), we include TF.IDF-weighted bag of words, part-of-speech tags, named entities as recognized by Alchemy API, sentiment scores, and sentence length (in tokens).

From (Gencheva et al., 2017), we adopt lexicon features, e.g., for bias (Recasens et al., 2013), for sentiment (Liu et al., 2005), for assertiveness (Hooper, 1974), and also for subjectivity.

We further use structural features, e.g., for location of the sentence within the debate/intervention, LDA topics (Blei et al., 2003), word embeddings (Mikolov et al., 2013), and discourse relations with respect to the neighboring sentences (Joty et al., 2015). More detail about the features can be found in the corresponding paper.

3.3 Model

In order to rank the English claims, we re-use the model from (Gencheva et al., 2017). In particular, we use a neural network with two hidden layers. We provide the features, which give information not only about the claim but also about its context, as an input to the network. The input layer is followed by the first hidden layer, which is composed of two hundred ReLU neurons (Glorot et al., 2011). The second hidden layer contains fifty neurons with the same ReLU activation function. Finally, there is a sigmoid unit, which classifies the sentence as check-worthy or not.

Apart from the class prediction, we also need to rank the claims based on the likelihood of their check-worthiness. For this, we use the probability that the model assigns to a claim to belong to the positive class. We train the model for 100 iterations using Stochastic Gradient Descent (LeCun et al., 1998).

3.4 Adaptation to Arabic

To handle Arabic along with English, we integrated some new tools. First, we had to add a language detector in order to use the appropriate sentence tokenizer for each language. For English, NLTK's (Loper and Bird, 2002) `sent_tokenize` handles splitting the text into sentences. However, for Arabic it can only split text based on the presence of the period (.) character. This is because other sentence endings — such as question marks— are different characters (e.g., the Arabic question mark is '؟', and not '?'). Hence, we used our custom regular expressions to split the Arabic text into sentences.

Next comes tokenization. For English, we used NLTK's tokenizer (Bird et al., 2009), while for Arabic we used Farasa's segmenter (Abdelali et al., 2016). For Arabic, tokenization is not enough; we also need word segmentation since conjunctions and clitics are commonly attached to the main word, e.g., ‫ه‬ + ‫بيت‬ + ‫و‬ ('and his house', lit. "and house his"). This causes explosion in the vocabulary size and data sparseness.

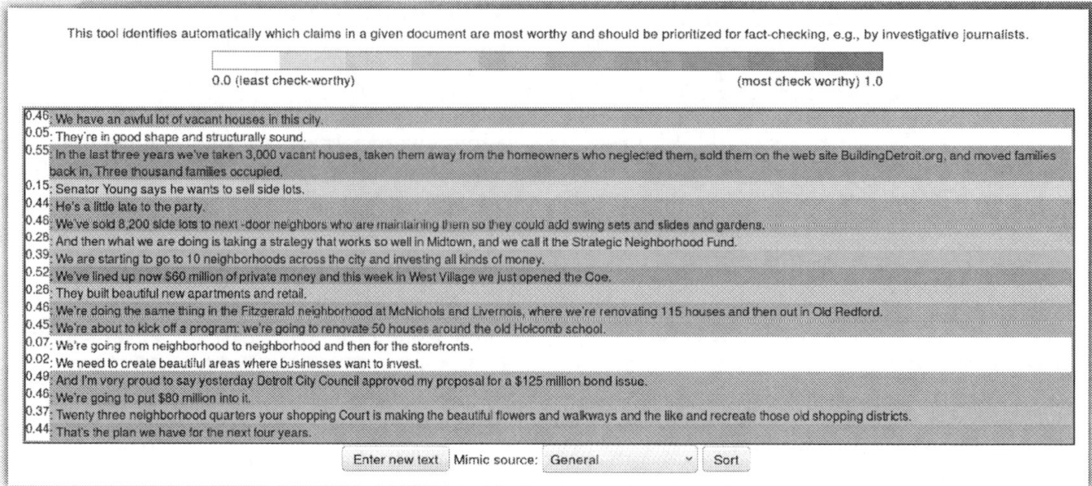

Figure 2: Screenshot of ClaimRank's output for an English presidential debate, in natural order.

We further needed a part-of-speech (POS) tagger for Arabic, for which we used Farasa (Abdelali et al., 2016), while we used NLTK's POS tagger for English (Bird et al., 2009). This yields different tagsets: for English, this is the Penn Treebank tagset (Marcus et al., 1993), while for Arabic this the Farasa tagset. Thus, we had to further map all POS tags to the same tagset: the Universal tagset (Petrov et al., 2012).

3.5 Evaluation

We train the system on five English political debates, and we test on two debates: either English or their Arabic translations. Note that, compared to our original model (Gencheva et al., 2017), here we use more debates: seven instead of four. Moreover, here we exclude some of the features, namely some debate-specific information (e.g., speaker, system messages), in order to be able to process any free text, and also discourse parse features, as we do not have a discourse parser for Arabic.

One of the most important components of the system that we had to port across languages were the word embeddings. We experimented with the following cross-language embeddings:
– *VecMap*: we used a parallel English-Arabic corpus of TED talks[1] (Cettolo et al., 2012) to generate monolingual embeddings (Arabic and English) using word2vec (Mikolov et al., 2013). Then we projected these embeddings into a joint vector space using VecMap (Artetxe et al., 2017).

– *MUSE embeddings*: In a similar fashion, we generated cross-language embeddings from the same TED talks using Facebook's supervised MUSE model (Lample et al., 2017) to project the Arabic and the English monolingual embeddings into a joint vector space.
– *Attract-Repel embeddings*: we used the pre-trained English-Arabic embeddings from Attract-Repel (Mrkšić et al., 2017).

Table 1 shows the system performance when predicting claims by any of the sources, using word2vec and the cross-language embeddings.[2] All results are well above a random baseline.

We can see some drop in MAP for English when using VecMap or MUSE, which is to be expected as the model needs to balance between preserving the original embeddings and projecting them into a joint space. The Attract-Repel vectors perform better for English, which is probably due to the monolingual synonymy/antonymy constraints that they impose (Vulić et al., 2017), thus yielding better vectors, even for English.

The overall MAP results for Arabic are competitive, compared to English. The best model is MUSE, while Attract-Repel is way behind, probably because, unlike VecMap and MUSE, its word embeddings are trained on unsegmented Arabic, which causes severe data sparseness issues.

---

[1]We used TED talks as they are conversational large corpora, which is somewhat close to the debates we train on.

[2]Note that these results are not comparable to those in (Gencheva et al., 2017) as we use a different evaluation setup: train/test split vs. cross-validation, debates that involve not only Hillary Clinton and Donald Trump, and we also disable the metadata and the discourse parse features.

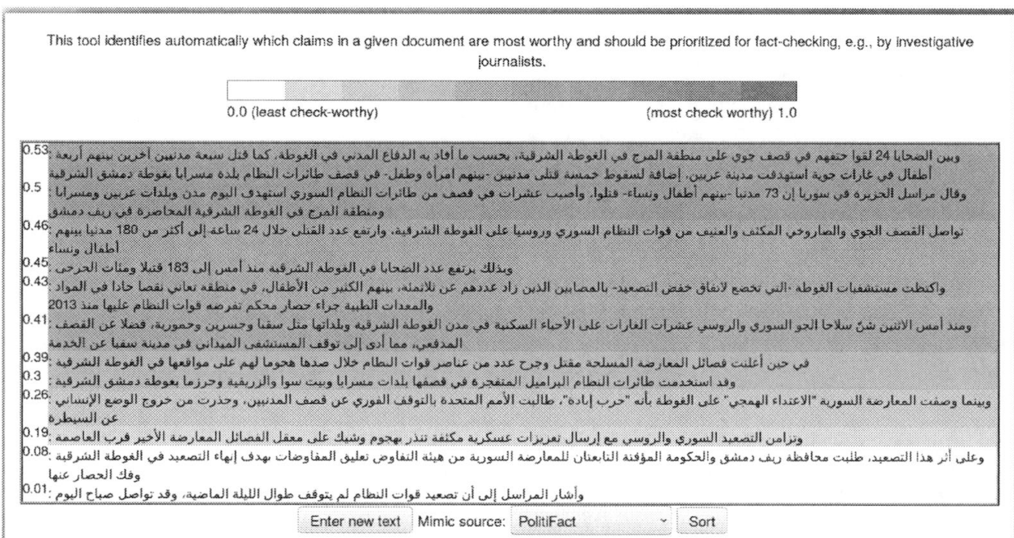

Figure 3: Screenshot of ClaimRank's output for an Arabic news article, sorted by score.

| System | **English** | | | | | | **Arabic** | | | | | |
	MAP	R-Pr	P@5	P@10	P@20	P@50	MAP	R-Pr	P@5	P@10	P@20	P@50
word2vec	0.323	0.330	0.80	0.60	0.45	0.38	—	—	—	—	—	—
VecMap	0.298	0.333	0.30	0.40	0.45	0.44	0.291	0.324	0.10	0.25	0.35	0.41
MUSE	0.319	0.332	0.40	0.45	0.50	0.49	0.302	0.331	0.10	0.25	0.38	0.48
Attract-Repel	0.342	0.385	0.40	0.45	0.50	0.46	0.263	0.312	0.10	0.15	0.30	0.41
Random	0.161	0.161	0.10	0.20	0.13	0.08						

Table 1: Performance when using different cross-language embeddings.

In the final system, we use MUSE vectors for both languages, which perform best overall: not only for MAP, but also P@20, and P@50, which are very important measures assuming that manual fact-checking can be done for up to 20 or up to 50 claims only (in fact, statistics show that eight out of our nine fact-checking organizations had no more than 50 claims checked per debate).

4 The System in Action

ClaimRank is available online.[3] Our systems' user interface consists of three views:
– *The text entry view*: composed of a text box, and a submit button.
– *The results view* shows the text split into sentences with scores reflecting the degree of check-worthiness, and each sentence has a color intensity that reflects its score range, as shown in Figure 2. The user can sort the results, or choose to mimic different media.
– *The sorted results view* shows the most check-worthy sentences first, as Figure 3 shows.

---

[3]http://claimrank.qcri.org

5 Conclusion and Future Work

We have presented ClaimRank —an online system for prioritizing check-worthy claims. Claim-Rank can help professional fact-checkers and journalists in their work as it can help them identify where they should focus their efforts first. The system learns from selections by nine reputable fact-checking organizations, and as a result, it can mimic the sentence selection strategies as applied by each and any of them, as well as for the union of them all.

While originally trained on a collection of political debates, ClaimRank can also work for other kinds of text, e.g., interviews or just regular news articles. Moreover, even though initially developed for English, the system was subsequently adapted to also support Arabic, using a combination of manual training data translation and cross-language embeddings.

In future work, we wold like to train the models on more political debates and speeches, as well as on other genres. We further plan to add support for more languages.

References

Ahmed Abdelali, Kareem Darwish, Nadir Durrani, and Hamdy Mubarak. 2016. Farasa: A fast and furious segmenter for Arabic. In *Proceedings of the Conference of the North American Chapter of the Association for Computational Linguistics*, NAACL-HLT '16, pages 11–16, San Diego, CA, USA.

Mikel Artetxe, Gorka Labaka, and Eneko Agirre. 2017. Learning bilingual word embeddings with (almost) no bilingual data. In *Proceedings of the 55th Annual Meeting of the Association for Computational Linguistics*, ACL '17, pages 451–462, Vancouver, Canada.

Steven Bird, Ewan Klein, and Edward Loper. 2009. *Natural Language Processing with Python*, 1st edition. O'Reilly Media, Inc.

David M Blei, Andrew Y Ng, and Michael I Jordan. 2003. Latent Dirichlet allocation. *Journal of Machine Learning Research*, 3(Jan):993–1022.

Mauro Cettolo, Christian Girardi, and Marcello Federico. 2012. WIT³: Web inventory of transcribed and translated talks. In *Proceedings of the 16th Conference of the European Association for Machine Translation*, EAMT '12, pages 261–268, Trento, Italy.

Pepa Gencheva, Preslav Nakov, Lluís Màrquez, Alberto Barrón-Cedeño, and Ivan Koychev. 2017. A context-aware approach for detecting worth-checking claims in political debates. In *Proceedings of the International Conference Recent Advances in Natural Language Processing*, RANLP '17, pages 267–276, Varna, Bulgaria.

Xavier Glorot, Antoine Bordes, and Yoshua Bengio. 2011. Deep sparse rectifier neural networks. In *Proceedings of the Fourteenth International Conference on Artificial Intelligence and Statistics*, PMLR '15, pages 315–323, Fort Lauderdale, FL, USA.

Naeemul Hassan, Chengkai Li, and Mark Tremayne. 2015. Detecting check-worthy factual claims in presidential debates. In *Proceedings of the 24th ACM International Conference on Information and Knowledge Management*, CIKM '15, pages 1835–1838, Melbourne, Australia.

Joan B. Hooper. 1974. *On Assertive Predicates*. Indiana University Linguistics Club. Indiana University Linguistics Club.

Shafiq Joty, Giuseppe Carenini, and Raymond T. Ng. 2015. CODRA: A novel discriminative framework for rhetorical analysis. *Comput. Linguist.*, 41(3):385–435.

Guillaume Lample, Ludovic Denoyer, and Marc'Aurelio Ranzato. 2017. Unsupervised machine translation using monolingual corpora only. *arXiv preprint arXiv:1711.00043*.

Yann LeCun, Léon Bottou, Yoshua Bengio, and Patrick Haffner. 1998. Gradient-based learning applied to document recognition. *Proceedings of the IEEE*, 86(11):2278–2324.

Bing Liu, Minqing Hu, and Junsheng Cheng. 2005. Opinion observer: Analyzing and comparing opinions on the web. In *Proceedings of the 14th International Conference on World Wide Web*, WWW '05, pages 342–351, New York, NY, USA.

Edward Loper and Steven Bird. 2002. NLTK: The natural language toolkit. In *Proceedings of the Workshop on Effective Tools and Methodologies for Teaching Natural Language Processing and Computational Linguistic*, ETMTNLP '02, pages 63–70, Philadelphia, PA, USA.

Mitchell P Marcus, Mary Ann Marcinkiewicz, and Beatrice Santorini. 1993. Building a large annotated corpus of English: The Penn Treebank. *Computational linguistics*, 19(2):313–330.

Tomas Mikolov, Ilya Sutskever, Kai Chen, Greg S Corrado, and Jeff Dean. 2013. Distributed representations of words and phrases and their compositionality. In *Advances in neural information processing systems*, NIPS '13, pages 3111–3119, Lake Tahoe, CA, USA.

Nikola Mrkšić, Ivan Vulić, Diarmuid Ó Séaghdha, Ira Leviant, Roi Reichart, Milica Gašić, Anna Korhonen, and Steve Young. 2017. Semantic specialisation of distributional word vector spaces using monolingual and cross-lingual constraints. *Transactions of the Association for Computational Linguistics*, 5:309–324.

Ayush Patwari, Dan Goldwasser, and Saurabh Bagchi. 2017. TATHYA: A multi-classifier system for detecting check-worthy statements in political debates. In *Proceedings of the ACM on Conference on Information and Knowledge Management*, CIKM '17, pages 2259–2262, Singapore.

Slav Petrov, Dipanjan Das, and Ryan McDonald. 2012. A universal part-of-speech tagset. In *Proceedings of the Eight International Conference on Language Resources and Evaluation*, LREC '12, pages 2089–2096, Istanbul, Turkey.

Marta Recasens, Cristian Danescu-Niculescu-Mizil, and Dan Jurafsky. 2013. Linguistic models for analyzing and detecting biased language. In *Proceedings of the 51st Annual Meeting of the Association for Computational Linguistics*, ACL '13, pages 1650–1659, Sofia, Bulgaria.

Ivan Vulić, Nikola Mrkšić, Roi Reichart, Diarmuid Ó Séaghdha, Steve Young, and Anna Korhonen. 2017. Morph-fitting: Fine-tuning word vector spaces with simple language-specific rules. In *Proceedings of the 55th Annual Meeting of the Association for Computational Linguistics*, ACL '17, pages 56–68, Vancouver, Canada.

360° Stance Detection

Sebastian Ruder, John Glover, Afshin Mehrabani, Parsa Ghaffari
Aylien Ltd., Dublin, Ireland
`{sebastian,john,afshin,parsa}@aylien.com`

Abstract

The proliferation of fake news and filter bubbles makes it increasingly difficult to form an unbiased, balanced opinion towards a topic. To ameliorate this, we propose 360° Stance Detection, a tool that aggregates news with multiple perspectives on a topic. It presents them on a spectrum ranging from support to opposition, enabling the user to base their opinion on multiple pieces of diverse evidence.

1   Introduction

The growing epidemic of fake news in the wake of the election cycle for the 45th President of the United States has revealed the danger of staying within our filter bubbles. In light of this development, research in detecting false claims has received renewed interest (Wang, 2017). However, identifying and flagging false claims may not be the best solution, as putting a strong image, such as a red flag, next to an article may actually entrench deeply held beliefs (Lyons, 2017).

A better alternative would be to provide additional evidence that will allow a user to evaluate multiple viewpoints and decide with which they agree. To this end, we propose 360° Stance Detection, a tool that provides a wide view of a topic from different perspectives to aid with forming a balanced opinion. Given a topic, the tool aggregates relevant news articles from different sources and leverages recent advances in stance detection to lay them out on a spectrum ranging from support to opposition to the topic.

Stance detection is the task of estimating whether the attitude expressed in a text towards a given topic is 'in favour', 'against', or 'neutral'. We collected and annotated a novel dataset, which associates news articles with a stance towards a specified topic. We then trained a state-of-the-art stance detection model (Augenstein et al., 2016) on this dataset.

The stance detection model is integrated into the 360° Stance Detection website as a web service. Given a news search query and a topic, the tool retrieves news articles matching the query and analyzes their stance towards the topic. The demo then visualizes the articles as a 2D scatter plot on a spectrum ranging from 'against' to 'in favour' weighted by the prominence of the news outlet and provides additional links and article excerpts as context.[1]

The interface allows the user to obtain an overview of the range of opinion that is exhibited towards a topic of interest by various news outlets. The user can quickly collect evidence by skimming articles that fall on different parts of this opinion spectrum using the provided excerpts or peruse any of the original articles by following the available links.

2   Related work

Until recently, stance detection had been mostly studied in debates (Walker et al., 2012; Hasan and Ng, 2013) and student essays (Faulkner, 2014). Lately, research in stance detection focused on Twitter (Rajadesingan and Liu, 2014; Mohammad et al., 2016; Augenstein et al., 2016), particularly with regard to identifying rumors (Qazvinian et al., 2011; Lukasik et al., 2015; Zhao et al., 2015). More recently, claims and headlines in news have been considered for stance detection (Ferreira and Vlachos, 2016), which require recognizing entailment relations between claim and article.

---

[1]The demo can be accessed here: `http://bit.do/ aylien-stance-detection-demo`. A screencast of the demo is available here: `https://www.youtube. com/watch?v=WYckOr2NhFM`.

Proceedings of NAACL-HLT 2018: Demonstrations, pages 31–35
New Orleans, Louisiana, June 2 - 4, 2018. ©2018 Association for Computational Linguistics

TOPIC	Wind farm
Headline	State House Puts Curbs On Wind Farms Pending Study
Article	The Tennessee House on Thursday voted to put curbs on wind farms pending a study. Senator Lamar Alexander said, "I am glad the Tennessee General Assembly is taking steps to prohibit the construction of some Tennessee wind farms and instead give the state a chance to study the issue. This will give Tennesseans the opportunity to evaluate whether we want our landscape littered with wind turbines that are over two times as tall as the skyboxes at the University of Tennessee football stadium and produce only a small amount of unreliable electricity."

Figure 1: Interface provided to annotators. Annotation instructions are not shown.

3 Dataset

3.1 Task definition

The objective of stance detection in our case is to classify the stance of an author's news article towards a given topic as 'in favour', 'against', or 'neutral'. Our setting differs from previous instantiations of stance detection in two ways: a) We focus on excerpts from news articles, which are longer and may be more complex than tweets; and b) we do not aim to classify a news article with regard to its agreement with a claim or headline but with regard to its stance towards a topic.

3.2 Data collection

We collect data using the AYLIEN News API[2], which provides search capabilities for news articles enriched with extracted entities and other metadata. As most extracted entities have a neutral stance or might not be of interest to users, we take steps to compile a curated list of topics, which we detail in the following.

Topics We define a topic to include named entities, but also more abstract, controversial keywords such as 'gun control' and 'abortion'. We compile a diverse list of topics that people are likely to be interested in from several sources: a) We retrieve the top 10 entities with the most mentions in each month from November 2015 to June 2017 and filter out entities that are not locations, persons, or organizations and those that are generally perceived as neutral; b) we manually curate a list of current important political figures; and c) we use DBpedia to retrieve a list of controversial topics. Specifically, we included all of the topics mentioned in the Wikipedia

Topic type	# topics	Examples
Popular	44	Arsenal F.C., Russia
Controversial	300	Abortion, Polygamy
Political	22	Ted Cruz, Xi Jinping
Total	366	

Table 1: Types and numbers of retrieved topics.

list of controversial issues[3] and converted them to DBpedia resource URIs (e.g. `http://en.wikipedia.org/wiki/Abortion` → `http://dbpedia.org/resource/Abortion`) in order to facilitate linking between topics and DBpedia metadata. We then used DBpedia types (Auer et al., 2007) to filter out all entities of type Place, Person and Organisation. Finally, we ranked the remaining topics based on their number of unique outbound edges within the DBpedia graph as a measure of prominence, and picked the top 300. We show the final composition of topics in Table 1. For each topic, we retrieve the most relevant articles using the News API from November 2015 to July 2017.

Annotation For annotation, we need to trade-off the complexity and cost of annotation with the agreement between annotators. Annotating entire news articles places a large cognitive load on the annotator, which leads to fatigue and inaccurate annotations. For this reason, we choose to annotate excerpts from news articles. In internal studies, we found that providing a context window of 2-3 sentences around the mention of the entity together with the headline provides suffi-

---

[2]`https://newsapi.aylien.com/`

[3]`https://en.wikipedia.org/wiki/Wikipedia:List_of_controversial_issues`

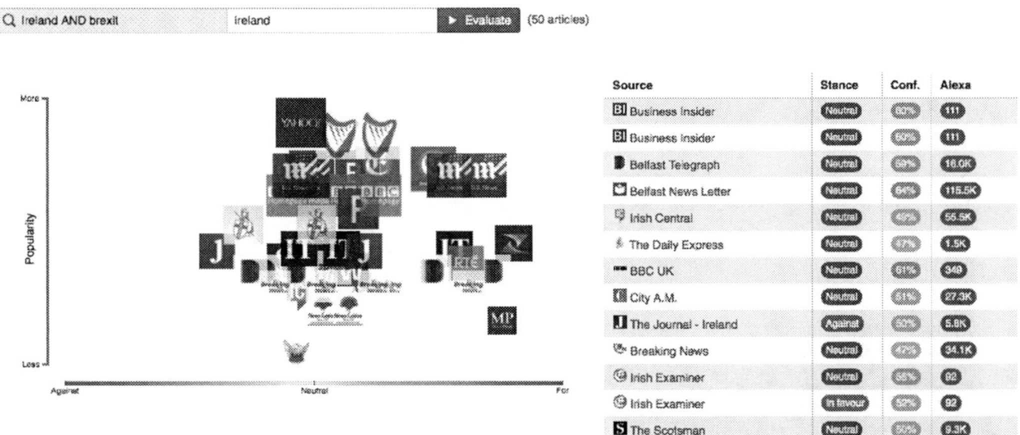

Figure 2: 360° Stance Detection interface. News articles about a query, i.e. 'Ireland AND brexit' are visualized based on their stance towards a specified topic, i.e. 'ireland' and the prominence of the source. Additional information is provided in a table on the right, which allows to skim article excerpts or follow a link to the source.

cient context to produce a reliable annotation. If the entity is not mentioned explicitly, we provide the first paragraph of the article and the headline as context. We annotate the collected data using CrowdFlower with 3 annotators per example using the interface in Figure 1. We retain all examples where at least 2 annotators agree, which amounts to 70.5% of all examples.

Final dataset The final dataset consists of 32,227 pairs of news articles and topics annotated with their stance. In particular, 47.67% examples have been annotated with 'neutral', 21.9% with 'against', 19.05% with 'in favour', and 11.38% with 'unrelated'. We use 70% of examples for training, 20% for validation, and 10% for testing according to a stratified split. As we expect to encounter novel and unknown entities in the wild, we ensure that entities do not overlap across splits and that we only test on unseen entities.

4   Model

We train a Bidirectional Encoding model (Augenstein et al., 2016), which has achieved state-of-the-art results for Twitter stance detection on our dataset. The model encodes the entity using a bidi-

rectional LSTM (BiLSTM)[4], which is then used to initialize a BiLSTM that encodes the article and produces a prediction. To reduce the sequence length, we use the same context window that was presented to annotators for training the LSTM. We use pretrained GloVe embeddings (Pennington et al., 2014) and tune hyperparameters on a validation set. The best model achieves a test accuracy of 61.7 and a macro-averaged test F1 score of 56.9.[5] It significantly outperforms baselines such as a bag-of-n-grams (accuracy: 46.3; F1: 44.2).

5   360° Stance Detection Demo

The interactive demo interface of 360° Stance Detection, which can be seen in Figure 2, takes two inputs: a news search query, which is used to retrieve news articles using News API, and a stance target topic, which is used as the target of the stance detection model. For good results, the stance target should also be included as a keyword in the news search query. Multiple keywords can be provided as the query by connecting them with

---

[4]We tried other encoding strategies, such as averaging pretrained embeddings, but this performed best.

[5]These scores are comparable to those achieved in (Augenstein et al., 2016). Compared to tweets, stance in news is often more subtle and thus more challenging to detect, while our dataset contains more diverse entities than previous ones.

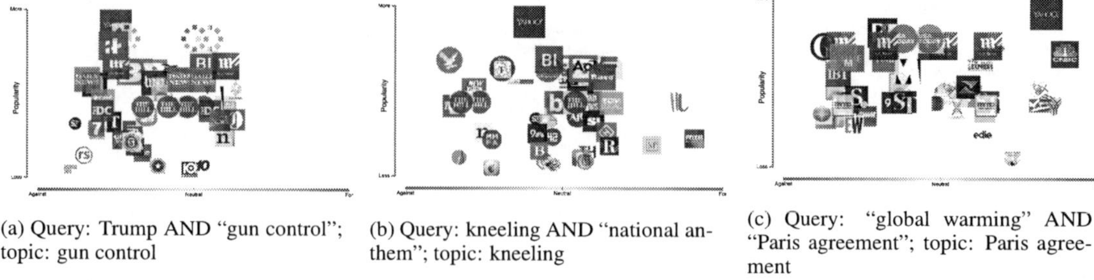

(a) Query: Trump AND "gun control"; topic: gun control

(b) Query: kneeling AND "national anthem"; topic: kneeling

(c) Query: "global warming" AND "Paris agreement"; topic: Paris agreement

Figure 3: 360° Stance Detection visualizations for example queries and topics.

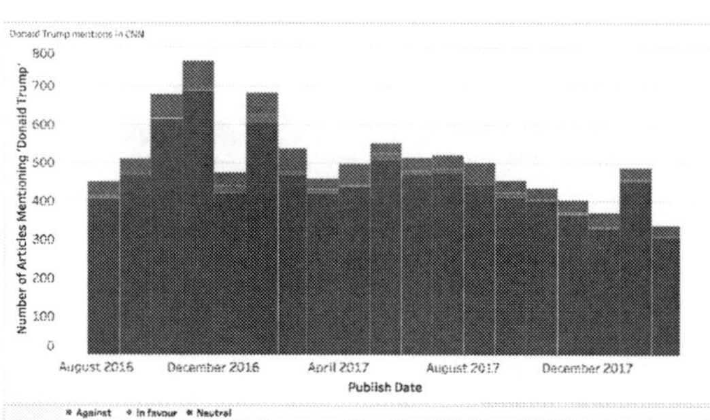

Figure 4: Visualization distribution of stance towards Donald Trump and number of CNN news articles mentioning Donald Trump from August 2016 to January 2018.

'AND' or 'OR' as in Figure 2.

When these two inputs are provided, the application retrieves a predefined number of news articles (up to 50) that match the first input, and analyzes their stance towards the target (the second input) using the stance detection model. The stance detection model is exposed as a web service and returns for each article-target entity pair a stance label (i.e. one of 'in favour', 'against' or 'neutral') along with a probability.[6]

The demo then visualizes the collected news articles as a 2D scatter plot with each (x,y) coordinate representing a single news article from a particular outlet that matched the user query. The x-axis shows the stance of the article in the range $[-1, 1]$. The y-axis displays the prominence of the news outlet that published the article in the range $[1, 1000000]$, measured by its Alexa ranking[7]. A table displays the provided information in a complementary format, listing the news outlets of the articles, the stance labels, confidence scores, and

prominence rankings. Excerpts of the articles can be scanned by hovering over the news outlets in the table and the original articles can be read by clicking on the source.

360° Stance Detection is particularly useful to gain an overview of complex or controversial topics and to highlight differences in their perception across different outlets. We show visualizations for example queries and three controversial topics in Figure 3. By extending the tool to enable retrieval of a larger number of news articles and more fine-grained filtering, we can employ it for general news analysis. For instance, we can highlight the volume and distribution of the stance of news articles from a single news outlet such as CNN towards a specified topic as in Figure 4.

6 Conclusion

We have introduced 360° Stance Detection, a tool that aims to provide evidence and context in order to assist the user with forming a balanced opinion towards a controversial topic. It aggregates news with multiple perspectives on a topic, annotates them with their stance, and visualizes them on a spectrum ranging from support to opposition, allowing the user to skim excerpts of the articles or read the original source. We hope that this tool will demonstrate how NLP can be used to help combat filter bubbles and fake news and to aid users in obtaining evidence on which they can base their opinions.

Acknowledgments

Sebastian Ruder is supported by the Irish Research Council Grant Number EBPPG/2014/30 and Science Foundation Ireland Grant Number SFI/12/RC/2289.

---

[6]We leave confidence calibration (Guo et al., 2017) for future work.

[7]https://www.alexa.com/

References

Sören Auer, Christian Bizer, Georgi Kobilarov, Jens Lehmann, Richard Cyganiak, and Zachary Ives. 2007. Dbpedia: A nucleus for a web of open data. In *The semantic web*, Springer, pages 722–735.

Isabelle Augenstein, Tim Rocktäschel, Andreas Vlachos, and Kalina Bontcheva. 2016. Stance Detection with Bidirectional Conditional Encoding. In *Proceedings of the 2016 Conference on Empirical Methods in Natural Language Processing.* http://arxiv.org/abs/1606.05464.

Adam Faulkner. 2014. Automated classification of stance in student essays: An approach using stance target information and the wikipedia link-based measure. *Science* 376(12):86.

William Ferreira and Andreas Vlachos. 2016. Emergent: a novel data-set for stance classification. In *Proceedings of the 2016 conference of the North American chapter of the association for computational linguistics: Human language technologies.* pages 1163–1168.

Chuan Guo, Geoff Pleiss, Yu Sun, and Kilian Q. Weinberger. 2017. On Calibration of Modern Neural Networks. *Proceedings of ICML 2017* http://arxiv.org/abs/1706.04599.

Kazi Saidul Hasan and Vincent Ng. 2013. Stance classification of ideological debates: Data, models, features, and constraints. In *Proceedings of the Sixth International Joint Conference on Natural Language Processing.* pages 1348–1356.

Michal Lukasik, Trevor Cohn, and Kalina Bontcheva. 2015. Classifying tweet level judgements of rumours in social media. *arXiv preprint arXiv:1506.00468* .

Tessa Lyons. 2017. News Feed FYI: Replacing Disputed Flags with Related Articles. https://bit.ly/2BTVuOx.

Saif Mohammad, Svetlana Kiritchenko, Parinaz Sobhani, Xiaodan Zhu, and Colin Cherry. 2016. Semeval-2016 task 6: Detecting stance in tweets. In *Proceedings of the 10th International Workshop on Semantic Evaluation (SemEval-2016).* pages 31–41.

Jeffrey Pennington, Richard Socher, and Christopher D. Manning. 2014. Glove: Global Vectors for Word Representation. *Proceedings of the 2014 Conference on Empirical Methods in Natural Language Processing* pages 1532–1543. https://doi.org/10.3115/v1/D14-1162.

Vahed Qazvinian, Emily Rosengren, Dragomir R Radev, and Qiaozhu Mei. 2011. Rumor has it: Identifying misinformation in microblogs. In *Proceedings of the Conference on Empirical Methods in Natural Language Processing.* Association for Computational Linguistics, pages 1589–1599.

Ashwin Rajadesingan and Huan Liu. 2014. Identifying users with opposing opinions in twitter debates. In *International conference on social computing, behavioral-cultural modeling, and prediction.* Springer, pages 153–160.

Marilyn A Walker, Pranav Anand, Robert Abbott, and Ricky Grant. 2012. Stance classification using dialogic properties of persuasion. In *Proceedings of the 2012 Conference of the North American Chapter of the Association for Computational Linguistics: Human Language Technologies.* Association for Computational Linguistics, pages 592–596.

William Yang Wang. 2017. "Liar , Liar Pants on Fire": A New Benchmark Dataset for Fake News Detection. In *Proceedings of the 55th Annual Meeting of the Association for Computational Linguistics (ACL 2017).*

Zhe Zhao, Paul Resnick, and Qiaozhu Mei. 2015. Enquiring minds: Early detection of rumors in social media from enquiry posts. In *Proceedings of the 24th International Conference on World Wide Web.* International World Wide Web Conferences Steering Committee, pages 1395–1405.

DebugSL: An Interactive Tool for Debugging Sentiment Lexicons

Andrew T. Schneider, John N. Male, Saroja Bhogadhi, Eduard C. Dragut
Temple University, Philadelphia, PA
Computer and Information Sciences Department
`atschneider, john.male, tug63697, edragut@temple.edu`

Abstract

We introduce `DebugSL`, a visual (Web) debugging tool for sentiment lexicons (SLs). Its core component implements our algorithms for the automatic detection of polarity inconsistencies in SLs. An inconsistency is a set of words and/or word-senses whose polarity assignments cannot all be simultaneously satisfied. `DebugSL` finds inconsistencies of small sizes in SLs and has a rich user interface which helps users in the correction process.

1 Introduction

The problem of Sentiment Analysis (SA) is that of identifying the polarity (*positive, negative, neutral*) of the speaker towards the topic of a given piece of text. SA techniques are facilitated by Sentiment Lexicons (SLs), which are lists of words or word-senses tagged with their *a priori* polarity probability values. A tag may be a single value, e.g., *positive*, or it may be a distribution. The large number of SLs and methods to generate them renders errors and disagreements inevitable (Liu, 2015; Feldman, 2013). Numerous works raise the issue of polarity disagreements between SLs and its negative impact on SA tasks (Potts, 2011; Emerson and Declerck, 2014; Liu, 2015). Schneider and Dragut (2015) gives examples of SLs that disagree on up to 78% of their annotations and shows that the accuracy of an SA task can improve by 8.5% by correcting a modest number of inconsistencies in an SL.

Dragut et al. (2012) introduces the Polarity Consistency Problem (PCP) which provides a framework for identifying inconsistent polarity annotations in SLs based on the interaction between words and their underlying shared senses (synsets). Dragut et al. (2015); Dragut and Fellbaum (2014); Schneider and Dragut (2015) further developed the theoretical basis of the PCP.

In this work we present `DebugSL`, an SL consistency checker and debugger system that implements the methods developed in those works for solving the PCP, in a user friendly environment. Given an SL as input, `DebugSL` automatically detects entries with potentially incorrect polarity tags and displays these entries in a bipartite graph to facilitate correction efforts. `DebugSL` interfaces with external sources, such as Dictionary.com, to assist in the debugging process.

2 Background

We give a brief overview of the PCP and our methods to solve it in this section. The interested reader is directed to Dragut et al. (2012, 2015); Dragut and Fellbaum (2014); Schneider and Dragut (2015) for full details.

2.1 Polarity Probability

Every word and synset is taken to have an underlying discrete probability distribution, called a **polarity distribution**, carrying the *a priori* probability it is used with a positive, negative, or neutral sense, P_+, P_- and P_0, respectively, with the requirements that $P_+, P_-, P_0 \geq 0$ and $\sum_p P_p = 1$. For instance, the synset *"worthy of reliance or trust"* of the adjective `reliable` has $P_+ = .375, P_- = .0$ and $P_0 = .625$ in the SL SentiWordNet (Baccianella et al., 2010). The polarity distribution of a word is a weighted sum over the polarity distributions of its senses. For word w: $P_p(w) = \sum_{s \in S(w)} f(w, s) \cdot P_p(s)$, where $P_p(s)$ is the polarity value of synset s with polarity $p \in \{+, -, 0\}$, $S(w)$ is the set of all synsets of w, and $f(w, s)$ denotes the weight between word w and sense s. The weights may be the word–synset usage frequencies; they may also be drawn from uniform, Zipfian, or geometric distributions. In all cases the weights are normalized so that $\sum_{s \in S(w)} f(w, s) = 1$ for all w.

Proceedings of NAACL-HLT 2018: Demonstrations, pages 36–40
New Orleans, Louisiana, June 2 - 4, 2018. ©2018 Association for Computational Linguistics

2.2 Word Polarity Value

Word SLs often only give a discrete annotation tag for a word, one of the values: *positive(+)*, *negative(-)*, or *neutral(0)*. We call this a **polarity value**. We determine polarity value for a word as follows:

$$\text{polarity}(w) = \begin{cases} + & \text{if } P_+ > P_- + P_0, \\ - & \text{if } P_- > P_+ + P_0, \\ 0 & \text{otherwise} \end{cases}$$

Schneider and Dragut (2015) discusses alternatives for these equations.

2.3 Polarity Consistency

In this context, the PCP amounts to the following question:

Given a set of words and polarity tags from an SL, does there exist an assignment of polarities to the word senses such that all of the word polarity values agree with the SL tags?

If the answer is **yes** we say the SL in question is *consistent*. If the answer is **no** we say the SL is *inconsistent*.

Figure 1 shows a network of 4 words with their annotation tags from (Opinion Finder) OF (Wilson et al., 2005) and their related synsets which comprise a connected component. w_3 : *pertinacity* and w_4 : *tenacity* are tagged $-$ and $+$, respectively. Since both words share only one synset, s_3, there is no polarity distribution for s_3 which can simultaneously satisfy the polarity value demands of both w_3 and w_4. Hence this component is inconsistent.

2.4 Solving the PCP via Linear Programming

Using the above definitions, the conversion to an LP problem follows a direct procedure. We refer the interested reader to Schneider and Dragut (2015) for the details.

`DebugSL` supports both discrete and continuous polarity distributions of the synsets. In the discrete case, the synset polarity distributions are restricted to the set $\{0,1\}$, i.e., exactly one of P_+, P_-, or P_0 is 1 and the other two are 0, for each synset; this corresponds to an integer LP problem. For the continuous case, each of P_+, P_-, or P_0 is in the range $[0,1]$, which corresponds to a general LP problem over real numbers. In the discrete case PCP is NP-complete, while for the continuous case the problem is solvable in polynomial time (Dragut et al., 2012; Schneider and Dragut, 2015).

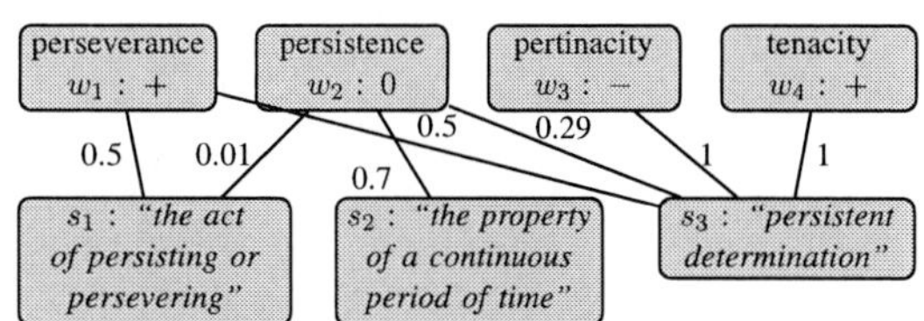

Figure 1: A network of 4 words and 3 synsets. Edges represent word–synset relations, weighted by frequency.

3 Supporting SL Debugging

A key capability of `DebugSL` is that of isolating a (small) subset of words/synsets that is polarity inconsistent, but becomes consistent if one element is removed; we call this an Irreducible Polarity Inconsistent Subset (IPIS). Fixing an SL via IPIS isolation proceeds iteratively: (1) isolate an IPIS, (2) determine a repair for this IPIS, (3) if the model is still infeasible, return to step 1. `DebugSL` can deterministically identify an IPIS, but it cannot deterministically decide which inconsistent words and/or senses to adjust as this is simply not an objective decision. Much like a software debugger, which can identify a known programming error, say the use of an undefined variable, but cannot assign a value to the variable, our debugger can identify inconsistent components, but it does not decide which elements to adjust. In Figure 1, minimally one of `pertinacity(-)` and `tenacity(+)` must be adjusted, but the decision as to which requires user feedback.

The example of Figure 1 belies the complexity of the PCP. `DebugSL` employs a divide and conquer approach, dividing an instance of PCP into the connected components of the bipartite word–synset graph, then solving for each component separately. Running `DebugSL` on OF generates 1178 such components for adjectives alone; the largest component has 914 unique words and 1880 unique synsets. Manually checking such SLs is unrealistic.

4 System Overview

`DebugSL` follows a four-step procedure to identify and reduce lexicon inconsistency. (1) The user uploads a formatted SL to the `DebugSL` system. (2) A server-side program uses the lexical database WordNet(WN) (Fellbaum, 1998) to form the underlying word–synset graph of the SL and checks for inconsistencies. (3) Inconsistent components are returned to the client and they are displayed

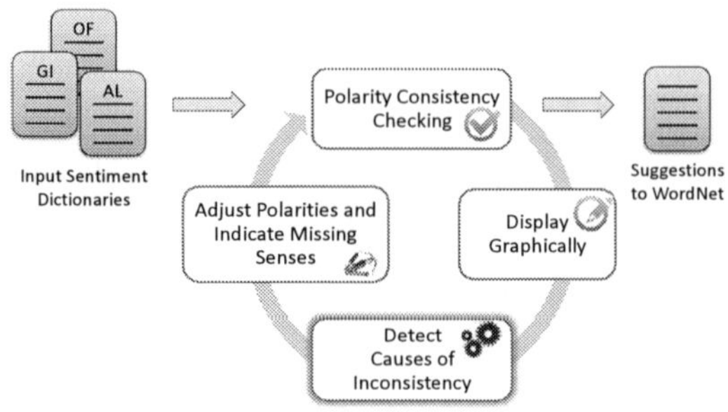

Figure 2: `DebugSL` process flow

graphically for inspection. (4) The user dynamically interacts with the components, such as looking up information on the words/synsets and adjusting their polarities. The user can repeat the process as desired.

1. Input. The user begins by uploading an SL to `DebugSL` and specifying various interface options, such as the part of speech and the version of WN to use. After the lexicon has been successfully uploaded, the user can download the (modified) lexicon, or save it in the system.

2. Lexicon Inconsistency Checking. A server-side Java program builds the connected components of word–synset linkage. `DebugSL` checks the consistency of each connected component. Inconsistent components are returned to the client.

3. Component Display. A JavaScript process receives the inconsistent components from the server and formats them to be understood by the graphing library SigmaJS which displays the inconsistent components to the user.

4. Interactive Viewing and User Analysis. The interactive viewing is essential to our tool because it allows a user to focus on a small set of inconsistent words or synsets, make adjustments, and re-run the program to see the effects.

5 Software

`DebugSL` is developed using web technologies. Client side work is completed using HTML 5, CSS, and JavaScript. The graphs are structured using the open source JavaScript library SigmaJS. The client-side program is programmed in Java and is called through a Java Servlet. For linear programming `DebugSL` employs the GUROBI LP solver (`www.gurobi.com`). Apache Tomcat is used as the local server.

5.1 Interactive Features

Customizable Polarity Display. `DebugSL` displays the word polarities from the uploaded SL on the word–synset graph. By default, the polarities are shown by node color: green, red, and grey for *positive*, *negative*, and *neutral*, respectively. These color choices are customizable. The user can switch to display polarities by symbols: $+$, $-$, and 0, instead, or use both symbols and colors.

Component and Word Selection. Inconsistent components are listed on the left represented by the first word of each component. An ellipsis indicates the presence of additional words. When a component is selected, its words are expanded into a sublist (Figure 3a on the left).

All Viewing and Progressive Viewing. Two modes of viewing the graph are available. In *All Viewing* mode all checked words and synsets are visible. Clicking on a word or synset hides any edges not associated with that word or synset.

Progressive Viewing mode allows the user to build the desired connected graph by progressively adding words. Clicking a word node hides other words and reveals its associated synsets. Clicking a revealed synset hides all but the associated words and edges. The user may use any selected word or synset as a base for building the graph. Holding shift allows words to be added progressively.

Dictionary Query. The user may look up the senses of any word from an online dictionary by right-clicking. This functionality is currently implemented to interface with three online dictionaries: Merriam-Webster (`www.merriam-webster.com`), Dictionary.com (`www.dictionary.com`), and the Free Dictionary (`www.thefreedictionary.com`). The dictionary appears to the right of the graph window with the results of the word lookup. Right-clicking a new word, automatically updates the dictionary area.

5.2 Identifying Missing Senses in WordNet

In some cases, when an inconsistency is identified, the user may decide that the polarity assignments are correct and the error is in fact due to a missing sense in WN. `DebugSL` allows the user to check for potentially missing senses in WN. As an example, the verbs "tantalize" and "taunt," have positive and negative polarities, respectively, in Opinion Finder (Wilson et al., 2005). They also have a shared, unique sense in WN. By our formula-

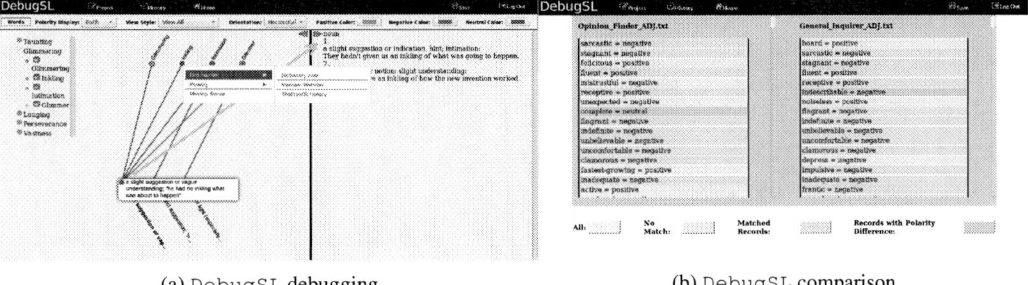

(a) <code>DebugSL</code> debugging   (b) <code>DebugSL</code> comparison

Figure 3: `DebugSL` screenshots

tion, this leads to a contradiction. In this case the Free Dictionary gives a second sense of tantalize that is missing from WN: *"to be strongly attractive to..."*. This sense conveys a positive polarity. Hence, tantalize conveys a positive sentiment when used with this sense, and the inconsistency is not due to a mislabeling in the SL.

When the user utilizes the online dictionary lookup feature, the dictionary senses (definitions) of the word are automatically matched to their corresponding best matching synsets in the WN graph, using the Levenshtein edit distance and the Gale-Shapley stable marriage matching algorithm (Gale and Shapley, 1962). If a relevant sense appears to be missing from WN, the user can log a note of the missing synset with us and we can, in turn, provide this information to the WN team (Dragut and Fellbaum, 2014).

6 Demonstration

We present two main scenarios to demonstrate the practical usefulness of `DebugSL`, screenshots of which are shown in Figure 3. The source code is available at `https://github.com/atschneid/DebugSL`.

1. Iterative SL Debugging: This commences with a user uploading an SL, $\mathcal{L}$. The user must turn a few knobs, e.g., select the part of speech, weighting scheme, and WN version. `DebugSL` displays the discovered sets of polarity inconsistencies on the left side. Let $\mathcal{I}$ be an IPIS the user has selected. This demo scenario has two paths:

Debugging. The user attempts to correct polarity values assigned to the entries in $\mathcal{I}$. Most IPISs consist of up to 4 words; very few have more than 8. This aids in holding the user's focus. The user can use the bipartite view in `DebugSL` to analyze the words and their sense and determine if some entries in $\mathcal{I}$ have wrong polarity tags. Upon iden-

tifying a mislabeled entry in $\mathcal{I}$, the user can edit its polarity value (see Figure 3a), then repeat the consistency check again on the revised SL, and analyze any new or remaining IPISs. At any time, the user can save, revisit, and eventually download the revised version of $\mathcal{L}$.

Missing Senses. If all the entries in $\mathcal{I}$ have the correct polarity tags, there remains the possibility that WN has incomplete information. `DebugSL` allows the user to compare the synsets of a word w in $\mathcal{I}$ with those of w in several online dictionaries (Figure 3a, see the popup menu in the center). The user selects a dictionary to reference and the senses of w from this dictionary will appear beside the graph. `DebugSL` matches the WN synsets with the dictionary senses (see Figure 3). The user can suggest via `DebugSL` a sense present in Dictionary.com for w that is missing in WN. We store all the suggestions.

2. Comparing Two SLs: This second demo scenario uncovers the disagreement between two SLs: typically one word annotating, S_w, (e.g., OF) and one synset annotating, S_s, (e.g., SentiWordNet). The formal procedure for this functionality is described at length in Schneider and Dragut (2015). The output is the collection of graphs of components with inconsistencies. `DebugSL` can also compare two word annotating SLs or two sense annotating SLs wherein `DebugSL` checks for agreement.

7 Conclusion

In this paper we have presented the system `DebugSL` and described its usage. The project source code is available at `https://github.com/atschneid/DebugSL` and a screencast can be viewed at `https://cis.temple.edu/~edragut/DebugSL.webm`. The system will be deployed online for use by the public.

References

Stefano Baccianella, Andrea Esuli, and Fabrizio Sebastiani. 2010. SentiWordNet 3.0: An Enhanced Lexical Resource for Sentiment Analysis and Opinion Mining. In *LREC*.

Eduard Dragut and Christiane Fellbaum. 2014. The role of adverbs in sentiment analysis. In *Proceedings of Frame Semantics in NLP: A Workshop in Honor of Chuck Fillmore (1929-2014)*.

Eduard Dragut, Hong Wang, Prasad Sistla, Clement Yu, and Weiyi Meng. 2015. Polarity consistency checking for domain independent sentiment dictionaries. *IEEE TKDE*, 27(3):838–851.

Eduard C. Dragut, Hong Wang, Clement Yu, Prasad Sistla, and Weiyi Meng. 2012. Polarity consistency checking for sentiment dictionaries. In *ACL*.

Guy Emerson and Thierry Declerck. 2014. Sentimerge: Combining sentiment lexicons in a bayesian framework. In *workshop at COLING*.

Ronen Feldman. 2013. Techniques and applications for sentiment analysis. *Commun. ACM*, 56(4).

Christiane Fellbaum. 1998. *WordNet: An On-Line Lexical Database and Some of its Applications*. MIT Press.

David Gale and Lloyd S. Shapley. 1962. College admissions and the stability of marriage. *AMM*, 69.

Bing Liu. 2015. *Sentiment Analysis: Mining Opinions, Sentiments, and Emotions*. Cambridge University Press.

Christopher Potts. 2011. Sentiment symposium tutorial: Lexicons.

Andrew T. Schneider and Eduard C. Dragut. 2015. Towards debugging sentiment lexicons. In *ACL*.

T. Wilson, J. Wiebe, and P. Hoffmann. 2005. Recognizing contextual polarity in phrase-level sentiment analysis. In *HLT/EMNLP*.

ELISA-EDL: A Cross-lingual Entity Extraction, Linking and Localization System

Boliang Zhang[1], Ying Lin[1], Xiaoman Pan[1], Di Lu[1], Jonathan May[2],
Kevin Knight[2], Heng Ji[1]
[1] Rensselaer Polytechnic Institute
{zhangb8,liny9,panx2,lud2,jih}@rpi.edu
[2] Information Sciences Institute
{jonmay,knight}@isi.edu

Abstract

We demonstrate ELISA-EDL, a state-of-the-art re-trainable system to extract entity mentions from low-resource languages, link them to external English knowledge bases, and visualize locations related to disaster topics on a world heatmap. We make all of our data sets[1], resources and system training and testing APIs[2] publicly available for research purpose.

1 Introduction

Our cross-lingual entity extraction, linking and localization system is capable of extracting named entities from unstructured text in any of 282 Wikipedia languages, translating them into English, and linking them to English Knowledge Bases (Wikipedia and Geonames). This system then produces visualizations of the results such as heatmaps, and thus it can be used by an English speaker for monitoring disasters and coordinating rescue and recovery efforts reported from incident regions in low-resource languages. In the rest of the paper, we will present a comprehensive overview of the system components (Section 2 and Section 3), APIs (Section 4), interface[3](Section 5), and visualization[4] (Section 6).

2 Entity Extraction

Given a text document as input, the entity extraction component identifies entity name mentions and classifies them into pre-defined types: Person (PER), Geo-political Entity (GPE), Organization (ORG) and Location (LOC). We consider name tagging as a sequence labeling problem, to tag each token in a sentence as the Beginning (B), Inside (I) or Outside (O) of an en-

tity mention with a certain type. Our model is based on a bi-directional long short-term memory (LSTM) networks with a Conditional Random Fields (CRFs) layer (Chiu and Nichols, 2016). It is challenging to perform entity extraction across a massive variety of languages because most languages don't have sufficient data to train a machine learning model. To tackle the low-resource challenge, we developed creative methods of deriving noisy training data from Wikipedia (Pan et al., 2017), exploiting non-traditional language-universal resources (Zhang et al., 2016) and cross-lingual transfer learning (Cheung et al., 2017).

3 Entity Linking and Localization

After we extract entity mentions, we link GPE and LOC mentions to GeoNames[5], and PER and ORG mentions to Wikipedia[6]. We adopt the name translation approach described in (Pan et al., 2017) to translate each tagged entity mention into English, then we apply an unsupervised collective inference approach (Pan et al., 2015) to link each translated mention to the target KB. Figure 2 shows an example output of a Hausa document. The extracted entity mentions *"Stephane Dujarric"* and *"birnin Bentiu"* are linked to their corresponding entries in Wikipedia and GeoNames respectively.

Compared to traditional entity linking, the unique challenge of linking to GeoNames is that it is very scarce, without rich linked structures or text descriptions. Only 500k out of 4.7 million entities in Wikipedia are linked to GeoNames. Therefore, we associate mentions with entities in the KBs in a collective manner, based on salience, similarity and coherence measures (Pan et al., 2015). We calculate topic-sensitive PageRank scores for 500k overlapping entities between

---

[1]https://elisa-ie.github.io/wikiann
[2]https://elisa-ie.github.io/api
[3]https://elisa-ie.github.io
[4]https://elisa-ie.github.io/heatmap

[5]http://www.geonames.org
[6]https://www.wikipedia.org

Proceedings of NAACL-HLT 2018: Demonstrations, pages 41–45
New Orleans, Louisiana, June 2 - 4, 2018. ©2018 Association for Computational Linguistics

APIs	Description
`/status`	Retrieve the current server status, including supported languages, language identifiers, and the state (offline, online, or pending) of each model.
`/status/{identifier}`	Retrieve the current status of a given language.
`/entity_discovery_and_linking/ {identifier}`	Main entry of the EDL system. Take input in either plain text or `*.ltf` format, tag names that are PER, ORG or LOC/GPE, and link them to Wikipedia.
`/name_transliteration/ {identifier}`	Transliterate a name to Latin script.
`/entity_linking/{identifier}`	Query based entity linking. Link each mention to KBs.
`/entity_linking_amr`	English entity linking for Abstract Meaning Representation (AMR) style input (Pan et al., 2015). AMR (Banarescu et al., 2013) is a structured semantic representation scheme. The rich semantic knowledge in AMR boosts linking performance.
`/localize/{identifier}`	Localize a LOC/GPE name based on GeoNames database.

Table 1: RUN APIs description.

APIs	Description
`/status`	An alias of `/status`
`/status/{identifier}`	Query the current status of a model being trained.
`/train/{identifier}`	Train a new name tagging model for a language. A model id is automatically generated and returned based on model name, and time stamp.

Table 2: TRAIN APIs description.

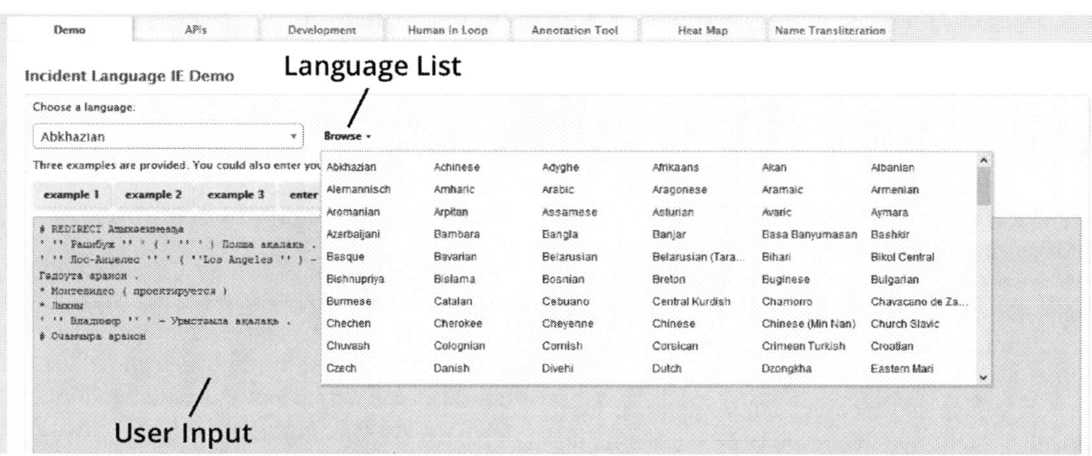

Figure 1: Cross-lingual Entity Extraction and Linking Interface

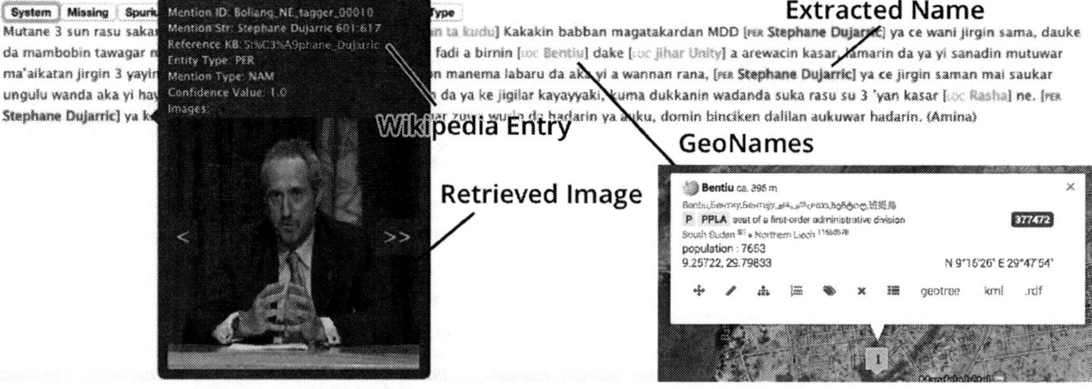

Figure 2: Cross-lingual Entity Extraction and Linking Testing Result Visualization

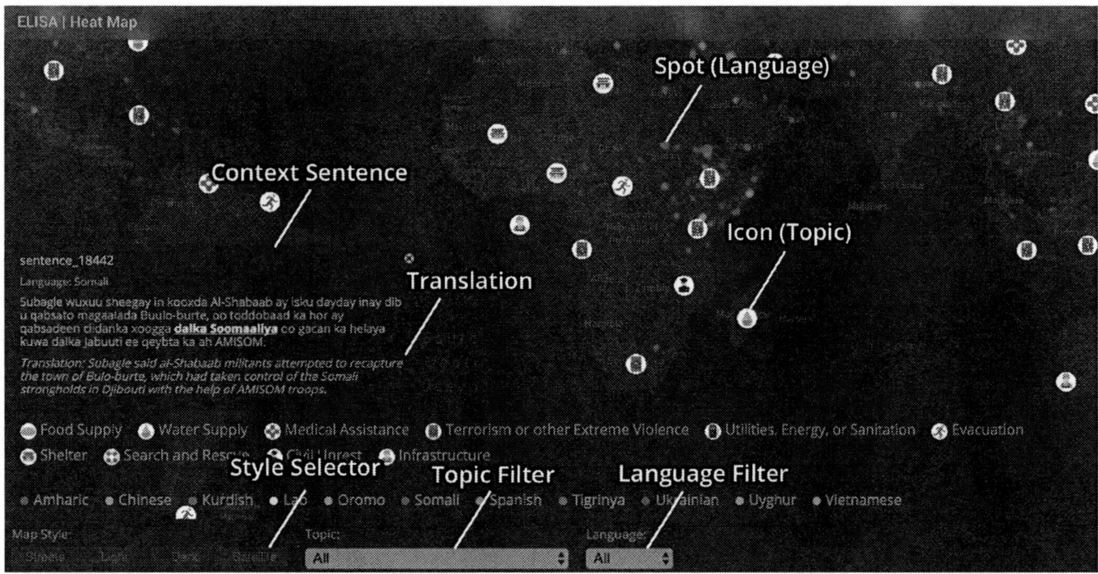

Figure 3: Heatmap Visualization

Language	F1 (%)	Language	F1 (%)
Arabic	51.9	Bengali	74.8
Chechen	58.9	Persian	58.4
Hausa	70.2	Hungarian	60.2
Oromo	81.3	Russian	63.7
Somali	67.6	Tamil	65.9
Thai	69.8	Tigrinya	73.2
Tagalog	78.7	Turkish	74.4
Uyghur	72.3	Uzbek	71.8
Vietnamese	68.5	Yoruba	50.1

Table 3: Name Tagging Performance on Low-Resource Languages

GeoNames and Wikipedia as their salience scores. Then we construct knowledge networks from source language texts, where each node represents a entity mention, and each link represents a sentence-level co-occurrence relation. If two mentions cooccur in the same sentence, we prefer their entity candidates in the GeoNames to share an administrative code and type, or be geographically close in the world, as measured in terms of latitude and longitude.

Table 3 shows the performance of our system on some representative low-resource languages for which we have ground-truth annotations from the DARPA LORELEI[7] programs, prepared by the Linguistic Data Consortium.

4 Training and Testing APIs

In this section, we introduce our back-end APIs. The back-end is a set of RESTful APIs built with Python Flask[8], which is a light weight framework that includes template rendering and server hosting capabilities. We use Swagger for documentation management. Besides the on-line hosted APIs, we also publish our Docker copy[9] at Dockerhub for software distribution.

In general, we categorize the APIs into two sections: RUN and TRAIN. The RUN section is responsible for running the pre-trained models for 282 languages, and the TRAIN section provides a re-training function for users who want to train their own customized name tagging models using their own datasets. We also published our training and test data sets, as well as resources related to at morphology analysis and name translation at: https://elisa-ie.github.io/wikiann. Table 1 and Table 2 present the detailed functionality and usages of the APIs of these two sections. Besides the core components as described in Section 2 and Section 3, we also provide the APIs of additional components, including a re-trainable name transliteration component (Lin et al., 2016) and a universal name and word translation component based on word alignment derived from cross-

---

[7]https://www.darpa.mil/program/low-resource-languages-for-emergent-incidents

[8]http://flask.pocoo.org
[9]https://hub.docker.com/r/elisarpi/elisa-ie/

lingual Wikipedia links (Pan et al., 2017). More detailed usages and examples can be found in our Swagger[10] documentation: `https://elisa-ie.github.io/api`.

5   Testing Interface

Figure 1 shows the test interface, where a user can select one of the 282 languages, enter a text or select an example document, and run the system. Figure 2 shows an output example. In addition to the entity extraction and linking results, we also display the top 5 images for each entity retrieved from Google Image Search[11]. In this way even when a user cannot read a document in a low-resource language, s/he will obtain a high-level summary of entities involved in the document.

6   Heatmap Visualization

Using disaster monitoring as a use case, we detect the following ten topics from the input multilingual data based on translating 117 English disaster keywords via PanLex[12]: (1) water supply, (2) food supply, (3) medical assistance, (4) terrorism or other extreme violence, (5) utilities, energy or sanitation, (6) evacuation, (7) shelter, (8) search and rescue, (9) civil unrest or widespread crime, and (10) infrastructure, as defined in the NIST LoreHLT2017 Situation Frame detection task[13]. If a sentence includes one of these topics and also a location or geo-political entity, we will visualize the entity on a world *heatmap* using Mapbox[14] based on its coordinates in the GeoNames database obtained from the entity linker. We also show the entire context sentence and its English translation produced from our state-of-the-art Machine Translation system for low-resource languages (Cheung et al., 2017). Figure 3 illustrates an example of the visualized heatmap.

We use different colors and icons to stand for different languages and frame topics respectively (e.g., the bread icon represents "food supply"). Users can also specify the language or frame topic or both to filter out irrelevant results on the map. By clicking an icon, its context sentence will be displayed in a pop-up with automatic translation

and highlighted mentions and keywords. We provide various map styles (light, dark, satellite, and streets) for different needs, as shown in Figure 4.

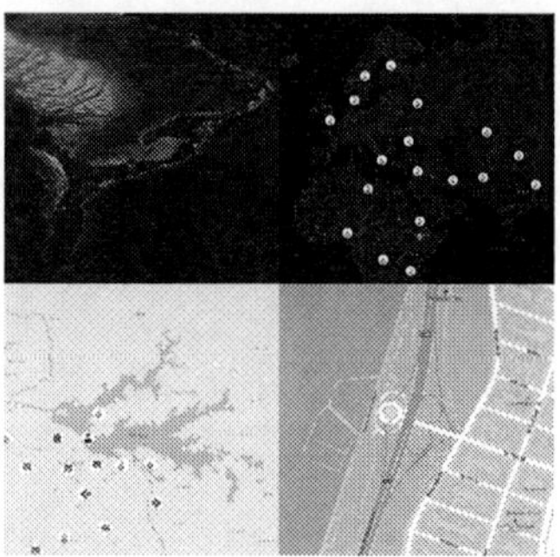

Figure 4: Different Map Styles

7   Related Work

Some recent work has also focused on low-resource name tagging (Tsai et al., 2016; Littell et al., 2016; Zhang et al., 2016; Yang et al., 2017) and cross-lingual entity linking (McNamee et al., 2011; Spitkovsky and Chang, 2011; Sil and Florian, 2016), but the system demonstrated in this paper is the first publicly available end-to-end system to perform both tasks and all of the 282 Wikipedia languages.

8   Conclusions and Future Work

Our publicly available cross-lingual entity extraction, linking and localization system allows an English speaker to gather information related to entities from 282 Wikipedia languages. In the future we will apply common semantic space construction techniques to transfer knowledge and resources from these Wikipedia languages to all thousands of living languages. We also plan to significantly expand entities to the thousands of fine-grained types defined in YAGO (Suchanek et al., 2007) and WordNet (Miller, 1995).

Acknowledgments

This work was supported by the U.S. DARPA LORELEI Program No. HR0011-15-C-0115. The views and conclusions contained in this document are those of the authors and should not be interpreted as representing the official policies, either expressed or implied, of the U.S. Government. The U.S. Government is authorized to reproduce and distribute reprints for Government purposes notwithstanding any copyright notation here on.

---

[10]`https://swagger.io`
[11]`https://images.google.com`
[12]`http://panlex.org`
[13]`https://www.nist.gov/itl/iad/mig/lorehlt-evaluations`
[14]`https://www.mapbox.com`

References

Laura Banarescu, Claire Bonial, Shu Cai, Madalina Georgescu, Kira Griffitt, Ulf Hermjakob, Kevin Knight, Philipp Koehn, Martha Palmer, and Nathan Schneider. 2013. Abstract meaning representation for sembanking. In *ACL Workshop on Linguistic Annotation and Interoperability with Discourse*.

Leon Cheung, Thamme Gowda, Ulf Hermjakob, Nelson Liu, Jonathan May, Alexandra Mayn, Nima Pourdamghani, Michael Pust, Kevin Knight, Nikolaos Malandrakis, Pavlos Papadopoulos, Anil Ramakrishna, Karan Singla, Victor Martinez, Colin Vaz, Dogan Can, Shrikanth Narayanan, Kenton Murray, Toan Nguyen, David Chiang, Xiaoman Pan, Boliang Zhang, Ying Lin, Di Lu, Lifu Huang, Kevin Blissett, Tongtao Zhang, Heng Ji, Ondrej Glembek, Murali Karthick Baskar, Santosh Kesiraju, Lukas Burget, Karel Benes, Igor Szoke, Karel Vesely, Jan "Honza" Cernocky, Camille Goudeseune, Mark Hasegawa Johnson, Leda Sari, Wenda Chen, and Angli Liu. 2017. ELISA system description for lorehlt 2017. In *Proc. LoReHLT2017*.

Jason P. C. Chiu and Eric Nichols. 2016. Named entity recognition with bidirectional LSTM-CNNs. *Transactions of the Association for Computational Linguistics* 4:357–370.

Ying Lin, Xiaoman Pan, Aliya Deri, Heng Ji, and Kevin Knight. 2016. Leveraging entity linking and related language projection to improve name transliteration. In *Proc. ACL2016 Workshop on Named Entities*.

Patrick Littell, Kartik Goyal, David Mortensen, Alexa Little, Chris Dyer, and Lori Levin. 2016. Named entity recognition for linguistic rapid response in low-resource languages: Sorani Kurdish and Tajik. In *Proc. of the 26th International Conference on Computational Linguistics (COLING2016)*.

Paul McNamee, James Mayfield, Dawn Lawrie, Douglas W. Oard, and David Doermann. 2011. Cross-language entity linking. In *Proc. of 5th International Joint Conference on Natural Language Processing (IJCNLP2011)*.

George A. Miller. 1995. WordNet: A lexical database for english. *Communications of the ACM* 38(11):39–41.

Xiaoman Pan, Taylor Cassidy, Ulf Hermjakob, Heng Ji, and Kevin Knight. 2015. Unsupervised entity linking with abstract meaning representation. In *Proc. the 2015 Conference of the North American Chapter of the Association for Computational Linguistics Human Language Technologies (NAACL-HLT 2015)*.

Xiaoman Pan, Boliang Zhang, Jonathan May, Joel Nothman, Kevin Knight, and Heng Ji. 2017. Cross-lingual name tagging and linking for 282 languages. In *Proc. the 55th Annual Meeting of the Association for Computational Linguistics (ACL2017)*.

Avirup Sil and Radu Florian. 2016. One for all: Towards language independent named entity linking. In *Proc. of the 54th Annual Meeting of the Association for Computational Linguistics (ACL2016)*.

Valentin I Spitkovsky and Angel X Chang. 2011. Strong baselines for cross-lingual entity linking. In *Proc. of the Text Analysis Conference (TAC2011)*.

Fabian M. Suchanek, Gjergji Kasneci, and Gerhard Weikum. 2007. Yago: a core of semantic knowledge. In *Proc. of the 16th international conference on World Wide Web (WWW2017)*.

Chen-Tse Tsai, Stephen Mayhew, and Dan Roth. 2016. Cross-lingual named entity recognition via wikification. In *Proc. of the 20th SIGNLL Conference on Computational Natural Language Learning (CoNLL2016)*.

Zhilin Yang, Ruslan Salakhutdinov, and William W Cohen. 2017. Transfer learning for sequence tagging with hierarchical recurrent networks. In *Proc. of the 5th International Conference on Learning Representations (ICLR2017)*.

Boliang Zhang, Xiaoman Pan, Tianlu Wang, Ashish Vaswani, Heng Ji, Kevin Knight, and Daniel Marcu. 2016. Name tagging for low-resource incident languages based on expectation-driven learning. In *Proc. of the 2016 Conference of the North American Chapter of the Association for Computational Linguistics: Human Language Technologies (NAACL-HLT 2016)*.

Entity Resolution and Location Disambiguation in the Ancient Hindu Temples Domain using Web Data

Ayush Maheshwari, Vishwajeet Kumar, Ganesh Ramakrishnan
Indian Institute of Technology Bombay
Mumbai, India
{ayushm,vishwajeet,ganesh}@cse.iitb.ac.in

J. Saketha Nath *
IIT Hyderabad
Hyderabad, India
saketha@iith.ac.in

Abstract

We present a system for resolving entities and disambiguating locations based on publicly available web data in the domain of ancient *Hindu Temples*. Scarce, unstructured information poses a challenge to Entity Resolution(ER) and snippet ranking. Additionally, because the same set of entities may be associated with multiple locations, Location Disambiguation(LD) is a problem. The mentions and descriptions of *temples*[1] exist in the order of hundreds of thousands, with such data generated by various users in various forms such as text (Wikipedia pages), videos (YouTube videos), blogs, *etc.* We demonstrate an integrated approach using a combination of grammar rules for parsing and unsupervised (clustering) algorithms to resolve entity and locations with high confidence. A demo of our system is accessible at `tinyurl.com/templedemos`[2]. Our system is open source and available on GitHub[3].

1 Introduction

Entity Resolution (ER) is the process of associating mentions of entities in text with a dictionary of entities. Here the dictionary might be either manually curated (such as Wikipedia) or constructed in an unsupervised manner (Bhattacharya and Getoor, 2007). It is a well studied problem with wide applications. This problem is of particular significance for domains in which the information available on the Web is relatively scarce.

In the domain of ancient *Hindu Temples*[4], which are present in the order of hundreds of thousands, the corresponding sources of information are often diverse and scarce. There are more than six hundred thousand temples in the country:however, sufficient information exists only for a few of them on the Web. Furthermore,

Figure 1: Sample descriptions (posts) from YouTube videos on various temples. Irrelevant posts are snippets which cannot be associated with any temple, whereas the relevant posts are about *Giriraj Dham, Ammachiveedu Muhurthi, Shivalokathyagar* and *Gorakhnath* temples respectively.

a significant fraction of such data ($\sim$60%), is generated by the crowd over social multi-media platforms such as YouTube and Twitter. This data is ridden with subjective evaluations, opinions, and speculations. See Figure 1 for examples which we contrast with relatively objective and factual passages. The irrelevant posts in Figure 1 are speculative, subjective/opinionated or irrelevant. Our initial challenge is to weed out such speculative information carefully while holding on to sparse, factual and historical information. Additionally, the problem becomes more complex when the information about the domain is either poorly structured or unstructured. In Figure 2 we present an example snippet containing multiple *temple names* and multiple *temple locations*. We observe that a snippet can sometimes contain multiple mentions of similar *temple names* and *temple locations*. Due to similar temple names present at multiple locations, we also face the problem of Location Disambiguation (LD).

In this work, we present a novel approach to perform ER and LD for ancient temples using text and multimedia content publicly available on the Web. We retrieve information about temples from various sources such as Google Maps, YouTube *etc.*, and preprocess it. Using

---

* This work was done while author was at IIT Bombay

[1] Throughout the paper by 'temples' we mean entities in the domain of ancient Hindu Temples.

[2] Demo of the Snippet Ranking system can be accessed at `tinyurl.com/entityr`

[3] `https://github.com/vishwajeet93/templeSearch`

[4] Note: Here *Temple* is an entity with two attributes *viz.*, 1) Temple Name and 2) Temple Location

46

Proceedings of NAACL-HLT 2018: Demonstrations, pages 46–50
New Orleans, Louisiana, June 2 - 4, 2018. ©2018 Association for Computational Linguistics

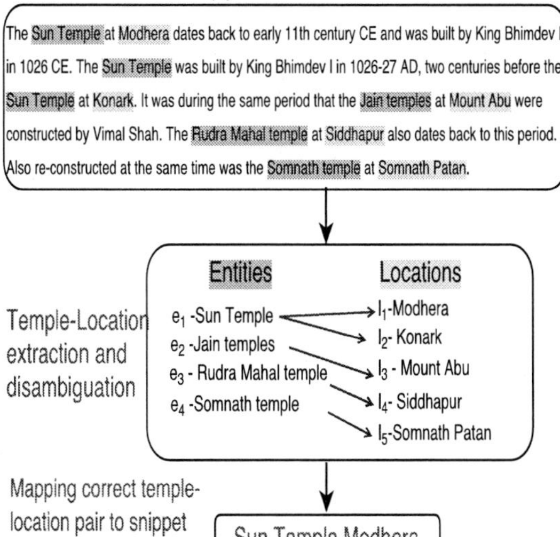

Figure 2: An example of temple name and location disambiguation. Snippet contain multiple mentions of same temple. Temple is present at multiple locations which makes disambiguation challenging.

this information, we extract videos present on YouTube about the temples along with its metadata such as title and description, and map videos to the corresponding temple. Next, we rank various textual snippets pertaining to the same temple on the basis of the relevance of each snippet. We demonstrate our approach through a system that accurately disambiguates videos to temples and ranks results in order of their relevance to a user query. We measure the effectiveness of our approach in terms of precision, recall and F-score. Our main contributions are as follows:

- A novel approach to perform ER and LD for temples using evidence from multiple snippets extracted from various web sources. Evidence may actually be subjective evaluations, opinions or speculations, not actual facts. We design heuristics with low false positive rates that help us filter out such misleading instances.
- A method to disambiguate temple and location names, and accurately associate relevant videos.
- A novel CNN-based(Convolutional Neural Network) technique to rank multiple snippets pertaining to the same temple by computing similarities.
- A system to search information (snippets, location, videos *etc.*) about temples.

2   Related Work

(Getoor and Machanavajjhala, 2013; Benjelloun et al., 2009; Wang et al., 2012) proposed to use crowd sourced

data to resolve entities. (Wang et al., 2012) propose a hybrid human-machine approach to determine the most relevant, matching entity pairs. Instead of directly asking users to resolve entities, the system adopts a two-step approach; the system estimates the most likely mentions for an entity. This information is presented to the users to verify matching pairs of entities.

(Inkpen et al., 2017) proposed a set of heuristic rules to disambiguate location names in Twitter[5] messages. Their heuristics rely on geographical (latitude-longitude, geographic hierarchy) and demographic information (population of a region). (Awamura et al., 2015) used spatial proximity and temporal consistency clues to disambiguation location names. Our approach jointly resolves entity and disambiguate location names using publicly available web data.

3   Our Approach

We propose a novel technique to address the problem of entity resolution and location disambiguation. To extract the basic location and video data related to each temple, we use the Google Maps[6] and YouTube API[7] respectively. We disambiguate the name and location of each temple using publicly available data on the Web and leverage Google Maps to assign videos to the correct temple.

The *temples names* and *temple locations* are extracted from the snippets using text processing techniques. Thereafter, we use the *K*-medoids algorithm[8] to cluster snippets belonging to the same temple. Given a new temple, we retrieve the set of snippets related to the temple. These snippets are fed as input to a CNN based ranking system to score and rank snippets based on the queried temple.

3.1   Data collection

Most information pertaining to temples, as available on the Web is in the form of videos uploaded by individuals on video sharing websites such as YouTube, blogs, and Wikipedia pages. In most cases, the content uploaded by a user either (i) does not contain the specific name or location of the temple or (ii) contains multiple temple names and locations. In contrast, moderated content on sites such as Wikipedia is well-organized and contains unambiguous information.

Additionally, descriptions of temples are splintered over personal websites, Google Maps[9] and government websites, just to name a few sources. We crawled the Web to fetch mentions of temple names. We extracted

---

[5]https://www.twitter.com
[6]https://developers.google.com/maps/
[7]https://developers.google.com/youtube/
[8]https://en.wikipedia.org/wiki/K-medoids
[9]https://maps.google.com

temples and their locations from place annotations available on Google Maps. Through this, we were able to enlist over four hundred thousand temples located across the country. We use *temple name* and *location* to extract information about the temples present in YouTube[10] videos.

3.2 Temple Name and Location Disambiguation

We manually designed and wrote rules for parsing the textual data (from sources mentioned earlier) and extracted temple names. For this, we employed the JAPE grammar in the GATE tool (Cunningham et al., 2002). For illustration, consider the sentence: *The **Shankaracharya temple** is housed in the **Srinagar** district on the hill known as Takht-e-Suleiman.* In this illustration, the temple name and location (highlighted in bold) are extracted using manually composed parsing rules based on JAPE grammar.

Owing to user subjectivity, consistency and quality of the content varies widely. In our case, snippets within the corpus are replete with distinct mentions of the same entity. There are multiple variants of a single *temple name* in a single snippet. For example, *Vaishno Devi Mandir, Vaishno Devi Temple* or *shrine of Mata Vaishno Devi* are variants of the same *temple name*. To correctly attribute multiple variants to a single *temple name* (such as *Vaishno Devi Temple*), we pre-process these mentions and map them to a canonical temple entity by following a two-step approach. First, we build a vocabulary containing spelling variants and synonyms. As an example, **sh** and **h** are commonly used interchangeably (eg: *Shiva* and *Siva*). Similarly, *temple* and *mandir* are used interchangeably as synonyms (the latter being a word from Samskrit). Second, we wrote JAPE Grammar rules to parse temple names into their canonical forms. For instance, *Vaishno* uniquely identifies variants of the *Vaishno Devi Temple*. We follow a similar technique to disambiguate locations.

3.3 Mapping Videos to Temple

For most queries, videos retrieved in the top search results are unrelated to the temple name and its location. This leads to the need to map videos to a correct temple. User generated content needs to be analyzed and filtered to remove unrelated videos. We achieve this by fetching the top-15 videos for each temple and extracting their title and description. We store each title and description pair into a document, say d. We repeat this for each video-temple pair to form a set of document $D = d_1, d_2, ..., d_n$. Below, we describe our approach to map videos to *temples* with high confidence.

1. Extract *temple name* and *temple location* from the document d_i using disambiguation methods.

Figure 3: Pseudo-code for temple name and location disambiguation and clustering algorithm for processing textual snippets.

2. Use Google Maps API to list *temple names* located around the extracted *temple location*. The *temple names* and *temple location* form a tuple t stored in set T.
3. For each element $t \in T$, we calculate TF-IDF score for tuple t over each document $d \in D$, where D is the indexed set of documents.
4. We rank documents based on TF-IDF scores for each query $t \in T$ and map the top ranked d to the temple.

3.4 Snippet Clustering

Textual snippets retrieved from publicly available data on the web are pre-processed to remove stop words before giving input to the text processing engine. We use a CNN-based ranking method, explained in Section 3.5, which produces a score matrix for each snippet in the cluster. We label each cluster using a snippet that we determine to be the centroid of that cluster and select the corresponding *Temple name* and *location* pair that identifies the cluster. The score matrix is finally sorted to determine the top-k snippets belonging to that cluster. Pseudo-code for the clustering algorithm is described in Figure 3.

3.5 Snippet Ranking

We use a CNN-based architecture to score and rank snippets such that the CNN assigns the highest score to the snippet having maximum overlap with the queried temple. More formally the similarity between query

---

q and snippet **s** is computed as:

$$sim(q,s) = \mathbf{q}^T W \mathbf{s} \qquad (1)$$

For our CNN model, we use the short text ranking system proposed by Severyn (Severyn and Moschitti, 2015). The convolution filter width is set to 5, the feature map size to 150, and the batch size to 50. We set the dropout parameter to 0.5. We initialized word vectors using pre-trained word embeddings. Before passing our input to the CNN, we pre-process the text and exclude plural nouns, cardinal numbers and foreign words from the snippets. Pre-processing helps us handle out of vocabulary words. We use the Stanford Part of Speech (POS) (Toutanova et al., 2003) tagger to annotate each word with its POS tag. As an example, consider the following input snippet: *Temple of Lord Somnath one of Jyotirlinga temple of Lord Shiva is situated near the town of Veraval in Western part of Gujarat whose present structure is built in 1951.* The PoS tagger annotates words like *Lord , Somnath, Shiva, Veraval, Gujarat* as proper nouns. We provide the query-temple pair as an input to the CNN which outputs the associated similarity score. The highest score represents the most relevant snippet for the temple.

4 Experiments and Results

4.1 Data Set

Our dataset[11] consists of more than four hundred thousand temple names with their locations extracted from Google Places. It also contains more than two hundred thousand videos fetched from YouTube.

Model (Values in %)	Ground Truth	
	Temple	∼Temple
Predicted as Temple	77	12
Predicted as ∼Temple	9	2

Precision = 0.863, Recall = 0.89, F = 0.876

Table 1: Precision, recall and F measure for the mapped entities

4.2 Results

We sample 1000 videos randomly from the complete video set to compute precision, recall and F-measure and evaluate the performance of videos mapped to the temple as shown in Table 1. 77% of YouTube videos are mapped to the correct temple with its location, 9% videos are mapped incorrectly. 12% videos are not mapped to any temple while 2% videos are false negatives. False negatives correspond to videos not relevant to a temple though retrieved from YouTube. Overall, we observe good performance in terms of precision

and recall numbers, despite the association of a single temple name with multiple locations and despite the presence of multiple temples in the same location.

5 Demonstration Details

When a user enters a query in the search box (annotated with Temple Search in Figure 4(b)), the system returns a list of temples. On selecting the temple, the system provides location annotations in the **Map** tab. The system also provides list of relevant videos for the query temple in the **Videos** tab (Figure 4(c)). In our Snippet ranking demo [12], the user can select a temple from the drop-down list and view the description of extracted snippets. Additionally, a user can view snippet clusters for a temple along with the snippet ranking score (as shown in Figure 4(a)).

6 Conclusion

In this paper, we focused on the problem of ER and LD in a domain where data is scarce, mostly unstructured and user generated. We presented a novel approach to disambiguate temple names and locations. We also addressed the problem of mapping videos to temples using ER and LD techniques. We leverage evidence from user generated content to map videos to their correct temple and rank snippets. We also presented a novel CNN-based technique for snippet clustering and ranking. Furthermore, we evaluated the effective-ness of our mapping techniques. In the future, we would like to resolve attributes such as the date of establishment, main deity, etc. from the ambiguous text.

References

Takashi Awamura, Daisuke Kawahara, Eiji Aramaki, Tomohide Shibata, and Sadao Kurohashi. 2015. Location name disambiguation exploiting spatial proximity and temporal consistency. In *Proceedings of the Third International Workshop on Natural Language Processing for Social Media*, pages 1–9.

Omar Benjelloun, Hector Garcia-Molina, David Menestrina, Qi Su, Steven Euijong Whang, and Jennifer Widom. 2009. Swoosh: a generic approach to entity resolution. *The VLDB JournalThe International Journal on Very Large Data Bases*, 18(1):255–276.

Indrajit Bhattacharya and Lise Getoor. 2007. Collective entity resolution in relational data. *ACM Transactions on Knowledge Discovery from Data (TKDD)*, 1(1):5.

Hamish Cunningham, Diana Maynard, Kalina Bontcheva, and Valentin Tablan. 2002. GATE: A Framework and Graphical Development Environment for Robust NLP Tools and Applications. In *Proceedings of*

---

[11]Our annotated data is available for further academic research on request

[12]`tinyurl.com/entityr`

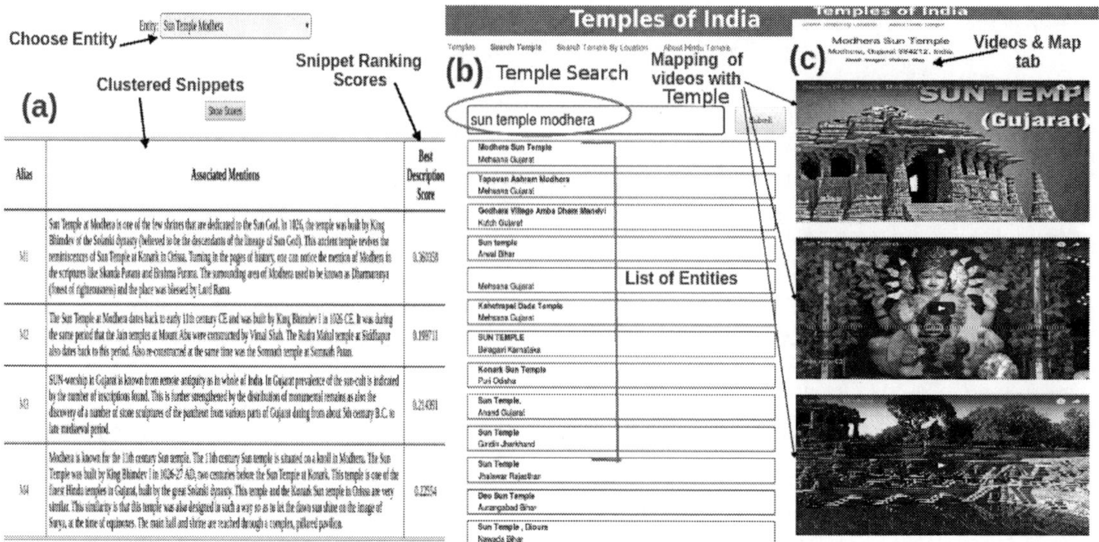

Figure 4: Snapshots of the system

the 40th Anniversary Meeting of the Association for Computational Linguistics (ACL'02).

Lise Getoor and Ashwin Machanavajjhala. 2013. Entity resolution for big data. In *Proceedings of the 19th ACM SIGKDD international conference on Knowledge discovery and data mining*, pages 1527–1527. ACM.

Diana Inkpen, Ji Liu, Atefeh Farzindar, Farzaneh Kazemi, and Diman Ghazi. 2017. Location detection and disambiguation from twitter messages. *Journal of Intelligent Information Systems*, 49(2):237–253.

Aliaksei Severyn and Alessandro Moschitti. 2015. Learning to rank short text pairs with convolutional deep neural networks. In *Proceedings of the 38th International ACM SIGIR Conference on Research and Development in Information Retrieval*, pages 373–382. ACM.

Kristina Toutanova, Dan Klein, Christopher D Manning, and Yoram Singer. 2003. Feature-rich part-of-speech tagging with a cyclic dependency network. In *Proceedings of the 2003 Conference of the North American Chapter of the Association for Computational Linguistics on Human Language Technology-Volume 1*, pages 173–180. Association for Computational Linguistics.

Jiannan Wang, Tim Kraska, Michael J Franklin, and Jianhua Feng. 2012. Crowder: Crowdsourcing entity resolution. *Proceedings of the VLDB Endowment*, 5(11):1483–1494.

Madly Ambiguous:
A Game for Learning about Structural Ambiguity and Why It's Hard for Computers

Ajda Gokcen
Department of Linguistics
University of Washington
Seattle, WA 98195
ajdag@uw.edu

Ethan Hill
IBM Watson Health
Cleveland, OH 44114
ehill@us.ibm.com

Michael White
Department of Linguistics
The Ohio State University
Columbus, OH 43210
mwhite@ling.osu.edu

Abstract

Madly Ambiguous is an open source, online game aimed at teaching audiences of all ages about structural ambiguity and why it's hard for computers. After a brief introduction to structural ambiguity, users are challenged to complete a sentence in a way that tricks the computer into guessing an incorrect interpretation. Behind the scenes are two different NLP-based methods for classifying the user's input, one representative of classic rule-based approaches to disambiguation and the other representative of recent neural network approaches. Qualitative feedback from the system's use in online, classroom, and science museum settings indicates that it is engaging and successful in conveying the intended take home messages.

1 Introduction

Madly Ambiguous is an open source,[1] in-browser online game[2] aimed at teaching audiences of all ages about structural ambiguity and some of the difficulties it poses for natural language processing. Users are introduced to the spunky Mr. Computer Head (Figure 1), a character who gives them an introduction to structural ambiguity and then challenges them to complete a sentence with a prepositional phrase attachment ambiguity in a way that he will misinterpret (Figures 4–5). After playing a round of the game, users may read more about how Mr. Computer Head and systems like him are trained to deal with tasks of ambiguity. Bringing Madly Ambiguous to fruition required an integration of NLP capabilities, cross-platform compatibility, and accessible pedagogical explanation of some fairly complex linguistic and computational concepts, the last of which proved to be the biggest challenge.

Figure 1: Mr. Computer Head, who acts as the opponent in the game, also narrates the introduction and explanation.

Madly Ambiguous has been developed as an outreach component of a project whose aim is to develop methods for avoiding ambiguity in natural language generation and for using disambiguating paraphrases to crowd source interpretations of structurally ambiguous sentences (Duan and White, 2014; Duan et al., 2016; White et al., 2017). The game was initially intended solely as an iPad demo outside of Ohio State's Language Sciences Research Lab, or "Language Pod," a fully functional research lab embedded within the Columbus Center of Science and Industry (COSI), one of the premier science centers in the country (Wagner et al., 2015). The COSI research pods are glass-enclosed research spaces where museum visitors can observe actual scientific research as it is occurring, creating excitement in children about science and encouraging scientific careers. Outside the pod, Ohio State graduate and undergraduate students (the "explainers") provide educational explanations to both adult and child COSI visitors about the work being conducted within the pod as well as language science in general. The explain-

---

[1] https://github.com/ajdagokcen/
madlyambiguous-repo
[2] http://madlyambiguous.osu.edu

Proceedings of NAACL-HLT 2018: Demonstrations, pages 51–55
New Orleans, Louisiana, June 2 - 4, 2018. ©2018 Association for Computational Linguistics

Figure 2: An illustration of why interpreting the sentence *Jane ate spaghetti with a fork* as the fork being part of the dish (instead of a utensil) is ridiculous and easy for a human to dismiss (albeit still a potential source of confusion for a computer).

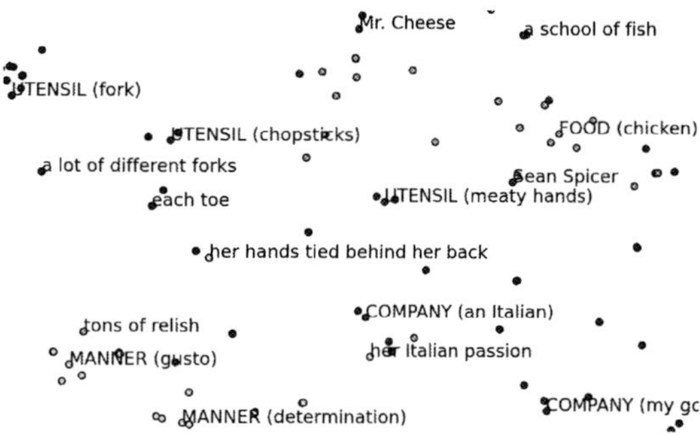

Figure 3: A zoomed-in view of a t-SNE plot showing some of the clusters of similar input phrases to the word2vec model. Phrases like "an Italian" and "her Italian passion" have different interpretations (COMPANY and MANNER, respectively), but are very close to one another on this plot, showing that even the more advanced method has its difficulties.

ers receive extensive training on how to talk about science to a general audience via courses offered at OSU and also from the COSI educational team.

The Language Pod organizers were enthusiastic about the development of Madly Ambiguous since they were aware of no general audience demos that dealt with syntax-related linguistic phenomena. After gathering feedback on the initial iPad version of Madly Ambiguous at COSI, it was completely redesigned as an in-browser demo that can be used on iPad, Android, and desktop browsers, both for informal science learning and undergraduate classroom use, as well as a stand-alone demo on the web. Qualitative feedback on the revamped Madly Ambiguous suggests that it is educational and engaging for all ages.

2 Design

2.1 Interface

Madly Ambiguous's interface is implemented using Node.js[3] as a single dynamic web page. It includes three primary sections: the introduction, the game, and the explanation of how it works. The introduction discusses the more general principles of structural ambiguity as well as the particular rules of the game, including interactive elements and humorous examples to make the instructions more interesting (Figure 2). The explanation of how it works can be read once the user has gone through at least one round of the game; it gives the basics of the two different methods the system uses for classifying the input, as described further in the next subsection.

The game itself has two phases of user interaction. First, users fill in the blank in the sentence, "Jane ate spaghetti with __ ." (See Figure 4.) The system gives a waiting screen depicting a contemplative Mr. Computer Head as it processes and classifies their input, and then displays the guess for users to confirm or deny based on their intended interpretation, as shown in Figure 5. Four different interpretations are possible, with one additional selection if the user feels none of the four capture the meaning. Once the user selects an answer, s/he is given the option to play again, possibly switching between basic and advanced mode.

As we discovered during trials of the initial version of the system, the main challenge of the interface was in presenting the different possible interpretations to users in a way that those with no prior understanding of linguistics could quickly grasp. In the current version, this is accomplished by presenting each option not just with a paraphrase of the sentence that captures the same meaning in a less ambiguous way, but also with a picture depicting the interpretation. Note that the pictures that accompany each meaning are based on the sentences in the introduction as opposed to the user's input, so even if the user enters a utensil such as *a silver spoon*, the picture for the UTENSIL interpretation always shows a fork.

Given the importance of illustrative pictures in making the demo accessible, along with the difficulty of staging such pictures, the current version includes only the sentence for which we have corresponding photos for each interpretation.

---

[3]https://nodejs.org

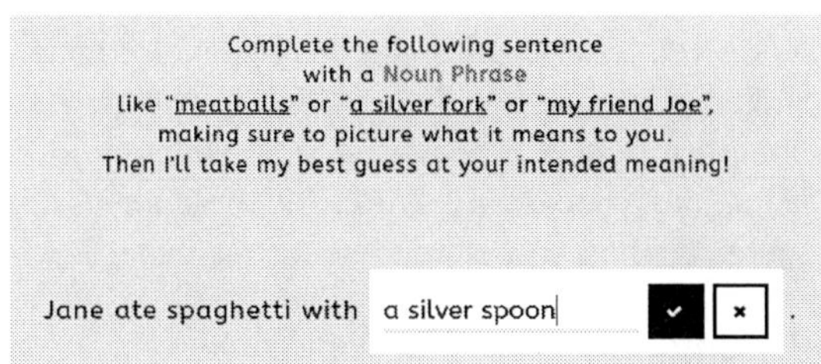

Figure 4: The main screen of the game, where users are asked to complete the ambiguous sentence in a way that the system will misinterpret.

2.2 The NLP

Behind the scenes, the system classifies the user's completion of the sentence "Jane ate spaghetti with __ " as having one of the following four semantic roles, as represented by keywords and paraphrases:

- UTENSIL: *Jane used __ to eat spaghetti.*
- PART: *Jane had spaghetti and __ .*
- MANNER: *Jane exhibited __ while eating spaghetti.*
- COMPANY: *Jane ate spaghetti in the presence of __ .*

There are two different methods of analysis that can be employed. *Basic mode* represents a classic rule-based approach to NLP, utilizing part-of-speech tagging, lemmatization, and WordNet (Miller, 1995) to arrive at an answer. This requires some heuristics based on the part-of-speech tags and lemmas in order to decide what the "most important" word of the input phrase is for cases like *Jane ate spaghetti with a bowl full of meatballs.* The most important word (or multiword phrase) is then looked up in WordNet and its hypernyms are used to choose the category, much as with how selectional restrictions have been traditionally used (e.g. Allen et al., 2001).

Advanced mode uses methods closer to the current state-of-the-art for modern NLP, namely word embeddings (Mikolov et al., 2013). The gensim implementation of word2vec (Řehůřek and Sojka, 2010) is used with vectors that have been pre-trained on the Google News corpus. A training set of phrases and interpretation labels is used to create clusters for each of the four interpretations. Inputs are then classified based on the nearest neighbor in the model to the average of all of the word vectors in the input phrase, not unlike in recent memory-based approaches to one-shot learning (Vinyals et al., 2016).

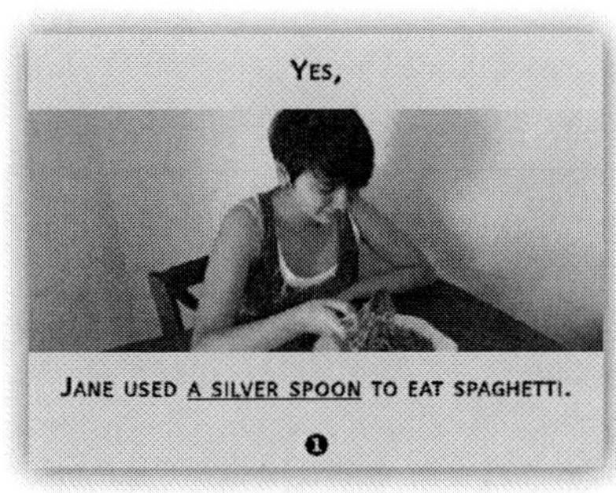

(scroll left or right for more options)

Figure 5: Once users complete the sentence, they're shown the system's guess for the sentence's meaning and can confirm or deny its veracity.

The explanation of how it works additionally covers common sources of interpretation errors. In basic mode, infrequent word senses listed in WordNet can cause confusion; for example, *trump* is listed as an archaic form of *trumpet*, leading Mr. Computer Head to conjecture that *President Trump* is a utensil. In advanced mode, the blending of unrelated senses in word embeddings can cause trouble; for example, as shown in the visualization of the clusters in Figure 3, the food and manner senses represented in the embedding for *relish* can lead to mistakes, as *tons of relish* is closer to one of the MANNER cluster centroids than the intended FOOD clusters.

3 Educational Objectives and Feedback

For informal science learning, like at COSI, the presentation of Madly Ambiguous can and should be tailored to different audiences. For all ages, the critical take home message is that sentences can have more than one meaning (even when the meaning of the words remains constant), and that while people are adept at using the context to determine what's intended, this can be very hard for computers.[4] Depending on the audience, the explainers might also skip the intro and jump right into the game with the pitch, *Hey, do you want to try to trick a computer?*

To separate the notion of intended meaning from the form of the sentence, users of the demo are encouraged to visualize the meaning they have in their head before clicking to see how Mr. Computer Head interprets their sentence completion. With more advanced audiences, the explainers will discuss how linguists use technical tools (like dependency trees) to analyze structural ambiguities and go over how the basic and advanced mode work. Finally, by discussing the kinds of errors the system makes, the explainers can broach the topic of why computers remain so much worse at ambiguity resolution than people. Classroom use can be similar, but with more background knowledge, students can be challenged to come up with ways to improve upon the system's current strategies.

Since the demo went live in Summer 2017, Mr. Computer Head's accuracy against user judgments is currently 64% for basic mode and 70% for advanced mode, well above the majority baseline of 29% despite most users trying hard to fool him.[5] Qualitatively, a high level of engagement with the demo can be observed by examining the lengths to which users go to win, cleverly coming up examples like *a cucumber dressed as a person* as COMPANY rather than FOOD, *pins and needles* as MANNER rather than UTENSIL, and *very British reserve* as MANNER rather than COMPANY, all of which fool Mr. Computer Head in one mode or the other.

Madly Ambiguous received more widespread community feedback after popular linguistics blog *All Things Linguistic* made a post about it, describing it as "a nice intro to automatic sentence processing" (McCulloch, 2017). From there the link was shared across Twitter, Facebook, and beyond. Translation platform Smartcat reached out to learn more about computational linguistics in a webcast interview (Banffy, 2017; Academy, 2017), while other computational linguistics pages like UW-CLMS discussed it on Facebook (CLMS, 2017).

Teachers of courses related to language and computers have also made posts about using Madly Ambiguous in the classroom, making comments such as, "I actually cannot believe I showed

---

[4]Indeed, PP-attachment ambiguities have remained a primary source of parser errors (Kummerfeld et al., 2012).

[5]To our surprise, the youngest users of Madly Ambiguous often want to *help* Mr. Computer Head get the right answer!

word2vec visualizations in a 100 level course – some people were at least nodding, and they are not all from [a] CS background. Absolutely loved using it as a pedagogical tool, and the students also seemed to have understood better" (Vajjala, 2017).

4   Summary and Future Work

In this paper we have introduced Madly Ambiguous, a game aimed at teaching audiences of all ages about structural ambiguity and demonstrating why it's hard for computers—an important lesson that serves to demystify natural language processing at a time when AI in general is arguably over-hyped, risking societal overreactions to the technology. Although Madly Ambiguous is complete and publicly available as-is, there are still more directions it could be taken in, as well as improvements to be made. Since the system saves the data from each round played, there are, as of February 2018, over 13,000 user inputs and judgments collected, which could be used as dynamic feedback for training future versions or possibly as data for other studies of structural ambiguity.

The game could be extended to include other sentences and types of structural ambiguity, such as with coordination (e.g., *The old dogs and cats went to the vet*, where *old* may modify *dogs and cats* or *dogs* alone). This may call for additional illustrative pictures, however. Other expansions might incorporate different successful vector-based methods into the word2vec mode to make it even more sophisticated. Compositional character models, as in Ling et al. (2015), could allow the system to meaningfully model even out-of-vocabulary words; syntactically/semantically compositional models as in Socher et al. (2012) could yield a single vector for multi-word phrases that composes the representations for each word rather than averaging them, potentially providing more separation between clusters. Another direction would be to dynamically generate explanations. It is an open source project, so anyone could contribute to the code!

Acknowledgments

We thank David King, Matt Metzger, and Kaleb White for their contributions to the interface and advanced mode functionality. The interactive demo materials were contributed by Laura Wagner and Victoria Sevich. Special thanks also to Kathryn Campbell-Kibler and Christy Doran for helpful suggestions, and to Yasemin Gokcen and Jessica Findsen for modeling with spaghetti as Jane and Mary. Madly Ambiguous was funded in part through NSF Grant 1319318.

References

Smartcat Academy. 2017. Computational linguistics. https://www.crowdcast.io/e/computational-linguistics.

James F Allen, Donna K Byron, Myroslava Dzikovska, George Ferguson, Lucian Galescu, and Amanda Stent. 2001. Toward conversational human-computer interaction. *AI magazine*, 22(4):27.

Octávio Banffy. 2017. Madly ambiguous linguistic game. https://community.smartcat.ai/topic/792-madly-ambiguous-linguistic-game/.

UW CLMS. 2017. Uw professional master's in computational linguistics: A fun game from ohio state. https://www.facebook.com/uwclma/posts/10155182653273246.

Manjuan Duan, Ethan Hill, and Michael White. 2016. Generating disambiguating paraphrases for structurally ambiguous sentences. In *Proceedings of the 10th Linguistic Annotation Workshop held in conjunction with ACL 2016 (LAW-X 2016)*, pages 160–170, Berlin, Germany. Association for Computational Linguistics.

Manjuan Duan and Michael White. 2014. That's Not What I Meant! Using Parsers to Avoid Structural Ambiguities in Generated Text. In *Proceedings of the 52nd Annual Meeting of the Association for Computational Linguistics (Volume 1: Long Papers)*, pages 413–423, Baltimore, Maryland. Association for Computational Linguistics.

Jonathan K. Kummerfeld, David Hall, James R. Curran, and Dan Klein. 2012. Parser showdown at the wall street corral: An empirical investigation of error types in parser output. In *Proceedings of the 2012 Joint Conference on Empirical Methods in Natural Language Processing and Computational Natural Language Learning*, pages 1048–1059, Jeju Island, South Korea. Association for Computational Linguistics.

Wang Ling, Chris Dyer, Alan W Black, Isabel Trancoso, Ramon Fermandez, Silvio Amir, Luis Marujo, and Tiago Luis. 2015. Finding function in form: Compositional character models for open vocabulary word representation. In *Proceedings of the 2015 Conference on Empirical Methods in Natural Language Processing*, pages 1520–1530.

Gretchen McCulloch. 2017. Madly ambiguous is a fill-in-the-blank game that teaches you about ambiguity while you try to trick a computer. http://allthingslinguistic.com/post/165950061882/madly-ambiguous-is-a-fill-in-the-blank-game-that.

Tomas Mikolov, Kai Chen, Greg Corrado, and Jeffrey Dean. 2013. Efficient estimation of word representations in vector space. *arXiv preprint arXiv:1301.3781*.

George A Miller. 1995. Wordnet: a lexical database for english. *Communications of the ACM*, 38(11):39–41.

Radim Řehůřek and Petr Sojka. 2010. Software Framework for Topic Modelling with Large Corpora. In *Proceedings of the LREC 2010 Workshop on New Challenges for NLP Frameworks*, pages 45–50, Valletta, Malta. ELRA. http://is.muni.cz/publication/884893/en.

Richard Socher, Brody Huval, Christopher D Manning, and Andrew Y Ng. 2012. Semantic compositionality through recursive matrix-vector spaces. In *Proceedings of the 2012 joint conference on empirical methods in natural language processing and computational natural language learning*, pages 1201–1211. Association for Computational Linguistics.

Sowmya Vajjala. 2017. Teaching Notes — Teaching about 'What is NLP?'. https://nishkalavallabhi.github.io/LandC5/.

Oriol Vinyals, Charles Blundell, Timothy P. Lillicrap, Koray Kavukcuoglu, and Daan Wierstra. 2016. Matching networks for one shot learning. *CoRR*, abs/1606.04080.

Laura Wagner, Shari R. Speer, Leslie C. Moore, Elizabeth A. McCullough, Kiwako Ito, Cynthia G. Clopper, and Kathryn Campbell-Kibler. 2015. Linguistics in a science museum: Integrating research, teaching, and outreach at the language sciences research lab. *Language and Linguistics Compass*, 9(10):420–431.

Michael White, Manjuan Duan, and David L. King. 2017. A simple method for clarifying sentences with coordination ambiguities. In *Proceedings of the 1st Workshop on Explainable Computational Intelligence (XCI 2017)*. Association for Computational Linguistics.

VnCoreNLP: A Vietnamese Natural Language Processing Toolkit

Thanh Vu[1], **Dat Quoc Nguyen**[2], **Dai Quoc Nguyen**[3], **Mark Dras**[4] and **Mark Johnson**[4]

[1]Newcastle University, United Kingdom; [2]The University of Melbourne, Australia;
[3]Deakin University, Australia; [4]Macquarie University, Australia
`thanh.vu@newcastle.ac.uk`, `dqnguyen@unimelb.edu.au`,
`dai.nguyen@deakin.edu.au`, `{mark.dras, mark.johnson}@mq.edu.au`

Abstract

We present an easy-to-use and fast toolkit, namely VnCoreNLP—a Java NLP annotation pipeline for Vietnamese. Our VnCoreNLP supports key natural language processing (NLP) tasks including word segmentation, part-of-speech (POS) tagging, named entity recognition (NER) and dependency parsing, and obtains state-of-the-art (SOTA) results for these tasks. We release VnCoreNLP to provide rich linguistic annotations to facilitate research work on Vietnamese NLP. Our VnCoreNLP is open-source and available at: `https://github.com/vncorenlp/VnCoreNLP`.

1 Introduction

Research on Vietnamese NLP has been actively explored in the last decade, boosted by the successes of the 4-year KC01.01/2006-2010 national project on Vietnamese language and speech processing (VLSP). Over the last 5 years, standard benchmark datasets for key Vietnamese NLP tasks are publicly available: datasets for word segmentation and POS tagging were released for the first VLSP evaluation campaign in 2013; a dependency treebank was published in 2014 (Nguyen et al., 2014); and an NER dataset was released for the second VLSP campaign in 2016. So there is a need for building an NLP pipeline, such as the Stanford CoreNLP toolkit (Manning et al., 2014), for those key tasks to assist users and to support researchers and tool developers of downstream tasks.

Nguyen et al. (2010) and Le et al. (2013) built Vietnamese NLP pipelines by wrapping existing word segmenters and POS taggers including: JVnSegmenter (Nguyen et al., 2006), vnTokenizer (Le et al., 2008), JVnTagger (Nguyen et al., 2010) and vnTagger (Le-Hong et al., 2010). However, these word segmenters and POS taggers are no longer considered SOTA models for Vietnamese (Nguyen and Le, 2016; Nguyen et al., 2016b).

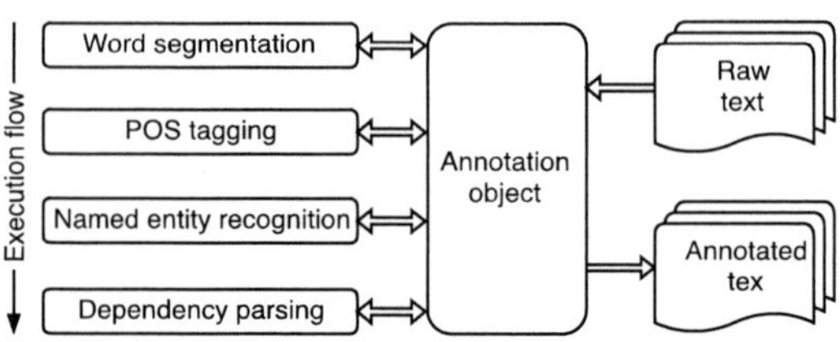

Figure 1: In pipeline architecture of VnCoreNLP, annotations are performed on an `Annotation` object.

Pham et al. (2017) built the NNVLP toolkit for Vietnamese sequence labeling tasks by applying a BiLSTM-CNN-CRF model (Ma and Hovy, 2016). However, Pham et al. (2017) did not make a comparison to SOTA traditional feature-based models. In addition, NNVLP is slow with a processing speed at about 300 words per second, which is not practical for real-world application such as dealing with large-scale data.

In this paper, we present a Java NLP toolkit for Vietnamese, namely VnCoreNLP, which aims to facilitate Vietnamese NLP research by providing rich linguistic annotations through key NLP components of word segmentation, POS tagging, NER and dependency parsing. Figure 1 describes the overall system architecture. The following items highlight typical characteristics of VnCoreNLP:

- **Easy-to-use** – All VnCoreNLP components are wrapped into a single .jar file, so users do not have to install external dependencies. Users can run processing pipelines from either the command-line or the Java API.

- **Fast** – VnCoreNLP is fast, so it can be used for dealing with large-scale data. Also it benefits users suffering from limited computation resources (e.g. users from Vietnam).

- **Accurate** – VnCoreNLP components obtain higher results than all previous published results on the same benchmark datasets.

56

2 Basic usages

Our design goal is to make VnCoreNLP simple to setup and run from either the command-line or the Java API. Performing linguistic annotations for a given file can be done by using a simple command as in Figure 2.

```
$ java -Xmx2g -jar VnCoreNLP.jar -fin
input.txt -fout output.txt
```

Figure 2: Minimal command to run VnCoreNLP.

Suppose that the file `input.txt` in Figure 2 contains a sentence "Ông Nguyễn Khắc Chúc đang làm việc tại Đại học Quốc gia Hà Nội." (Mr$_{\text{Ông}}$ Nguyen Khac Chuc is$_{\text{đang}}$ working$_{\text{làm_việc}}$ at$_{\text{tại}}$ Vietnam National$_{\text{quốc_gia}}$ University$_{\text{đại_học}}$ Hanoi$_{\text{Hà_Nội}}$). Table 1 shows the output for this sentence in plain text form.

1	Ông	Nc	O	4	sub
2	Nguyễn_Khắc_Chúc	Np	B-PER	1	nmod
3	đang	R	O	4	adv
4	làm_việc	V	O	0	root
5	tại	E	O	4	loc
6	Đại_học	N	B-ORG	5	pob
7	Quốc_gia	N	I-ORG	6	nmod
8	Hà_Nội	Np	I-ORG	6	nmod
9	.	CH	O	4	punct

Table 1: The output in file `output.txt` for the sentence 'Ông Nguyễn Khắc Chúc đang làm việc tại Đại học Quốc gia Hà Nội." from file `input.txt` in Figure 2. The output is in a 6-column format representing word index, word form, POS tag, NER label, head index of the current word, and dependency relation type.

Similarly, we can also get the same output by using the API as easy as in Listing 1.

```
VnCoreNLP pipeline = new VnCoreNLP() ;
Annotation annotation = new Annotation("
    Ông Nguyễn Khắc Chúc đang làm việc
    tại Đại học Quốc gia Hà Nội.");
pipeline.annotate(annotation);
String annotatedStr = annotation.
    toString();
```

Listing 1: Minimal code for an analysis pipeline.

In addition, Listing 2 provides a more realistic and complete example code, presenting key components of the toolkit. Here an annotation pipeline can be used for any text rather than just a single sentence, e.g. for a paragraph or entire news story.

3 Components

This section briefly describes each component of VnCoreNLP. Note that our goal is not to develop

```
import vn.pipeline.*;
import java.io.*;
public class VnCoreNLPExample {
 public static void main(String[] args)
    throws IOException {
  // "wseg", "pos", "ner", and "parse"
     refer to as word segmentation, POS
     tagging, NER and dependency
     parsing, respectively.
  String[] annotators = {"wseg", "pos",
     "ner", "parse"};
  VnCoreNLP pipeline = new VnCoreNLP(
     annotators);
  // Mr Nguyen Khac Chuc is working at
     Vietnam National University, Hanoi
     . Mrs Lan, Mr Chuc's wife, is also
     working at this university.
  String str = "Ông Nguyễn Khắc Chúc
     đang làm việc tại Đại học Quốc gia
     Hà Nội. Bà Lan, vợ ông Chúc, cũng
     làm việc tại đây.";
  Annotation annotation = new Annotation
     (str);
  pipeline.annotate(annotation);
  PrintStream outputPrinter = new
     PrintStream("output.txt");
  pipeline.printToFile(annotation,
     outputPrinter);
  // Users can get a single sentence to
     analyze individually
  Sentence firstSentence = annotation.
     getSentences().get(0);
 }
}
```

Listing 2: A simple and complete example code.

new approach or model for each component task. Here we focus on incorporating existing models into a single pipeline. In particular, except a new model we develop for the language-dependent component of word segmentation, we apply traditional feature-based models which obtain SOTA results for English POS tagging, NER and dependency parsing to Vietnamese. The reason is based on a well-established belief in the literature that for a less-resourced language such as Vietnamese, we should consider using feature-based models to obtain fast and accurate performances, rather than using neural network-based models (King, 2015).

- **wseg** – Unlike English where white space is a strong indicator of word boundaries, when written in Vietnamese white space is also used to separate syllables that constitute words. So word segmentation is referred to as the key first step in Vietnamese NLP. We have proposed a transformation rule-based learning model for Vietnamese word segmentation, which obtains better segmentation accuracy and speed than all previous word segmenters. See details in Nguyen et al. (2018).

- **pos** – To label words with their POS tag, we apply MarMoT which is a generic CRF framework and a SOTA POS and morphological tagger (Mueller et al., 2013).[1]

- **ner** – To recognize named entities, we apply a dynamic feature induction model that automatically optimizes feature combinations (Choi, 2016).[2]

- **parse** – To perform dependency parsing, we apply the greedy version of a transition-based parsing model with selectional branching (Choi et al., 2015).[3]

4   Evaluation

We detail experimental results of the word segmentation (**wseg**) and POS tagging (**pos**) components of VnCoreNLP in Nguyen et al. (2018) and Nguyen et al. (2017b), respectively. In particular, our word segmentation component gets the highest results in terms of both segmentation F1 score at 97.90% and speed at 62K words per second.[4] Our POS tagging component also obtains the highest accuracy to date at 95.88% with a fast tagging speed at 25K words per second, and outperforms BiLSTM-CRF-based models. Following subsections present evaluations for the NER (**ner**) and dependency parsing (**parse**) components.

4.1   Named entity recognition

We make a comparison between SOTA feature-based and neural network-based models, which, to the best of our knowledge, has not been done in any prior work on Vietnamese NER.

Dataset: The NER shared task at the 2016 VLSP workshop provides a set of 16,861 manually annotated sentences for training and development, and a set of 2,831 manually annotated sentences for test, with four NER labels PER, LOC, ORG and MISC. Note that in both datasets, words are also supplied with gold POS tags. In addition, each word representing a full personal name are separated into syllables that constitute the word. So this annotation scheme results in an unrealistic scenario for a pipeline evaluation because: (**i**)

gold POS tags are not available in a real-world application, and (**ii**) in the standard annotation (and benchmark datasets) for Vietnamese word segmentation and POS tagging (Nguyen et al., 2009), each full name is referred to as a word token (i.e., all word segmenters have been trained to output a full name as a word and all POS taggers have been trained to assign a label to the entire full-name).

For a more realistic scenario, we merge those contiguous syllables constituting a full name to form a word.[5] Then we replace the gold POS tags by automatic tags predicted by our POS tagging component. From the set of 16,861 sentences, we sample 2,000 sentences for development and using the remaining 14,861 sentences for training.

Models: We make an empirical comparison between the VnCoreNLP's NER component and the following neural network-based models:

- BiLSTM-CRF (Huang et al., 2015) is a sequence labeling model which extends the BiLSTM model with a CRF layer.

- BiLSTM-CRF + CNN-char, i.e. BiLSTM-CNN-CRF, is an extension of BiLSTM-CRF, using CNN to derive character-based word representations (Ma and Hovy, 2016).

- BiLSTM-CRF + LSTM-char is an extension of BiLSTM-CRF, using BiLSTM to derive the character-based word representations (Lample et al., 2016).

- BiLSTM-CRF$_{+POS}$ is another extension to BiLSTM-CRF, incorporating embeddings of automatically predicted POS tags (Reimers and Gurevych, 2017).

We use a well-known implementation which is optimized for performance of all BiLSTM-CRF-based models from Reimers and Gurevych (2017).[6] We then follow Nguyen et al. (2017b, Section 3.4) to perform hyper-parameter tuning.[7]

Main results: Table 2 presents F1 score and speed of each model on the test set, where VnCoreNLP obtains the highest score at 88.55% with a fast speed at 18K words per second. In particular, VnCoreNLP obtains 10 times faster speed than

---

[1] http://cistern.cis.lmu.de/marmot/

[2] https://emorynlp.github.io/nlp4j/components/named-entity-recognition.html

[3] https://emorynlp.github.io/nlp4j/components/dependency-parsing.html

[4] All speeds reported in this paper are computed on a personal computer of Intel Core i7 2.2 GHz.

[5] Based on the gold label PER, contiguous syllables such as "Nguyễn/B-PER", "Khắc/I-PER" and "Chúc/I-PER" are merged to form a word as "Nguyễn_Khắc_Chúc/B-PER."

[6] https://github.com/UKPLab/emnlp2017-bilstm-cnn-crf

[7] We employ pre-trained Vietnamese word vectors from https://github.com/sonvx/word2vecVN.

Model	F1	Speed
VnCoreNLP	**88.55**	**18K**
BiLSTM-CRF	86.48	2.8K
+ CNN-char	88.28	1.8K
+ LSTM-char	87.71	1.3K
BiLSTM-CRF$_{+POS}$	86.12	–
+ CNN-char	88.06	–
+ LSTM-char	87.43	–

Table 2: F1 scores (in %) on the test set w.r.t. gold word-segmentation. "**Speed**" denotes the processing speed of the number of words per second (for VnCoreNLP, we include the time POS tagging takes in the speed).

	Model	LAS	UAS	Speed
Gold POS	VnCoreNLP	**73.39**	79.02	–
	VnCoreNLP$_{-NER}$	73.21	78.91	–
	BIST-bmstparser	73.17	**79.39**	–
	BIST-barchybrid	72.53	79.33	–
	MSTParser	70.29	76.47	–
	MaltParser	69.10	74.91	–
Auto POS	VnCoreNLP	**70.23**	76.93	8K
	VnCoreNLP$_{-NER}$	70.10	76.85	**9K**
	jPTDP	69.49	**77.68**	700

Table 3: LAS and UAS scores (in %) computed on all tokens (i.e. including punctuation) on the test set w.r.t. gold word-segmentation. "**Speed**" is defined as in Table 2. The subscript "–NER" denotes the model without using automatically predicted NER labels as features. The results of the MSTParser (McDonald et al., 2005), MaltParser (Nivre et al., 2007), and BiLSTM-based parsing models BIST-bmstparser and BIST-barchybrid (Kiperwasser and Goldberg, 2016) are reported in Nguyen et al. (2016a). The result of the jPTDP model for Vietnamese is mentioned in Nguyen et al. (2017b).

the second most accurate model BiLSTM-CRF + CNN-char.

It is initially surprising that for such an isolated language as Vietnamese where all words are not inflected, using character-based representations helps producing 1+% improvements to the BiLSTM-CRF model. We find that the improvements to BiLSTM-CRF are mostly accounted for by the PER label. The reason turns out to be simple: about 50% of named entities are labeled with tag PER, so character-based representations are in fact able to capture common family, middle or given name syllables in 'unknown' full-name words. Furthermore, we also find that BiLSTM-CRF-based models do not benefit from additional predicted POS tags. It is probably because BiLSTM can take word order into account, while without word inflection, all grammatical information in Vietnamese is conveyed through its fixed word order, thus explicit predicted POS tags with noisy grammatical information are not helpful.

4.2 Dependency parsing

Experimental setup: We use the Vietnamese dependency treebank VnDT (Nguyen et al., 2014) consisting of 10,200 sentences in our experiments. Following Nguyen et al. (2016a), we use the last 1020 sentences of VnDT for test while the remaining sentences are used for training. Evaluation metrics are the labeled attachment score (LAS) and unlabeled attachment score (UAS).

Main results: Table 3 compares the dependency parsing results of VnCoreNLP with results reported in prior work, using the same experimental setup. The first six rows present the scores with gold POS tags. The next two rows show scores of VnCoreNLP with automatic POS tags which are produced by our POS tagging component. The last

row presents scores of the joint POS tagging and dependency parsing model jPTDP (Nguyen et al., 2017a). Table 3 shows that compared to previously published results, VnCoreNLP produces the highest LAS score. Note that previous results for other systems are reported without using additional information of automatically predicted NER labels. In this case, the LAS score for VnCoreNLP without automatic NER features (i.e. VnCoreNLP$_{-NER}$ in Table 3) is still higher than previous ones. Notably, we also obtain a fast parsing speed at 8K words per second.

5 Conclusion

In this paper, we have presented the VnCoreNLP toolkit—an easy-to-use, fast and accurate processing pipeline for Vietnamese NLP. VnCoreNLP provides core NLP steps including word segmentation, POS tagging, NER and dependency parsing. Current version of VnCoreNLP has been trained without any linguistic optimization, i.e. we only employ existing pre-defined features in the traditional feature-based models for POS tagging, NER and dependency parsing. So future work will focus on incorporating Vietnamese linguistic features into these feature-based models.

VnCoreNLP is released for research and educational purposes, and available at: `https://github.com/vncorenlp/VnCoreNLP`.

References

Jinho D. Choi. 2016. Dynamic Feature Induction: The Last Gist to the State-of-the-Art. In *Proceedings of NAACL-HLT*. pages 271–281.

Jinho D. Choi, Joel Tetreault, and Amanda Stent. 2015. It Depends: Dependency Parser Comparison Using A Web-based Evaluation Tool. In *Proceedings of ACL-IJCNLP*. pages 387–396.

Zhiheng Huang, Wei Xu, and Kai Yu. 2015. Bidirectional LSTM-CRF models for sequence tagging. *arXiv preprint* arXiv:1508.01991.

Benjamin Philip King. 2015. *Practical Natural Language Processing for Low-Resource Languages*. Ph.D. thesis, The University of Michigan.

Eliyahu Kiperwasser and Yoav Goldberg. 2016. Simple and Accurate Dependency Parsing Using Bidirectional LSTM Feature Representations. *Transactions of the Association for Computational Linguistics* 4:313–327.

Guillaume Lample, Miguel Ballesteros, Sandeep Subramanian, Kazuya Kawakami, and Chris Dyer. 2016. Neural Architectures for Named Entity Recognition. In *Proceedings of NAACL-HLT*. pages 260–270.

Hong Phuong Le, Thi Minh Huyen Nguyen, Azim Roussanaly, and Tuong Vinh Ho. 2008. A hybrid approach to word segmentation of Vietnamese texts. In *Proceedings of LATA*. pages 240–249.

Ngoc Minh Le, Bich Ngoc Do, Vi Duong Nguyen, and Thi Dam Nguyen. 2013. VNLP: An Open Source Framework for Vietnamese Natural Language Processing. In *Proceedings of SoICT*. pages 88–93.

Phuong Le-Hong, Azim Roussanaly, Thi Minh Huyen Nguyen, and Mathias Rossignol. 2010. An empirical study of maximum entropy approach for part-of-speech tagging of Vietnamese texts. In *Proceedings of TALN*.

Xuezhe Ma and Eduard Hovy. 2016. End-to-end Sequence Labeling via Bi-directional LSTM-CNNs-CRF. In *Proceedings of ACL (Volume 1: Long Papers)*. pages 1064–1074.

Christopher D. Manning, Mihai Surdeanu, John Bauer, Jenny Finkel, Steven J. Bethard, and David McClosky. 2014. The Stanford CoreNLP natural language processing toolkit. In *Proceedings of ACL 2014 System Demonstrations*. pages 55–60.

Ryan McDonald, Koby Crammer, and Fernando Pereira. 2005. Online Large-margin Training of Dependency Parsers. In *Proceedings of ACL*. pages 91–98.

Thomas Mueller, Helmut Schmid, and Hinrich Schütze. 2013. Efficient Higher-Order CRFs for Morphological Tagging. In *Proceedings of EMNLP*. pages 322–332.

Cam-Tu Nguyen, Trung-Kien Nguyen, et al. 2006. Vietnamese Word Segmentation with CRFs and SVMs: An Investigation. In *Proceedings of PACLIC*. pages 215–222.

Cam-Tu Nguyen, Xuan-Hieu Phan, and Thu-Trang Nguyen. 2010. JVnTextPro: A Java-based Vietnamese Text Processing Tool. http://jvntextpro.sourceforge.net/.

Dat Quoc Nguyen, Mark Dras, and Mark Johnson. 2016a. An empirical study for Vietnamese dependency parsing. In *Proceedings of ALTA*. pages 143–149.

Dat Quoc Nguyen, Mark Dras, and Mark Johnson. 2017a. A Novel Neural Network Model for Joint POS Tagging and Graph-based Dependency Parsing. In *Proceedings of the CoNLL 2017 Shared Task*. pages 134–142.

Dat Quoc Nguyen, Dai Quoc Nguyen, Son Bao Pham, Phuong-Thai Nguyen, and Minh Le Nguyen. 2014. From Treebank Conversion to Automatic Dependency Parsing for Vietnamese. In *Proceedings of NLDB*. pages 196–207.

Dat Quoc Nguyen, Dai Quoc Nguyen, Thanh Vu, Mark Dras, and Mark Johnson. 2018. A Fast and Accurate Vietnamese Word Segmenter. In *Proceedings of LREC*. page to appear.

Dat Quoc Nguyen, Thanh Vu, Dai Quoc Nguyen, Mark Dras, and Mark Johnson. 2017b. From Word Segmentation to POS Tagging for Vietnamese. In *Proceedings of ALTA*. pages 108–113.

Phuong Thai Nguyen, Xuan Luong Vu, et al. 2009. Building a Large Syntactically-Annotated Corpus of Vietnamese. In *Proceedings of LAW*. pages 182–185.

Tuan-Phong Nguyen and Anh-Cuong Le. 2016. A Hybrid Approach to Vietnamese Word Segmentation. In *Proceedings of RIVF*. pages 114–119.

Tuan Phong Nguyen, Quoc Tuan Truong, Xuan Nam Nguyen, and Anh Cuong Le. 2016b. An Experimental Investigation of Part-Of-Speech Taggers for Vietnamese. *VNU Journal of Science: Computer Science and Communication Engineering* 32(3):11–25.

Joakim Nivre, Johan Hall, et al. 2007. MaltParser: A language-independent system for data-driven dependency parsing. *Natural Language Engineering* 13(2):95–135.

Thai-Hoang Pham, Xuan-Khoai Pham, Tuan-Anh Nguyen, and Phuong Le-Hong. 2017. NNVLP: A Neural Network-Based Vietnamese Language Processing Toolkit. In *Proceedings of the IJCNLP 2017 System Demonstrations*. pages 37–40.

Nils Reimers and Iryna Gurevych. 2017. Reporting Score Distributions Makes a Difference: Performance Study of LSTM-networks for Sequence Tagging. In *Proceedings of EMNLP*. pages 338–348.

CNNs for NLP in the Browser: Client-Side Deployment and Visualization Opportunities

Yiyun Liang, Zhucheng Tu, Laetitia Huang, and Jimmy Lin
David R. Cheriton School of Computer Science
University of Waterloo
{yiyun.liang, michael.tu, laetitia.huang, jimmylin}@uwaterloo.ca

Abstract

We demonstrate a JavaScript implementation of a convolutional neural network that performs feedforward inference completely in the browser. Such a deployment means that models can run completely on the client, on a wide range of devices, without making backend server requests. This design is useful for applications with stringent latency requirements or low connectivity. Our evaluations show the feasibility of JavaScript as a deployment target. Furthermore, an in-browser implementation enables seamless integration with the JavaScript ecosystem for information visualization, providing opportunities to visually inspect neural networks and better understand their inner workings.

1 Introduction

Once trained, feedforward inference using neural networks (NNs) is straightforward: just a series of matrix multiplications, application of non-linearities, and other simple operations. With the rise of model interchange formats such as ONNX, we now have clean abstractions that separate model training from model inference. In this context, we explore JavaScript as a deployment target of neural networks for NLP applications. To be clear, we are *not* concerned with training, and simply assume the existence of a pre-trained model that we wish to deploy for inference.

Why JavaScript? We provide two compelling reasons. First, JavaScript is the most widely deployed platform in the world since it resides in every web browser. An implementation in JavaScript means that a NN can be embedded in any web page for client-side execution on any device that has a browser—from laptops to tablets to mobile phones to even potentially "smart home" gadgets. Performing inference on the client also obviates the need for server requests and the associated latencies. With such a deployment, NLP applications that have high demands on responsiveness (e.g., typeahead prediction, grammar correction) or suffer from low connectivity (e.g., remote locations or developing countries) can take advantage of NN models. Such a deployment also protects user privacy, since user data does not leave the client. Second, the browser has emerged as the dominant platform for information visualization, and JavaScript-based implementations support seamless integration with modern techniques and existing toolkits (e.g., D3.js). This provides opportunities to visually inspect neural networks.

We demonstrate a prototype implementation of a convolutional neural network for sentence classification, applied to sentiment analysis—the model of Kim (2014)—in JavaScript, running completely inside a web browser. Not surprisingly, we find that inference performance is significantly slower compared to code running natively, but the browser is nevertheless able to take advantage of GPUs and hardware acceleration on a variety of platforms. Our implementation enables simple visualizations that allow us to gain insights into what semantic n-gram features the model is extracting. This is useful for pedagogy (teaching students about neural networks) as well as research, since understanding a model is critical to improving it. Overall, our visualizations contribute to an emerging thread of research on *interpretable* machine learning (Lipton, 2016).

2 Background and Related Work

Browser-based neural networks are by no means new. Perhaps the best illustration of their potential is the work of Smilkov et al. (2016a), who illustrate backpropagation on simple multi-layer perceptrons with informative visualizations. This

Proceedings of NAACL-HLT 2018: Demonstrations, pages 61–65
New Orleans, Louisiana, June 2 - 4, 2018. ©2018 Association for Computational Linguistics

work, however, can be characterized as focusing on toy problems and useful primarily for pedagogy. More recently, Google Brain introduced TensorFlow.js (formerly deeplearn.js), an open-source library that brings NN building blocks to JavaScript. We take advantage of this library in our implementation.

Our work overcomes a technical challenge that to date remains unaddressed—working with word embeddings. Most NNs for NLP applications begin by converting an input sentence into an embedding matrix that serves as the actual input to the network. Embeddings can be quite large, often gigabytes, which makes it impractical to store directly in a web page. Following Lin (2015), we overcome this challenge by using an HTML standard known as IndexedDB, which allows word vectors to be stored locally for efficient access (more details below).

3 Technical Implementation

The convolutional neural network of Kim (2014) is a sentence classification model that consists of convolutions over a single sentence input embedding matrix with a number of feature maps and pooling followed by a fully-connected layer with dropout and softmax output. Since it has a straightforward architecture, we refer the reader to Kim's original paper for details. The starting point for this work is a PyTorch reimplementation of the model, which achieves accuracy comparable to the original reported results.[1]

Since our demonstration focuses on inference performance, we simply used a pre-trained model for sentiment analysis based on the Stanford Sentiment Treebank. We manually exported all weights from PyTorch and hand-coded the model architecture in TensorFlow.js, which at startup imports these weights. Since Kim CNN has a relatively simple architecture, this implementation is straightforward, as TensorFlow.js provides primitives that are quite similar to those in PyTorch. Because our implementation is pure JavaScript, the entire model can be directly included in the source of any web page, and, for example, connect to text entry boxes for input and DOM-manipulating code for output. However, there is one additional technical hurdle to overcome:

Nearly all neural networks for NLP applications make use of pre-trained word vectors to build an input representation (the embedding matrix) as the first step in inference. For a non-toy vocabulary, these word vectors consume many gigabytes. It is impractical to embed these data directly within a web page or as an external resource due to memory limitations, since all JavaScript code and associated resources are loaded into memory. Even if this were possible, all data would need to be reloaded every time the user refreshes the browser tab, leading to long wait times and an awkward user experience.

To address this challenge, we take advantage of IndexedDB, which is a low-level API for client-side storage of arbitrary amounts of data. Since IndexedDB is an HTML5 standard, it does not require additional plug-ins (assuming a standards-compliant browser). Although IndexedDB has a rich API, for our application we use it as a simple key–value store, where the key is a word and the value is its corresponding word vector. In Google's Chrome browser (which we use for our experiments), IndexedDB is supported by LevelDB, an on-disk key–value store built on the same basic design as the Bigtable tablet stack (Chang et al., 2006). In other words, inside every Chrome browser there is a modern data management platform that is directly accessible via JavaScript.

With IndexedDB, prior to using the model for inference, the user must first download and store the word embeddings locally. For convenience, the model weights are treated the same way. Note that this only needs to be performed once, and all data are persisted on the client until storage is explicitly reclaimed. This means that after a one-time setup, model inference happens locally in the browser, without any need for external connectivity. This enables tight interaction loops that do not depend on unpredictable server latencies.

4 Performance Evaluation

The first obvious question we tackle is the performance of our JavaScript implementation. How much slower is it than model inferencing performed natively? We evaluated in-browser inference on a 2015 MacBook Pro laptop equipped with an Intel Core i5-5257U processor (2 cores), running MacOS 10.13. We compared performance with the desktop machine used to train the model, which has an Intel Core i7-6800K processor (6 cores) and an NVIDIA GeForce GTX 1080

---

[1] https://github.com/castorini/Castor

	Latency (ms) / batch			
	1	32	64	128
PyTorch				
Desktop GPU (Ubuntu 16.04)	2.9	3.0	3.1	3.1
Desktop CPU (Ubuntu 16.04)	4.3	43	86	130
Chrome Browser				
Desktop GPU (Ubuntu 16.04)	30	56	100	135
Desktop CPU (Ubuntu 16.04)	783	47900	110000	253000
MacBook Pro GPU (MacOS 10.13)	33	180	315	702
MacBook Pro CPU (MacOS 10.13)	779	56300	126000	297000
iPad Pro (iOS 11)	170	472	786	1283
Nexus 6P (Android 8.1.0)	103	541	1117	1722
iPhone 6 (iOS 11)	400	1336	3055	7324

Table 1: Latency of our CNN running in Chrome on different devices for a batch of N sentences.

GPU (running Ubuntu 16.04). Our model was implemented using PyTorch v0.3.0 running CUDA 8.0. All experiments were performed on the Stanford Sentiment Treebank validation set. Due to the asynchronous nature of JavaScript execution in the browser, the TensorFlow.js API applies inference to batches of input sentences at a time. Thus, we measured latency per batch for batches of 1, 32, 64, and 128 sentences.

Evaluation results are shown in Table 1. The first block of the table shows the performance of PyTorch running on the desktop, with and without GPU acceleration. As expected, the GPU is able to exploit parallelism for batch inferencing, but on individual sentences, the CPU is only slightly slower. In the bottom block of the table, we report results of running our JavaScript implementation in Google Chrome (v64). We compared the desktop and the laptop, with and without GPU acceleration. For the most common case (inference on a single sentence), the browser is about an order of magnitude slower with the GPU. Without the GPU, performance drops by another $\sim 25\times$.

The above figures include only inference time. Loading the word vectors takes 7.4, 214, 459, and 1184 ms, for batch sizes of 1, 32, 64, and 128, respectively, on the MacBook Pro. As explained previously, using IndexedDB requires a one-time download of the word vectors and the model weights. This step takes approximately 16s on our MacBook Pro for 16,271 word vectors (for simplicity, we only download the vocabulary needed for our experiments). Loading the model itself takes approximately one second.

Because our implementation is in JavaScript, our model runs in any device that has a web browser. To demonstrate this, we evaluated performance on a number of other devices we had

convenient access to: an iPad Pro with an Apple A10X Fusion chip, a Nexus 6P with a Qualcomm Snapdragon 810 octa-core CPU, and an iPhone 6 with an Apple A8 chip. These results are also shown in Table 1. As expected, performance on these devices is lower than our laptop, but interestingly, batch inference on these devices is faster than batch inference in the browser without GPU acceleration. This indicates that hardware acceleration is a standard feature on many devices today. These experiments illustrate the feasibility of deploying neural networks on a wide range of devices, exploiting the ubiquity of JavaScript.

5   Visualization of Feature Maps

Another major advantage of in-browser JavaScript implementations of neural networks is seamless integration with modern browser-based information visualization techniques and toolkits (e.g., D3.js), which we describe in this section. Visualizations are useful for two purposes: First, they serve as intuitive aids to teach students how neural networks function. Although there are plenty of pedagogical resources for deep learning, nothing beats the convenience of an interactive neural network directly embedded in a web page that students can manipulate. Second, contributing to growing interest in "interpretable" machine learning (Lipton, 2016), visualizations can help us understand how various network components contribute to producing the final predictions.

Although there are many examples of neural network visualizations (Smilkov et al., 2016a; Bau et al., 2017; Olah et al., 2018), they mostly focus on vision applications, where inputs and feature maps are much easier to interpret visually. The fundamental challenge with NLP applications is that word embeddings (and by extension, feature maps) exist in an abstract semantic space that has no inherent visual meaning. How to best visualize embeddings remains an open question (Smilkov et al., 2016b; Rong and Adar, 2016).

Nevertheless, feature maps in CNNs can be thought of as n-gram feature detectors. For our sentiment analysis application (and more generally, sentence classification), we designed visualizations to answer two related questions: First, given a sentence, what feature maps are highly activated and where? Second, given a particular feature map, what token sequence activates it in a corpus of sentences?

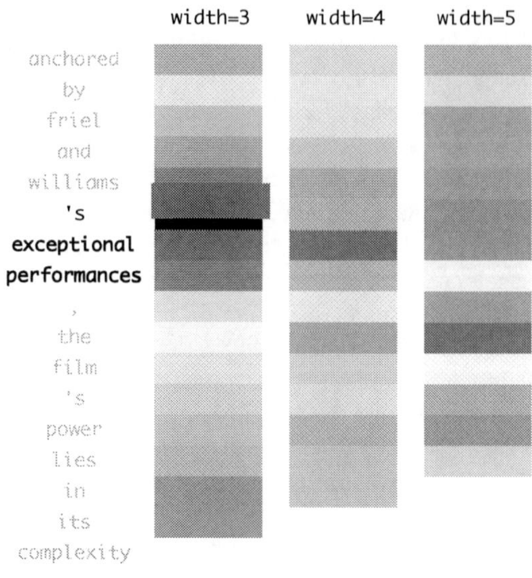

Figure 1: Visualization of feature map activations.

```
Filter 12 (width = 3, bias = 0.01)
4/4   ... this chamber drama  is superbly acted by the deeply appealing ...
3/4                            a superbly acted and funny gritty fable of ...
3/4   a rigorously structured  and exquisitely filmed drama about a father ...
4/4                            uses sharp humor and insight into human ...
4/4   ... friel and williams  's exceptional performances , the film 's ...
4/4   ... of elling , and  gets fine performances from his two leads ...
4/4                            an exquisitely crafted and acted tale .
4/4   ... mueller , the film  gets great laughs , but never at the ...
3/4   ... glides through on  some solid performances and witty dialogue .
3/4   ... and buoyed by  three terrific performances , far from ...
```

Figure 2: Visualization of the n-grams that a particular feature map most highly activates on.

The visualization in Figure 1 is designed to answer the first question. Running down the left edge is the sentence that we are examining; examples in this section are taken from the development set of the Stanford Sentiment Treebank. Each column represents feature maps of a particular width; each cell is aligned with the first token from the corresponding n-gram of the sentence over which the feature map applies. The heatmap (i.e., blue saturation) corresponds to maximum activation across all feature maps on that particular n-gram in the sentence. In our interactive visualization, when we mouse over a cell, it becomes enlarged and slightly offset to indicate focus, and the corresponding n-gram in the sentence is highlighted in bold. For this sentence, we see that filters of width three are most highly activated by the n-gram sequence ['s exceptional performance]. There are multiple ways to use color to summarize the activation of the feature maps, but we have found MAX to be the most insightful. From this visualization, we can see that feature maps of widths four and five activate on different parts of the sentence.

From the visualization in Figure 1, we see that *some* feature map activates highly on the n-gram ['s exceptional performance]. But which one? To answer this question, we can pivot over to the visualization shown in Figure 2, where we see that the answer is Filter 12: we show the n-grams that trigger the highest activation from sentences in the development set. The n-grams are aligned in a keyword-in-context format for easy browsing. To the left of each sentence we show x/y, where x is the ground truth label and y is the predicted label. Here, we clearly see that all the n-grams are related to positive aspects of performances, and this gives us some insight into the semantics captured by this feature map. From this visualization, we can click on any sentence and pivot back to the sentence-focused visualization in Figure 1.

6   Future Work and Conclusions

We describe a JavaScript implementation of a convolutional neural network that runs completely in the browser. Unsurprisingly, in-browser inference is significantly slower. However, for many applications, such a performance tradeoff may be worthwhile given the advantages of a JavaScript implementation—the ability to embed a neural network in any web page, the ability to run on a wide variety of devices and without internet connectivity, and opportunities for visualizations that help us interpret the model.

Ongoing work focuses on better integration of model training and browser deployment. Currently, porting a PyTorch model into JavaScript requires tediously rewriting the model into TensorFlow.js by hand. Although the library supports reading TensorFlow models, importers for PyTorch do not exist yet, as far as we are aware. Provided that the right adaptors are built, the ONNX model interchange format could provide an interlingua to support seamless integration, enabling a future where running neural networks in JavaScript becomes routine.

Acknowledgments. This research was supported by the Natural Sciences and Engineering Research Council (NSERC) of Canada.

References

David Bau, Bolei Zhou, Aditya Khosla, Aude Oliva, and Antonio Torralba. 2017. Network dissection: Quantifying interpretability of deep visual representations. In *Proceedings of the 2017 IEEE Conference on Computer Vision and Pattern Recognition (CVPR 2017)*, pages 6541–6549, Honolulu, Hawaii.

Fay Chang, Jeffrey Dean, Sanjay Ghemawat, Wilson C. Hsieh, Deborah A. Wallach, Michael Burrows, Tushar Chandra, Andrew Fikes, and Robert Gruber. 2006. Bigtable: A distributed storage system for structured data. In *Proceedings of the 7th USENIX Symposium on Operating System Design and Implementation (OSDI 2006)*, pages 205–218, Seattle, Washington.

Yoon Kim. 2014. Convolutional neural networks for sentence classification. In *Proceedings of the 2014 Conference on Empirical Methods in Natural Language Processing (EMNLP 2014)*, pages 1746–1751, Doha, Qatar.

Jimmy Lin. 2015. Building a self-contained search engine in the browser. In *Proceedings of the ACM International Conference on the Theory of Information Retrieval (ICTIR 2015)*, pages 309–312, Northampton, Massachusetts.

Zachary C. Lipton. 2016. The mythos of model interpretability. *arXiv:1606.03490*.

Chris Olah, Arvind Satyanarayan, Ian Johnson, Shan Carter, Ludwig Schubert, Katherine Ye, and Alexander Mordvintsev. 2018. The building blocks of interpretability. *Distill*.

Xin Rong and Eytan Adar. 2016. Visual tools for debugging neural language models. In *Proceedings of the ICML 2016 Workshop on Visualization for Deep Learning*, New York, New York.

Daniel Smilkov, Shan Carter, D. Sculley, Fernanda B. Viégas, and Martin Wattenberg. 2016a. Direct-manipulation visualization of deep networks. In *Proceedings of the ICML 2016 Workshop on Visualization for Deep Learning*, New York, New York.

Daniel Smilkov, Nikhil Thorat, Charles Nicholson, Emily Reif, Fernanda B. Viégas, and Martin Wattenberg. 2016b. Embedding projector: Interactive visualization and interpretation of embeddings. *arXiv:1611.05469*.

Generating Continuous Representations of Medical Texts

Graham Spinks
Department of Computer Science
KU Leuven, Belgium
graham.spinks@cs.kuleuven.be

Marie-Francine Moens
Department of Computer Science
KU Leuven, Belgium
sien.moens@cs.kuleuven.be

Abstract

We present an architecture that generates medical texts while learning an informative, continuous representation with discriminative features. During training the input to the system is a dataset of captions for medical X-Rays. The acquired continuous representations are of particular interest for use in many machine learning techniques where the discrete and high-dimensional nature of textual input is an obstacle. We use an Adversarially Regularized Autoencoder to create realistic text in both an unconditional and conditional setting. We show that this technique is applicable to medical texts which often contain syntactic and domain-specific shorthands. A quantitative evaluation shows that we achieve a lower model perplexity than a traditional LSTM generator.

1 Introduction

The main focus of this paper is the generation of realistic samples with a similar quality to those in a training set of medical texts. At the same time, an informative, continuous representation is created from the textual input.

Obtaining a good representation for medical texts may prove vital to building more sophisticated generative, discriminative or semantic models for the field. One of the obstacles is the discrete nature of text that makes it difficult to employ in many machine learning algorithms. This is the case for Generative Adversarial Networks (GANs), which are not adequate to generate text as it is difficult to backpropagate the error to discrete symbols (Goodfellow, 2016).

The ability of GANs to learn the underlying distribution, rather than repeating examples in the training data, has led to the successful generation of intricate high-resolution samples in computer vision (Zhang et al., 2017). Conditional GANs in particular, where the class or label is passed to both generator and discriminator, implicitly learn relevant ancillary information which leads to more detailed outputs (Gauthier, 2014; Mirza and Osindero, 2014). If we had a better understanding of how to train GANs with discrete data, some of those developments might be directly applicable to detailed text generation applications—such as image caption generation, machine translation, simplification of text, and text summarization—especially when dealing with noisy texts.

Another impediment is the nature of clinical data, which is often unstructured and not well-formed, yet commonly has a high and important information density. Textual reports often don't follow regular syntax rules and contain very specific medical terminology. Moreover, the amount of training data is often limited and each physician has a personal writing style. Simply reusing pre-trained continuous representations, such as vector-based word embeddings (Turian et al., 2010), is therefore not always feasible for medical datasets.

The approach to text generation has mainly been dominated by Long Short-Term Memory networks (LSTMs). While LSTMs are successful in creating realistic samples, no actionable smooth representation is created of the text and thus there are limited possibilities to manipulate or employ the representations in additional applications that require continuous inputs. While the creation of continuous representations of text usually involves an autoencoder, the results mostly lack enough semantic information to be particularly useful in an alternate task.

Kim et al. (2017) have shown how to achieve text generation with a continuous representation by implementing an Adversarially Regularized Autoencoder (ARAE). They combine the training of a rich discrete space autoencoder with recurrent neural networks (RNNs) and the training of

Proceedings of NAACL-HLT 2018: Demonstrations, pages 66–70
New Orleans, Louisiana, June 2 - 4, 2018. ©2018 Association for Computational Linguistics

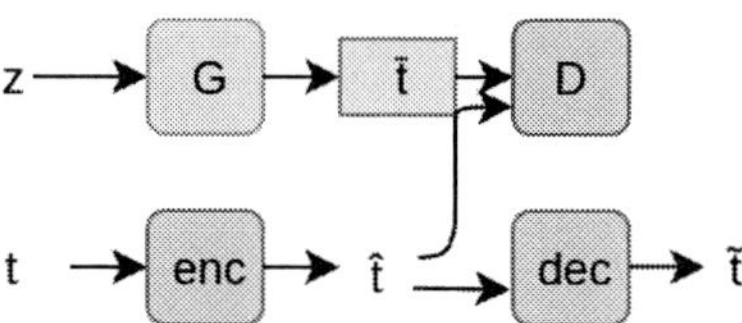

Figure 1. Overview of the ARAE architecture. The encoder *enc* creates a new continuous representation $\hat{t}$ from the input text t. The decoder *dec* tries to reconstruct the original text. Conjointly a generator G and discriminator D are trained in an adversarial setup. z is a random normal noise vector.

more simple, fully connected networks to generate samples in the continuous space. With adversarial (GAN) training, both the distribution of the generated as well as the encoded samples are encouraged to converge. The outcome is that a smooth representation is learned as well as a generator that can build realistic samples in the continuous space.

In this paper, we explore this methodology in the context of medical texts, more specifically captions for chest X-Rays. Analogous to conditional GANs, we also extend the network of Kim et al. (2017) by generating samples conditioned on categorical, medical labels (for example 'healthy'). We refer to this method as conditional ARAE. In a quantitative evaluation, the perplexity of the conditional ARAE outperforms both the unconditional ARAE as well as a traditional LSTM.

2   Methodology

For this demo we use the chest X-Ray dataset from the Indiana University hospital network (Demner-Fushman et al., 2015). The dataset consists of 7470 X-Ray images for 3851 patients with corresponding textual findings. In this paper, the images are not used. We retain a maximum of 30 words per caption and pad shorter sentences. All words are transformed to lowercase and those with a frequency below 5 are removed and replaced by an out-of-vocabulary marker. The dataset also contains Medical Subject Headings (MeSH) which are essentially labels that indicate the main diagnoses for each patient report.

2.1   GAN

In a GAN, the loss is defined as a two-player minmax game between the generator (G) and the discriminator (D). The discriminator gradually improves its capacity to distinguish a sample from

the real distribution from one of the generated distribution. The generator is trained on its ability to fool the discriminator into classifying its output as real data. The loss function can be described as:

$$\min_G \max_D \mathcal{L}_{GAN}(D,G) = \mathbb{E}_{x \sim p_d}[log(D(x))] +$$
$$\mathbb{E}_{z \sim p_z}[log(1 - D(G(z)))] \quad (1)$$

where x represents a sample from the real data distribution p_d and z is a noise vector sampled from the distribution p_z, typically a random normal distribution, which serves as the input for G. In a traditional GAN, the discriminator and generator are trained alternately in the hope that their performance improves each iteration. The setup of a traditional GAN is essentially illustrated by the top row in figure 1, where $\hat{t}$ would be a sample x from the real distribution and z is the noise vector.

To ensure convergence while training a GAN, we use an improved loss function, the Earth-Mover distance (EM) (Arjovsky et al., 2017). The formulation of a GAN in equation 1 minimizes the Kullback-Leibler divergence (KL-divergence) between the real and generated distributions. This formulation leads to infinite losses when the distribution of the generator maps to zero probability in the support of the real distribution. The Earth-Mover distance defines a more sensible distance measure for the convergence of two distributions x and y as specified in equation 2. It can be interpreted as a measure of the minimal amount of effort that is needed to move the mass of one distribution to match that of another.

$$W(P_r, P_g) = \inf_{\gamma \in \Pi(P_r, P_g)} \mathbb{E}_{(x,y) \sim \gamma}\big[\,\|x - y\|\,\big] \quad (2)$$

where $\Pi(P_r, P_g)$ is the set of all joint distributions γ with marginal distributions P_r and P_g. Computing the EM distance exactly is not tractable but Arjovsky et al. (2017) show that the Wasserstein GAN (WGAN) formulation (equation 3) leads to a theoretically sound and practical optimization of the EM distance if the parameters of D are restricted to a set of 1-Lipschitz functions, which in practice requires the weights to be constrained to an interval [-c,c]. In our experiments, c was set to 1 rather than a smaller value as we observe faster convergence during training.

$$\min_G \max_D \mathcal{L}_W(D,G) = \mathbb{E}_{x \sim p_d}[D(x)] -$$
$$\mathbb{E}_{z \sim p_z}[D(G(z))] \quad (3)$$

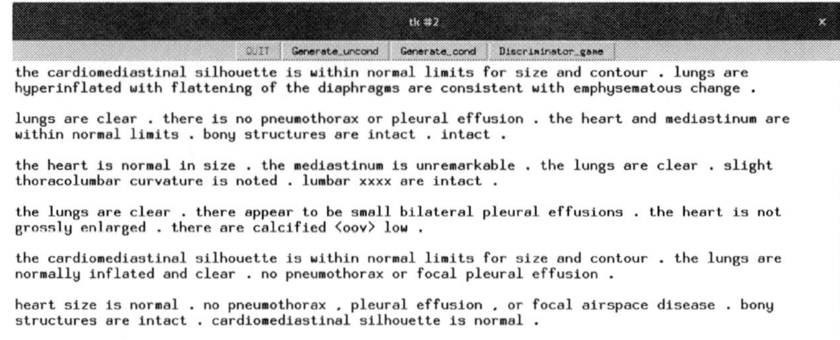

Figure 2. A screenshot of the demo. Random unconditional samples are generated from a noise vector z.

2.2 ARAE

In the traditional setup, GANs need to be fully differentiable to function. The error cannot adequately backpropagate when a series of discrete input variables are used. To alleviate this problem, an Adversarially Regularized Autoencoder (ARAE) is used (Kim et al., 2017). The input text is mapped to a continuous representation $\hat{t}$ with a discrete, word-based autoencoder. The encoder enc maps a text t onto $\hat{t}$ while the decoder implements the conditional probability distribution $p(t|\hat{t})$. Both encoder and decoder are single-layer LSTMs. The loss is computed as the cross-entropy over the word reconstruction (equation 4).

$$\mathcal{L}_{rec}(enc, dec) = -log(p(t)|enc(t)))\qquad(4)$$

The discriminator of the ARAE now tries to determine which samples derive from the real distribution of encoded texts, $\hat{t}$, and which are generated from a noise distribution, z. While D improves, the encoder enhances the representation $\hat{t}$ to contain more discriminative information. To avoid divergence between encoder and decoder, only a portion λ of the loss is backpropagated to enc. In our program we set λ to 0.05. The loss for the ARAE can then be described by equation 5.

$$\min_{G} \max_{D,enc} \mathcal{L}_W(D, G, enc) =$$
$$\mathbb{E}_{t\sim p_d}[D(enc(t))] - \mathbb{E}_{z\sim p_z}[D(G(z))]\qquad(5)$$

Both discriminator and generator are fully connected networks. The continuous representation is built with an autoencoder consisting of an LSTM for both encoder and decoder. The entire training process now consists of three steps: train the autoencoder on its reconstruction, train the discriminator and encoder to maximize the ability of the network to discriminate between real and generated samples, and finally, train the generator to try to fool the discriminator.

1. $\displaystyle \min_{enc,dec} \mathcal{L}_{rec}$

2. $\displaystyle \min_{D,enc} \mathcal{L}_D = \max_{D,enc} \mathcal{L}_W(D, G, enc)$

3. $\displaystyle \min_{G} \mathcal{L}_G = \min_{G} \mathcal{L}_W(D, G, enc)$

The outcome of this setup is both the creation of continuous representations as well as the generation of realistic captions. The architecture is illustrated in figure 1.

2.3 Conditional ARAE

Additionally, the above setup of the ARAE is extended to allow content generation conditioned on input labels. From the MeSH labels in the dataset, we create three simple categories of diagnoses: normal, cardiomegaly and other (which includes a vast array of diagnoses ranging from pleural effusion, opacity, degenerative disease, and so on).

During the training of the conditional ARAEs, the class or label is passed to both generator and discriminator. The formulation in equation (5) is supplemented by mentioning the conditional variable c in $G(z, c)$ and $D(enc(t), c)$. During training the discriminator is presented with real samples $\hat{t}$ in combination with real labels c_r as well as in combination with wrong labels c_w that don't match the samples. Finally it is also presented with fake samples $\bar{t}$ in combination with the labels c_r. The discriminator is encouraged to learn that only the first combination is correct, while the generator tries to create samples that fool the discriminator given designated labels.

68

label	generated caption
normal (+)	heart size within normal limits . no alveolar consolidation , no findings of pleural effusion or pulmonary edema . no pneumothorax . no pleural effusions .
normal (-)	stable appearance of previous xxxx sternotomy . clear lungs bilaterally . redemonstration of disc disease of the thoracic spine . no pneumothorax or pleural effusion . clear lung volumes .
cardiomegaly (+)	heart size is enlarged . stable tortuous aorta . no pneumothorax , pleural effusion or suspicious airspace opacity . prior granulomatous disease .
cardiomegaly (-)	clear lungs . no infiltrates or suspicious pulmonary opacity . no pleural effusion or pneumothorax . cardiomediastinal silhouette within normal limits . calcified granulomas calcified granulomas .
other (+)	he heart size and pulmonary vascularity appear within normal limits . right pleural effusion is present and appears increased . the osseous structures appear intact .
other (-)	heart size and mediastinal contours are normal in appearance . no **oov** airspace consolidation . no pleural effusion or pneumothorax . the visualized bony structures are unremarkable in appearance .

Table 1. Examples of captions generated by the the conditional ARAE from a random vector z and a class label. For each label an example of a correct (+) caption and a wrong (-) caption is given respectively.

	LSTM	ARAE (uncondit.)	ARAE (condit.)
perplexity	150.0	148.4	125.4

Table 2. Perplexity scores for each of the models.

3 Demonstration

In figure 2 some captions are presented that are generated by the ARAE. Both during training and generation, sampling is performed with a temperature of 0.1. These examples qualitatively demonstrate that it is possible to generate text that mimics the complexity of medical reports.

In table 1 we show some randomly chosen results for a network that produces text conditional on the class label. It becomes apparent that for the different labels, the network will produce wrong captions as well, especially for the label 'cardiomegaly' which has significantly less training examples. Empirically, the training is difficult and diverges a lot. We attribute the difficult convergence to two main factors. Firstly, despite the simple labels, the texts in different categories contain a large amount of overlap. Secondly, the conditional ARAE has many objective functions and four different networks (enc, dec, G, D) to optimize and balance in order to learn both what an informative representation looks like as well as how to generate it.

In order to assess the performance of the system, we also train a baseline language model that consists of a 1-layer LSTM. The perplexity of the different models are presented in table 2. From the results we see that while both ARAE models achieve a lower perplexity than the LSTM, the conditional ARAE performs significantly better.

We built a demo interface with the main goal of illustrating the quality and the diversity of the generated text[1]. Upon starting the demo, the trained ARAE networks can be loaded by pressing 'Load_models'. Once loaded, the user can interact in three ways. Firstly, sentences can be generated without conditional labels from a random noise vector by pressing 'Generate_uncond'. Secondly, sentences can be generated from a random noise vector conditioned on one of the three labels (normal, cardiomegaly, other) by pressing 'Generate_cond'. Finally, when pressing 'Discriminator_game', a game starts where the user can attempt to fool the discriminator by inputting a short caption that might belong to an X-Ray. When the user presses 'enter', the system outputs whether the discriminator classifies it as a real caption or not. A screenshot of the interface is shown in figure 2 where unconditional sentences were generated.

4 Conclusion

With an Adversarially Regularized Autoencoder, a continuous text representation is learned of medical captions that can be useful in further applications. GANs are models that learn the underlying distribution while generating detailed continuous data. Therefore the successful training of a GAN on discrete data in the ARAE setup forebodes success for text generation as well. We illustrate the potential of GANs for discrete inputs by extending the ARAE architecture to create text conditioned on simple class labels, similar to conditional GANs. A quantitative evaluation shows that the conditional ARAE achieves a lower perplexity than both the unconditional ARAE and an LSTM baseline.

---

[1]Demo available at https://liir.cs.kuleuven.be/software.php

References

Martin Arjovsky, Soumith Chintala, and Léon Bottou. 2017. Wasserstein gan. *arXiv preprint arXiv:1701.07875*.

Dina Demner-Fushman, Marc D Kohli, Marc B Rosenman, Sonya E Shooshan, Laritza Rodriguez, Sameer Antani, George R Thoma, and Clement J McDonald. 2015. Preparing a collection of radiology examinations for distribution and retrieval. *Journal of the American Medical Informatics Association*, 23(2):304–310.

Jon Gauthier. 2014. Conditional generative adversarial nets for convolutional face generation. *Class Project for Stanford CS231N: Convolutional Neural Networks for Visual Recognition, Winter semester*, 2014(5):2.

Ian Goodfellow. 2016. Nips 2016 tutorial: Generative adversarial networks. *arXiv preprint arXiv:1701.00160*.

Yoon Kim, Kelly Zhang, Alexander M Rush, Yann LeCun, et al. 2017. Adversarially regularized autoencoders for generating discrete structures. *arXiv preprint arXiv:1706.04223*.

Mehdi Mirza and Simon Osindero. 2014. Conditional generative adversarial nets. *arXiv preprint arXiv:1411.1784*.

Joseph Turian, Lev Ratinov, and Yoshua Bengio. 2010. Word representations: a simple and general method for semi-supervised learning. In *Proceedings of the 48th Annual Meeting of the Association for Computational Linguistics*, pages 384–394. Association for Computational Linguistics.

Han Zhang, Tao Xu, Hongsheng Li, Shaoting Zhang, Xiaolei Huang, Xiaogang Wang, and Dimitris Metaxas. 2017. Stackgan: Text to photo-realistic image synthesis with stacked generative adversarial networks. In *IEEE Int. Conf. Comput. Vision (ICCV)*, pages 5907–5915.

Vis-Eval Metric Viewer: A Visualisation Tool for Inspecting and Evaluating Metric Scores of Machine Translation Output

David Steele and **Lucia Specia**
Department of Computer Science
University of Sheffield
Sheffield, UK
`dbsteele1,l.specia@sheffield.ac.uk`

Abstract

Machine Translation systems are usually evaluated and compared using automated evaluation metrics such as BLEU and METEOR to score the generated translations against human translations. However, the interaction with the output from the metrics is relatively limited and results are commonly a single score along with a few additional statistics. Whilst this may be enough for system comparison it does not provide much useful feedback or a means for inspecting translations and their respective scores. Vis-Eval Metric Viewer (VEMV) is a tool designed to provide visualisation of multiple evaluation scores so they can be easily interpreted by a user. VEMV takes in the source, reference, and hypothesis files as parameters, and scores the hypotheses using several popular evaluation metrics simultaneously. Scores are produced at both the sentence and dataset level and results are written locally to a series of HTML files that can be viewed on a web browser. The individual scored sentences can easily be inspected using powerful search and selection functions and results can be visualised with graphical representations of the scores and distributions.

1 Introduction

Automatic evaluation of Machine Translation (MT) hypotheses is key for system development and comparison. Even though human assessment ultimately provides more reliable and insightful information, automatic evaluation is faster, cheaper, and often considered more consistent.

Many metrics have been proposed for MT that compare system translations against human references, with the most popular being BLEU (Papineni et al., 2002), METEOR (Denkowski and Lavie, 2014), TER (Snover et al., 2006), and, more recently, BEER (Stanojevic and Sima'an, 2014). These and other automatic metrics are often criti-

cised for providing scores that can be non-intuitive and uninformative, especially at the sentence level (Zhang et al., 2004; Song et al., 2013; Babych, 2014). Additionally, scores across different metrics can be inconsistent with each other. This inconsistency can be an indicator of linguistic properties of the translations which should be further analysed. However, multiple metrics are not always used and any discrepancies among them tend to be ignored.

Vis-Eval Metric Viewer (VEMV) was developed as a tool bearing in mind the aforementioned issues. It enables rapid evaluation of MT output, currently employing up to eight popular metrics. Results can be easily inspected (using a typical web browser) especially at the segment level, with each sentence (source, reference, and hypothesis) clearly presented in interactive score tables, along with informative statistical graphs. No server or internet connection is required. Only readily available packages or libraries are used locally.

Ultimately VEMV is an accessible utility that can be run quickly and easily on all the main platforms.

Before describing the technical specification of the VEMV tool and its features in Section 3, we give an overview of existing metric visualisation tools in Section 2.

2 Related Tools

Several tools have been developed to visualise the output of MT evaluation metrics that go beyond displaying just single scores and/or a few statistics.

Despite its criticisms and limitations, BLEU is still regarded as the *de facto* evaluation metric used for rating and comparing MT systems. It was one of the earliest metrics to assert a high enough correlation with human judgments.

Interactive BLEU (iBleu) (Madnani, 2011) is

71

Proceedings of NAACL-HLT 2018: Demonstrations, pages 71–75
New Orleans, Louisiana, June 2 - 4, 2018. ©2018 Association for Computational Linguistics

a visual and interactive scoring environment that uses BLEU. Users select the source, reference, and hypothesis files using a graphical user interface (GUI) and these are scored. The dataset BLEU score is shown alongside a bar chart of sentence scores. Users can select one of the sentences by clicking on the individual bars in the chart. When a sentence is selected its source and hypothesis translation is also shown, along with the standard BLEU statistics (e.g. score and n-gram information for the segment). Whilst iBLEU does provide some interactivity, using the graph itself to choose the sentences is not very intuitive. In addition the tool provides results for only one metric.

METEOR is another popular metric used to compute sentence and dataset-level scores based on reference and hypothesis files. One of its main components is to word-align the words in the reference and hypothesis. The Meteor-X-Ray tool generates graphical output with visualisation of word alignments and scores. The alignments and score distributions are used to generate simple graphs (output to PDF). Whilst the graphs do provide extra information there is little in the way of interactivity.

MT-ComparEval (Klejch et al., 2015) is a different evaluation visualisation tool, available to be used online[1] or downloaded locally. Its primary function is to enable users, via a GUI, to compare two (or more) MT system outputs, using BLEU as the evaluation metric. It shows results at both the sentence and dataset level highlighting confirmed, improving, and worsening n-grams for each MT system with respect to the other. Sentence-level metrics (also n-gram) include precision, recall, and F-Measure information as well as score differences between MT systems for a given sentence. Users can upload their own datasets to view sentence-level and dataset scores, albeit with a very limited choice of metrics. The GUI provides some interaction with the evaluation results and users can make a number of preference selections via check boxes.

The Asiya Toolkit (Giménez et al., 2010) is a visualisation tool that can be used online or as a stand-alone tool. It offers a comprehensive suite of metrics, including many linguistically motivated ones. Unless the goal is to run a large number of metrics, the download version is not very practical. It relies on many external tools such as syn-

tactic and semantic parsers. The online tool[2] aims to offer a more practical solution, where users can upload their translations. The tool offers a module for sentence-level inspection through interactive tables. Some basic dataset-level graphs are also displayed and can be used to compare system scores.

In comparison to the other software described here, VEMV is a light yet powerful utility, which offers a wide enough range of metrics and can be easily extended to add other metrics. It has a very specific purpose in that it is designed for rapid and simple use locally, without the need for servers, access to the internet, uploads, or large installs. Users can quickly get evaluation scores from a number of mainstream metrics and view them immediately in easily navigable interactive score tables. We contend that currently there is no other similar tool that is lightweight and offers this functionality and simplicity.

3 Vis-Eval Metric Viewer Software & Features

This section provides an overview of the VEMV software and outlines the required input parameters, technical specifications, and highlights a number of the useful features.

3.1 The Software

VEMV is essentially a multi-metric evaluation tool that uses three tokenised text files (source, reference, and hypothesis) as input parameters and scores the hypothesis translation (MT system output) using up to eight popular metrics: BLEU, MT-Eval[3] (MT NIST & MT BLEU), METEOR, BEER, TER, Word Error Rate (WER), and Edit Distance (E-Dist).[4] All results are displayed via easily navigable web pages that include details of all sentences and scores (shown in interactive score tables - Figure 1). A number of graphs showing various score distributions are also created.

The key aims of VEMV are to make the evaluation of MT system translations easy to undertake and to provide a wide range of feedback that helps the user to inspect how well their system performed, both at the sentence and dataset level.

---

[2]At the time of writing the online version did not work.
[3]https://www.nist.gov/
[4]A WER like metric that calculates the Levenshtein (edit) distance between two strings, but at the character level.

POS ✔ REF Length ✔ Sentence ✔ Sen Bleu ✔ MT Bleu ✔ MT Nist ✔ METEOR ✔ BEER ✔ TER ✔ WER ✔ Edit Dist

POS	REF Length	Sentence	Sen Bleu	MT Bleu	MT NIST	MET-EOR	BEER	TER	WER (Score)	E Dist (Score)
1	9 (44)	SRC: 你有那个症状多长时间了？ REF: how long have you been having that symptom ? HYP: how long have you been that symptom ?	0.6102	0.6102	11.1177 (0.7713)	0.4613	0.818	0.1111	1 (0.8889)	7 (0.8409)
2	11 (41)	SRC: 我在哪坐去波士顿的巴士？ REF: where can i catch a bus to go to boston ? HYP: where do i get the bus for boston ?	0.1886	0.096	3.6523 (0.2529)	0.3052	0.4682	0.5455	6 (0.4545)	16 (0.6098)

Figure 1: A screenshot of an interactive score table showing two example sentences and their respective scores.

3.2 Input and Technical Specification

VEMV is written in Python 3 (also compatible with Python 2.7). To run the tool, the following software needs to be installed:

- Python $>=$ 2.7 (required)

- NLTK[5] $>=$ 3.2.4 (required)

- Numpy (required)

- Matplotlib / Seaborn (optional - for graphs)

- Perl (optional - for MT BLEU, MT NIST)

- Java (optional - for METEOR, BEER, TER)

With the minimum required items installed the software will generate scores for standard BLEU, WER, and E-Dist. The optional items enable a user to run a wider range of metrics and produce nearly 200 graphs during evaluation.

The input commands to run the software can be typed directly into the command-line on any platform, or passed as arguments in an interactive development environment (IDE) such as Spyder.[6]

Once the software has been run (see Section 3.5), a folder containing all of the generated HTML, text, and image files is produced. A user will typically explore the output by opening the 'main.html' file in a browser (Chrome, Firefox, and Opera have been tested) and navigating it like with any (offline) website. The text files contain the output for the various metric scores and can be inspected in detail. The graphs are output as image files (PNGs), which are primarily viewed in the HTML pages, but can also be used separately for reports (e.g. Figure 3 in Section 3.4)

---

[5] http://www.nltk.org
[6] https://github.com/spyder-ide/spyder/releases

3.3 Main Features

Here we outline some key features of the Vis-Eval Metric Viewer tool:

Scoring with multiple evaluation metrics

Currently VEMV uses eight evaluation metrics to score individual sentences and the whole document. All results are shown side by side for comparison purposes and can be inspected at a granular level (Figure 1).

A glance at the two sentences in Figure 1 already provides numerous points for analysis. For example, the MT in sentence 2 is a long way from the reference and receives low metric scores. However, whilst not identical to the reference, the MT is correct and could be interchanged with the reference without losing meaning. For sentence 1 the MT is only a single word away from the reference and receives good scores, (much higher than sentence 2) although the meaning is incorrect. The interactive display enables the user to easily examine such phenomena in a given dataset.

Clear and easily navigable output

The main output is shown as a series of web pages and can be viewed in modern browsers. The browsers themselves also have a number of powerful built-in functions, such as page search, which are applicable to any of the output pages, adding an extra layer of functionality.

The output consists of easily navigable interactive score tables and graphs, logically organised across web pages. The tool includes its own search facility (for target and source sentences) and the option to show or hide metric scores to aid clarity, especially useful for comparing only a selection of metrics. All of the segment level metric scores can be sorted according to the metric of interest.

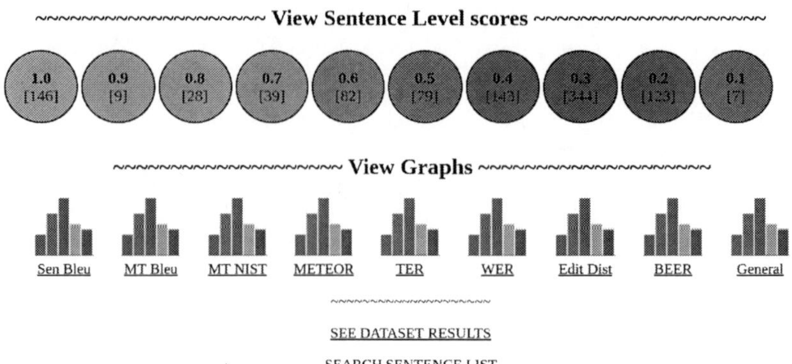

Figure 2: A screenshot of the VisEval Metric Viewer main page.

Results saved locally

Once scored, the generated text files, images, and HTML pages are saved locally in a number of organised folders. The majority of the text files are made up from the standard raw output of the metrics themselves. The image files are statistical graphs produced from the metric scores. Both the text and image files can be inspected directly on a metric by metric basis and used for reference. The VEMV tool brings together the text and images in the HTML files to form the main viewable output.

Runtime user options

The minimal default settings will quickly produce scores for standard BLEU, WER and E-Dist. Numerous parameters can be set on the command line enabling the user to choose any or all of the additional metrics and whether or not to generate graphs.

A number of the metrics (especially BLEU and METEOR) have a plethora of parameters, which can be selected. To avoid the need for complex command line inputs the metric level parameters can be placed in an easily editable text based configuration file, which in turn is passed to the command line.

In addition, the user can choose which metric will be the dominant one for sorting and display purposes (the default is BLEU) and there is an option for selecting how many score bins or pages to use to show the sentences. The default is 100 pages (one for every percentage point), but some users may prefer fewer pages (e.g. 10 or 20) in order to simplify the main interface and general navigation.

An accessibility flag has also been added. It removes some of the colour formatting from the displays making it easier for users with visual impairments (e.g colour blindness).

3.4 Viewing the Actual Output

Figure 2 shows the main page of the software. In this case all eight metrics were used as shown by the mini graph icons. Each of these mini graph icons act as a link. Ten score bins (circular icons) were selected as a parameter.

Users can click on any of the links/icons to navigate to the various pages. Clicking on the circular icons opens the sentence level score pages (Figure 1) showing individual sentences with a given score. Clicking on the mini graph icons takes the user to the graph display web pages for the respective metrics or the general document wide statistics. Figure 3, for example, is a metric graph showing the distribution of standard BLEU scores for the dataset. In this case the chart in Figure 3 would be accessed by clicking on the very left hand mini graph icon on the main page shown in Figure 2.

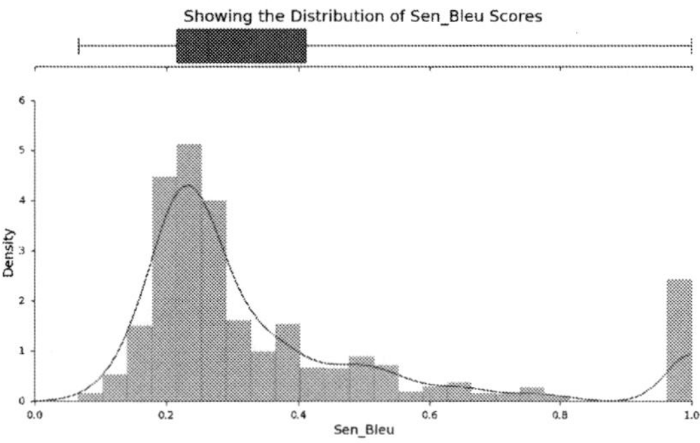

Figure 3: A graph showing the distribution of standard BLEU scores.

3.5   Downloading and Running the Tool

Vis-Eval Metric Viewer can currently be downloaded from the following location on GitHub: `https://github.com/David-Steele/VisEval_Metric_Viewer`.

The associated README file provides instructions on how to get started with using the tool, and what to do if you run into any problems.

In terms of hardware requirements, a computer with at least 2GB of RAM and 300MB of available storage is needed to run the software.

A short video demonstration of these and other features of the Vis-Eval Metric Viewer software can be found online at: `https://youtu.be/nUmdlXGYeMs`.

4   Conclusion and Future Work

The Vis-Eval Metric Viewer tool was designed with three main aims:

- To provide a useful tool that is easy to install (using readily available packages), and simple to use and run on a local machine without the need for a server or internet connection.

- To offer a single place for scoring translations using multiple popular metrics.

- To provide in depth visual feedback making it easy to examine segment level metric scores.

The tool offers a light weight solution that makes it easy to compare multiple-metric scores in a clear manner. Feedback can be interactively explored and searched rapidly with ease, whilst numerous graphs provide additional information. The tool can be run locally on any platform. All results are saved in self-contained folders for easy access.

We plan to add the following functionalities to VEMV in the future:

- Dynamic graphs, enabling users to select (in real time) variables to compare, and other features such as zooming in/out.

- Inclusion of a few additional popular lightweight evaluation metrics. The modular design of the software means that adding new metrics is a relatively trivial process.

- Using the saved output from the tool to compare multiple MT systems against one another.

References

Bogdan Babych. 2014. Automated mt evaluation metrics and their limitations. *Tradumàtica*, (12):464–470.

Michael Denkowski and Alon Lavie. 2014. Meteor universal: Language specific translation evaluation for any target language. In *Proceedings of the Ninth Workshop on Statistical Machine Translation*, pages 376–380, Baltimore, Maryland, USA. Association for Computational Linguistics.

Giménez, Jesús Màrquez, and Lluís. 2010. Asiya: An open toolkit for automatic machine translation (meta-)evaluation. *The Prague Bulletin of Mathematical Linguistics*, 94:77–86.

Ondřej Klejch, Eleftherios Avramidis, Aljoscha Burchardt, and Martin Popel. 2015. MT-compareval: Graphical evaluation interface for machine translation development. *The Prague Bulletin of Mathematical Linguistics*, (104):63–74.

Nitin Madnani. 2011. ibleu: Interactively debugging & scoring statistical machine translation systems. In *Proceedings of the Fifth IEEE International Conference on Semantic Computing*, pages 213–214.

Kishore Papineni, Salim Roukos, Todd Ward, and Wei-Jing Zhu. 2002. Bleu: A method for automatic evaluation of machine translation. In *Proceedings of the 40th Annual Meeting on Association for Computational Linguistics*, pages 311–318, Stroudsburg, PA, USA. Association for Computational Linguistics.

Matthew Snover, Bonnie Dorr, Richard Schwartz, Linnea Micciulla, and John Makhoul. 2006. A study of translation edit rate with targeted human annotation. In *In Proceedings of Association for Machine Translation in the Americas*, pages 223–231.

Xingyi Song, Trevor Cohn, and Lucia Specia. 2013. BLEU deconstructed: Designing a better MT evaluation metric. *International Journal of Computational Linguistics and Applications*, (4):29–44.

Milos Stanojevic and Khalil Sima'an. 2014. Beer: Better evaluation as ranking. In *Proceedings of the Ninth Workshop on Statistical Machine Translation*, pages "414–419". "Association for Computational Linguistics".

Ying Zhang, Stephan Vogel, and Alex Waibel. 2004. Interpreting bleu/nist scores: How much improvement do we need to have a better system. In *Proceedings of Language Resources and Evaluation*, pages 2051–2054.

Know Who Your Friends Are:
Understanding Social Connections from Unstructured Text

Léa A. Deleris, Francesca Bonin, Elizabeth Daly, Stéphane Deparis,
Yufang Hou, Charles Jochim, Yassine Lassoued and Killian Levacher
IBM Research - Ireland
Dublin , Ireland
`lea.deleris, fbonin, edaly, stephane.deparis`
`yhou, charlesj, ylassoued, killian.levacher @ie.ibm.com`

Abstract

Having an understanding of interpersonal relationships is helpful in many contexts. Our system seeks to assist humans with that task, using textual information (e.g., case notes, speech transcripts, posts, books) as input. Specifically, our system first extracts qualitative and quantitative information elements (which we call signals) about interactions among persons, aggregates those to provide a condensed view of relationships and then enables users to explore all facets of the resulting social (multi-)graph through a visual interface.

1 Introduction

The social network of a person plays a vital role in their well being providing access to assistance, resources, support (Wellman and Wortley, 1990) and even influencing health (Christakis and Fowler, 2007). Understanding the quality of the social relationships, beyond the simple existence of a relationship or its demographic nature (family or not), provides a better perspective on the context and is essential in a variety of situations that extends beyond social media such as criminal investigations (identifying suspects and acolytes), sales (connecting to the right persons in target companies), political analysis (understanding the evolution of alliances) and human resources (improving team dynamics). For instance, Yose et al. (2018) analysed a medieval text to get novel insights into the hostilities during the battle of Clontarf of 1014.

The initial motivation for this work comes from the domain of social care. One essential task for care workers is to identify who plays a supportive or disruptive role in a patient's environment at a given time. Problems emerge when details get lost within notes of the multiple persons composing the care team. Significant details may have been recorded but are locked inside free-text narratives, requiring other parties to invest a great deal of time to gain a full understanding of the situation.

In this paper, we present a system designed to assist humans with the understanding of interpersonal relationships. Specifically, the system takes as input a collection of texts and automatically extracts a multigraph representation of the relationships (and their quality). From that information, we provide an interface to enable users to gain insights into the relationships, from aggregated information to fine-grained analysis of temporal patterns and emotions.

2 Background

Our work builds upon two areas: social graph identification and qualitative relationship analysis. Most of the research within the former attempts to build ontologies of relations between individuals based on information extracted from text (e.g., social networks, dialogues, novels) (Hauffa et al., 2011). Mori et al. (2006) try to enhance social network extraction from the web, considering a range of entities beyond just persons. They identify the nature of entities (e.g., person, firm, geopolitical entity) and their relations (e.g., mayor of).

The second area instead explores how to construct a qualitative representation of the relationship between individuals. Bracewell et al. (2011) for example determine the collegiality between two persons, as exhibited in a text. Srivastava et al. (2016) attempt to identify the polarity of relations (cooperative or conflictual) between characters in narrative summaries, using textual and structural features. Iyyer et al. (2016) model how the fictional relationship between two characters changes over time using deep recurrent autoencoders.

Altogether, while the first field enables the extraction of complex multi-party social graphs, links representing interpersonal relationships within

Proceedings of NAACL-HLT 2018: Demonstrations, pages 76–80
New Orleans, Louisiana, June 2 - 4, 2018. ©2018 Association for Computational Linguistics

these graphs often lack a more nuanced representation (Hauffa et al., 2011). On the other hand, techniques from qualitative relationship analysis lead to a more extensive understanding of relationships yet they are typically applied to minimal settings consisting of two or three individuals at most. Our work brings both fields together by producing larger multi-party social graphs with qualitative links identified between the individuals.

3 Modeling Relationships

We model *interpersonal relationships*, or simply *relationships* between two *entities* by analyzing a list of associated *relationship signals* (hereafter *signals*) which are extracted by an NLP system. At this point, we focus on four kinds of *signals*:

- Direct Speech - A person addressing another one without mentioning him/her, e.g., *Phoebe* (to *Monica*): *"The weather is nice today"*.

- Direct Reference - A person addressing another one and mentioning him/her explicitly, e.g., *Phoebe* (to *Monica*): *"I hate you"*.

- Indirect Reference - A person mentioning a third party, i.e., someone who is not present, e.g., *Phoebe*: *"I like Rachel"*.

- Third-Party Reference - The description, by a third-party, of any kind of relation between two entities, e.g., *Phoebe*: *"Ross has been in love with Rachel forever"*.

While we focus in our examples on humans, entities could also include corporations, governmental organizations, products, brands and animals (e.g., *"Toyota allies with Intel in bid to overtake GM."*).

For each detected signal, our system seeks to present a qualitative description including **sentiment**, **emotion** such as anger, disgust, joy, etc., other qualitative aspects such as **intensity**, **formality**, **cooperative vs. adversarial** along with information about the context such as **geographical location**, settings (**one-on-one vs. group discussion**), whether **face-to-face** or **remote**, whether **synchronous** or **asynchronous** interactions.

In turn, through a model to aggregate those signals together and over time, this enables us to attach qualitative metrics to *relationships* for instance **sentiment and emotions** – so as to differentiate between supportive relationships and negative relationships – but also **volatility** of sentiment and emotions, **intensity/frequency** [1] and **recency**.

The logic underneath the aggregation model can vary by situation, but is typically based on weighted counts of the various signals. For instance, in the sentence *"You, Frankie, you are a liar"*, the system would extract at the atomic level one direct speech signal from the speaker towards Frankie and three direct references as well. When aggregating, it may be that the three direct references are counted as one rather than three, being all from the same utterance and that the direct reference takes priority over the direct speech signal which could be discarded. However, in some scenario, it may be relevant to keep track at the level of each atomic signal. Our system provides the flexibility to design bespoke models of how signals map to relationships. From an engineering perspective, we rely on Solr[2] to index each signal with all inferred facets such as entities, sentiment and type.

4 NLP System

Our system combines NLP tools to perform *entity mention resolution* and then extracts signals between these entities.[3] Our entity mention resolution borrows from named-entity recognition, mention detection, coreference resolution, and entity linking. We address more than just named entities (i.e., we are interested in all (person) entity mentions), and look at not only coreferred ones. To get a complete picture of the connection for a person, we want to identify all possible references to them, whether named entities (e.g., Ross Geller, Ross) or not (e.g., him, you, that guy, his son, the professor).

Entity Mention Detection. We use named-entity recognition and coreference resolution to identify mentions of entities (people) in the text and supplement that with tools for identifying common roles (e.g., professions), titles, or relations (e.g., brother or neighbor).

Entity Linking and Resolution. We leverage social graph information to resolve the detected entity mentions. This involves, for example, making use of family relationships to find or disambiguate new mentions of entities in the text. When no social graph is provided, this step includes building the graph from a knowledge source or to bootstrap social graph creation using the output of the

---

[1] Granovetter observes that "the more frequently persons interact with one another, the stronger their sentiments of friendship for one another are apt to be" (Granovetter, 1973)

[2] http://lucene.apache.org/solr/

[3] As mentioned, we focus primarily on person entities.

entity mention detection. For those cases, further named-entity disambiguation may be needed (Pabico, 2014; Han and Zhao, 2009).

Relationship Signal Detection. Using the resolved entity mentions we detect relationship signals between entities and characterize the signal type (Section 3). In addition, we perform targeted sentiment and emotion analysis between entities.

Figure 1 illustrates how the different modules are articulated. The dashed arrow going from the graph-based mention resolution towards the text-level mention detection module indicates that information from the graph can further contribute in disambiguating and enriching the text-level mention detection steps (for instance pronoun resolution).

The output of the NLP extraction pipeline comprises a list of entity mentions and a list of relationship signals between those entities. These contribute to enrich our understanding of the social graph among the entities (or create one if none were provided as input). From this combined information we draw the relationship graph.

5 Visual Interface Features

Our current system enables users to (i) Aggregate information (over time, over sentiment categories), (ii) Visualize temporal relations over time and (iii) Scrutinize each atomic signal underneath each relationship (with the possibility of editing or correcting it). Another task that we are considering enabling is the ability to reason over the graph (knowledge propagation e.g., if A "admires" B and B "admires" C, it is likely that A "admires" C).

Our current interface hinges on three primary views. **Network overview** (Fig. 2) which provides a snapshot of the social relationships using visual cues to summarise them graphically. The average sentiment is indicated through the color of the links, red for negative, green for positive where thickness gives an indication of the strength, the thicker the link, the more positive or negative the sentiment. The UI supports visualising the network as an overview or over specific time intervals. Next version will include a representation of intensity (through dashes) along with an indication of volatility by replacing the line with a sinusoidal curve. Recency will be captured through the placement relative to the ego node, people who more recently interacted with the person are closer.

The **Personal network view** (Fig. 3) supports a view of the two-hop interpersonal relationships of the individual along with a summary view of the person in terms of general emotions expressed (donut chart in the bottom right quadrant of the screen). The view can show the overall sentiment and intensity of how they interact with others.

Finally, the **Relationship view** (Fig. 4) consists of a stream graph presenting the five primary emotions, anger, disgust, joy, fear and sadness as they change over time. It can be used to see the intensity of the relationships either by type, sentiment or emotions. Drill down support is provided where the user may hover over peak areas of interest in the graph to inspect the snippets of text from the input corpus that support the inferred emotions. The emotions are directional where the upper part of the stream graph represents the signals from Entity X to Entity Y and the lower part of the graph represents Entity Y towards Entity X.

6 Demo Flow

Ideally, we would have relied on anonymized careworker notes to demonstrate our system. However, privacy restrictions made access to such notes challenging and for our proof of concept, we have used the transcripts from the Friends TV series, whose theme, i.e. the interactions among a core group of friends is well aligned with our objective. We specifically focus on the first two seasons and leverage the character identification corpus created by Chen and Choi (2016), which includes entity annotation of personal mentions[4].

A natural starting page for an analysis is the (messy) social graph for all characters over all episodes of Season 1. Fig. 2 shows the overall social network when narrowing down to Season 1 Episode 2. From this place, a user can further dive into one specific character (selecting a node), or rather explore a relationship (selecting a link).

Assuming the user selects to focus on *Ross* then his personal network view (Fig. 3) would be displayed. The dominating emotion conveyed in this episode is joy, both in quantity and in strength (represented through length of the arc and radius respectively), followed by sadness and fear. In this episode, *Ross* learns from his now-lesbian ex-wife *Carol* that she is pregnant with his child. In terms of relationship, the graph shows mostly negative sentiments towards other characters, especially *Barry*, though positive ones towards *Rachel*.

---

[4]https://github.com/emorynlp/character-mining

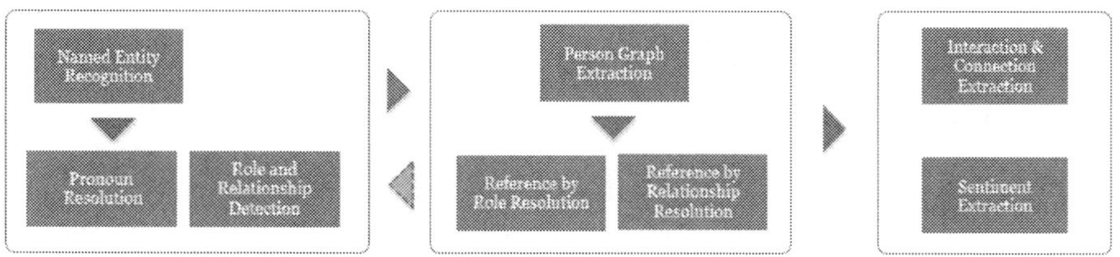

Figure 1: Overview of the NLP Interaction Extraction System

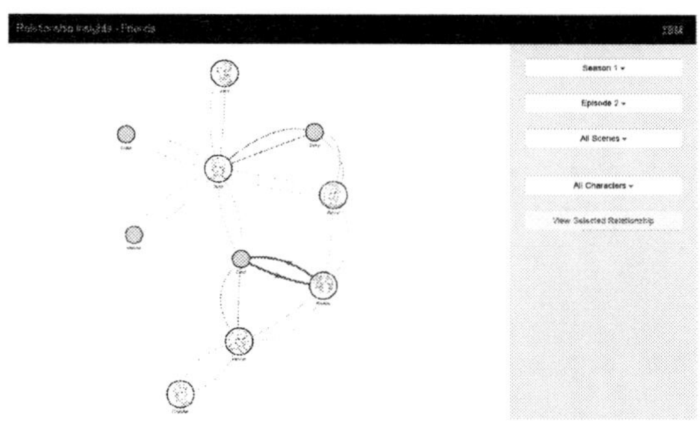

Figure 2: Overview of Social Relationships [S1E2]

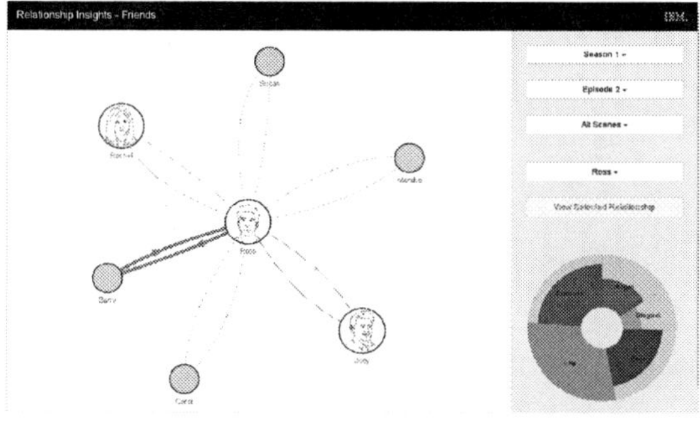

Figure 3: Personal Network for Ross [S1E2]

Selecting a relationship (eg. the one between Ross and Rachel) the user will be shown a stream graph as in Fig. 4. The graph shows the five primary emotions as they change over time during the series. The x axis represents the progressive episodes' numbers and the y axis the intensity of the emotion. Above the x axis the relation Ross towards Rachel is shown, below the relation Rachel towards Ross. We can observe the distinctive asymmetry of the relationship. For instance, in Episode 11, there is no specific emotion from *Rachel* towards *Ross* though quite a mix of emotions expressed by *Ross* towards *Rachel*. In this episode, *Ross* is jealous of *Rachel's* boyfriend *Paolo* and confides his feelings and love troubles towards *Rachel* to *Chandler's*

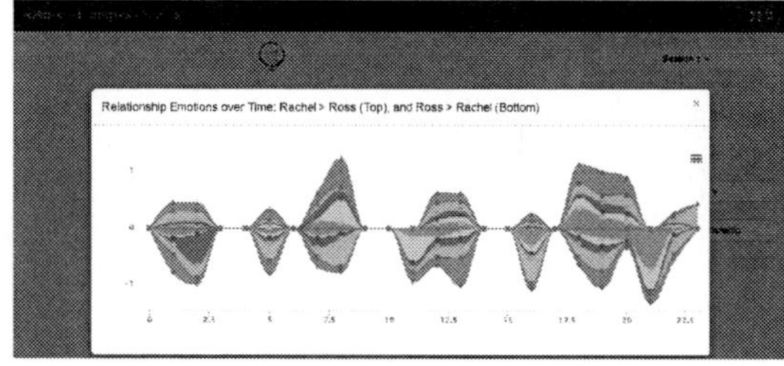

Figure 4: Stream graph of Relationship over time between Ross and Rachel [Season 1]

mother. In Episode 16, sentiments of anger, fear and disgust are present in Ross towards Rachel, but not viceversa.

As part of the actual demonstration, we will challenge users with a short information retrieval task aimed at illustrating the types of questions that our approach supports. For fact-based questions, we will give participants a set amount of time (i.e. 2 minutes) and will maintain a leaderboard of the fastest information finders (with participants' consent). Sample questions would be *"Whose mother did Ross kiss during season 1?"*, or *"How long did Rachel go out with Paolo?"*. For questions that require interpretation (e.g. *'Does Chandler like Frankie?"*), we would let participants tell us their opinion before and after using the tool and ask them if the system was helpful in gaining confidence about their final answer.

7 Conclusion

This paper presents a system to support the analysis and understanding of interpersonal relationships. Relationships are described along multiple quantitative and qualitative dimensions which are automatically populated from relationship signals extracted from text by a NLP system. The associated interface enables a user to quickly focus on a specific person or pair of persons and to investigate how the relationship evolves over time.

References

David B Bracewell, Marc Tomlinson, Ying Shi, Jeremy Bensley, and Mary Draper. 2011. Who's playing well with others: Determining collegiality in text. In *Proceedings of the 5th IEEE International Conference on Semantic Computing (ICSC 2011)*, pages 21–26. IEEE.

Yu-Hsin Chen and Jinho D. Choi. 2016. Character identification on multiparty conversation: Identifying mentions of characters in TV shows. In *Proceedings of the SIGDIAL 2016 Conference, The 17th Annual Meeting of the Special Interest Group on Discourse and Dialogue*, pages 90–100. The Association for Computer Linguistics.

Nicholas A Christakis and James H Fowler. 2007. The spread of obesity in a large social network over 32 years. *New England journal of medicine*, 357(4):370–379.

Mark S Granovetter. 1973. The strength of weak ties. *American journal of sociology*, pages 1360–1380.

Xianpei Han and Jun Zhao. 2009. Named entity disambiguation by leveraging wikipedia semantic knowledge. In *Proceedings of the 18th ACM Conference on Information and Knowledge Management*, CIKM '09, pages 215–224, New York, NY, USA. ACM.

Jan Hauffa, Gottlieb Bossert, Nadja Richter, Florian Wolf, Nora Liesenfeld, and Georg Groh. 2011. Beyond foaf: Challenges in characterizing social relations. In *Privacy, Security, Risk and Trust (PASSAT) and 2011 IEEE Third International Conference on Social Computing (SocialCom), 2011 IEEE Third International Conference on*, pages 790–795. IEEE.

Mohit Iyyer, Anupam Guha, Snigdha Chaturvedi, Jordan Boyd-Graber, and Hal Daumé III. 2016. Feuding families and former friends: Unsupervised learning for dynamic fictional relationships. In *Proceedings of the 2016 Conference of the North American Chapter of the Association for Computational Linguistics: Human Language Technologies*, pages 1534–1544.

Junichiro Mori, Takumi Tsujishita, Yutaka Matsuo, and Mitsuru Ishizuka. 2006. Extracting relations in social networks from the web using similarity between collective contexts. *The Semantic Web-ISWC 2006*, pages 487–500.

Jaderick P. Pabico. 2014. An analysis of named entity disambiguation in social networks. *Asia Pacific Journal of Multidisciplinary Research*, 2(4).

Shashank Srivastava, Snigdha Chaturvedi, and Tom M Mitchell. 2016. Inferring interpersonal relations in narrative summaries. In *Proceedings of the Thirtieth AAAI Conference on Artificial Intelligence*, pages 2807–2813.

Barry Wellman and Scot Wortley. 1990. Different strokes from different folks: Community ties and social support. *American journal of Sociology*, pages 558–588.

Joseph Yose, Ralph Kenna, Máirín MacCarron, and Pádraig MacCarron. 2018. Network analysis of the viking age in ireland as portrayed in cogadh gaedhel re gallaibh. *Royal Society Open Science*, 5(1):171024.

RiskFinder: A Sentence-level Risk Detector for Financial Reports

Yu-Wen Liu[†], Liang-Chih Liu[*], Chuan-Ju Wang[‡], Ming-Feng Tsai[†∧]
[†]Dept. of Computer Science, National Chengchi University
[*]Dept. of Information and Finance Management, National Taipei University of Technology
[‡]Research Center of Information Technology Innovation, Academia Sinica
[∧]MOST Joint Research Center for AI Technology and All Vista Healthcare
`g10435@cs.nccu.edu.tw`, `lcliu@ntut.edu.tw`,
`cjwang@citi.sinica.edu.tw`, `mftsai@nccu.edu.tw`

Abstract

This paper presents a web-based information system, RiskFinder, for facilitating the analyses of soft and hard information in financial reports. In particular, the system broadens the analyses from the word level to sentence level, which makes the system useful for practitioner communities and unprecedented among financial academics. The proposed system has four main components: 1) a Form 10-K risk-sentiment dataset, consisting of a set of risk-labeled financial sentences and pre-trained sentence embeddings; 2) metadata, including basic information on each company that published the Form 10-K financial report as well as several relevant financial measures; 3) an interface that highlights risk-related sentences in the financial reports based on the latest sentence embedding techniques; 4) a visualization of financial time-series data for a corresponding company. This paper also conducts some case studies to showcase that the system can be of great help in capturing valuable insight within large amounts of textual information. The system is now online available at `https://cfda.csie.org/RiskFinder/`.

1 Introduction

A great deal of mass media outlets such as newspapers and magazines, or financial reports required by authorities such as the SEC[1]-mandated Form-10Q and Form-10K, play an important role in disseminating information to participants in financial markets. The spread of this information may quickly or slowly influence the sentiment of market participants and thus reshape their perspectives on economic numbers, such as stock prices and interest rate levels. This information comes in two types: soft information, usually referring to textual information such as opinions and market commentary;

---

[1] Securities and Exchange Commission

and hard information, that is, numerical information such as historical time series of stock prices.

Due to the strong relation between the textual information and numerical measures, there has been a growing body of studies in the fields of finance and data science that adopt the techniques of natural language processing (NLP) and machine learning to examine the interaction between these two types of information (e.g., Kogan et al., 2009; Tsai et al., 2016; Tsai and Wang, 2017; Rekabsaz et al., 2017). For example, Loughran and McDonald (2011) and Jegadeesh and Wu (2013) investigate how the disclosures of finance sentiment or risk keywords in SEC-mandated financial reports affect investor expectations about a company's future stock prices. Moreover, Kogan et al. (2009) and Tsai and Wang (2017) exploit sentiment analysis of 10-K reports for financial risk analysis. Furthermore, in Liu et al. (2016), a web-based information system, FIN10K, is proposed for financial report analysis and visualization.

However, these studies and systems all focus on word-level analyses, which likely yield biased results or explanations because the usage of words in finance context, especially in financial reports, is usually complicated and sometimes includes tricks to hide original sentiment (Liu et al., 2016). One of the prominent examples is the negations of positive words to frame negative statements (Loughran and McDonald, 2016); moreover, we also find that the word "offset" is usually used to hide negative information with positive sentiment words. Therefore, to advance the understanding of financial textual information, this paper further constructs an information system based on sentence-level analysis to assist practitioners to capture more precise and meaningful insight within large amounts of textual information in finance.

There have been several studies proposed to produce distributed representations of words, such as

Proceedings of NAACL-HLT 2018: Demonstrations, pages 81–85
New Orleans, Louisiana, June 2 - 4, 2018. ©2018 Association for Computational Linguistics

word2vec (Mikolov et al., 2013). In recent years, there have also been several studies that extend the proportion from word level to sentence, paragraph, or even document level, such as doc2vec (Mikolov et al., 2013), FastText (Bojanowski et al., 2017), and Siamese-CBOW (Kenter et al., 2016). Following the fruitful progress of these techniques of word and sentence embeddings, this paper presents a web-based information system, RiskFinder, that broadens the content analysis from the word level to sentence level for financial reports.

The proposed system contains four main parts: 1) a Form 10-K risk-sentiment dataset, consisting of a set of risk-labeled financial sentences and pre-trained sentence embeddings; 2) metadata that summarizes the basic information about each financial report; 3) an interface that highlights risk-related sentences in the financial reports; 4) a visualization of financial time-series data associated with the corresponding financial reports. In the proposed system, we use the 10-K Corpus (Liu et al., 2016) which contains 40,708 financial reports from year 1996 to 2013. In addition to the 10-K corpus, we also construct a set of labeled financial sentences with respect to financial risk by involving 8 financial specialists including accountants and financial analysts to ensure the quality of the labeling. With the labeled sentences and the large collection of financial reports, we apply FastText (Bojanowski et al., 2017) and Siamese-CBOW (Kenter et al., 2016) to sentence-level textual analysis. Due to the superior performance of FastText, the system highlights high risk sentences in those reports via using FastText. For comparison purposes, the system shows the numbers of these highlighted high-risk sentences for the selected report, and we at the same time display the time-aligned relevant quantitative information such as the historical stock prices of the selected company to visualize its financial risk, which considerably facilitates case studies in the field of finance and accounting. Finally, we publish the pre-trained sentence vectors trained on the 10-K corpus and our constructed labeled sentences.

2   System Description

Figure 1 illustrates the user interface of the proposed RiskFinder system. In the system, there are 4 major components for risk detection, the details of which are provided in the following subsections.

2.1   Form 10-K Risk-sentiment Dataset

The first component is the collection of the Form 10-K risk-sentiment dataset. This work provides the financial risk-sentiment dataset that consists of two types of data: a set of risk-labeled financial sentences and the pre-trained sentence embeddings. There are in total 432 labeled financial sentences in the dataset, which were selected from the MD&A[2] sections of the 10-K corpus. When selecting the candidate sentences, we first used the six financial sentiment lexicons proposed by Loughran and McDonald (2011) to filter sentences and randomly chose 24 sentences per year for annotation, yielding in total 432 sentences for 18 years (1996 to 2013). To construct the risk-labeled dataset, eight financial specialists including accountants, financial analysts and consultants participated in the annotation task to ensure the quality of the labeling. In the annotation process, each of the candidate sentences was labeled by three different annotators, and then the rule of majority was used to determine the degree of risk of the sentence. A total of 138 sentences out of the 432 sentences are identified as high-risk sentences, and Cronbach's alpha, which is regarded as an indicator to determine the internal consistency, showed the reliability of 0.784. In addition, the dataset also includes the pre-trained sentence vectors, each of which is a 100-dimension real-valued vector, trained by FastText and Siamese-CBOW on the 10-K corpus.[3]

2.2   The Metadata

The second component of the proposed system is the metadata of the companies in the Form 10-K corpus. A user can first select the company in the list (1) (e.g., AEP INDUSTRIES INC in Figure 1). Following the selection, the MD&A section of the report and all fiscal years of the chosen company are then automatically loaded in the window (2) and timeline (3), respectively. A user can select their interesting fiscal year in timeline (3). Then, our system simultaneously displays in table (4) the following metadata which summarizes the basic information of the corresponding company:

1. the company name;
2. the company's CUSIP number, which facilitates the retrieval of information associated

---

[2]Management Discussion and Analysis of Financial Condition and Results of Operations

[3]The dataset is available at `https://cfda.csie.org/RiskFinder/` upon publication.

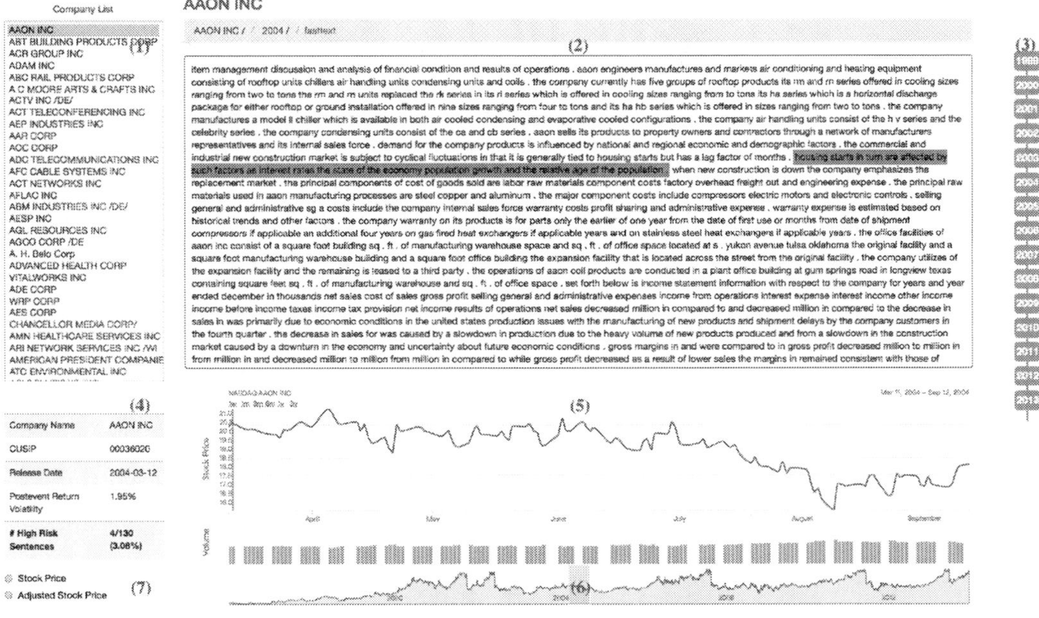

Figure 1: The user interface of the RiskFinder system

	Siamese-CBOW	FastText
Accuracy	0.656	0.813
Precision	0.776	0.774
Recall	0.438	0.621
F1-measure	0.558	0.684

Table 1: Performance for risk sentence classification

with this company from other widely used databases (e.g., Compustat and CRSP[4]);

3. the report release date;

4. the annualized post-event return volatilities;[5]

5. the number and the percentage of highlighted risk-related sentences in this report.

2.3 Risk-related Sentence Detection

To examine a company's financial risk given the textual information in its financial reports on Form 10-K, the proposed system focuses on the sentence-level investigation into the MD&A section, which is considered a major part where the firm managements are most likely to reveal information (Loughran and McDonald, 2011). To obtain representative sentence representations, we adopt two sentence embedding techniques to con-

duct sentence-level textual analyses: FastText, a linear classifier that enables efficient sentence classification and yields performance on par with other deep learning classifiers, and Siamese-CBOW, a neural network architecture that obtains word embeddings, directly optimized for sentence representations. Since Siamese-CBOW, the second approach, produces only sentence embedding (by simply averaging the word embedding of each word in a sentence), we then employ a logistic regression to construct a binary classifier to detect high-risk sentences. Table 1 tabulates the performance tested on the 87 sentences in terms of accuracy, precision, recall, and F1-measure with 4-fold cross-validation. Note that the 432 sentences are split into the training data and the testing data with 345 and 87 sentences, respectively, where the proportions of high-risk sentences are kept the same in training and testing sets. Due to the significant superior performance of FastText, we adopt it to highlight high-risk sentences in the reports in the proposed system. Furthermore, the number and percentage of highlighted high-risk sentences in each report are summarized in table (4) of Figure 1.

2.4 Visualization for Financial Measures

Our system attempts to facilitate the analysis of textual information and capture more insight into the financial risk associated with the announcement

---

[4]CRSP is the abbreviation for the Center for Research in Security Prices.

[5]The postevent return volatility is the root-mean square error from a Fama-French three-factor model (Loughran and McDonald, 2011; Tsai et al., 2016).

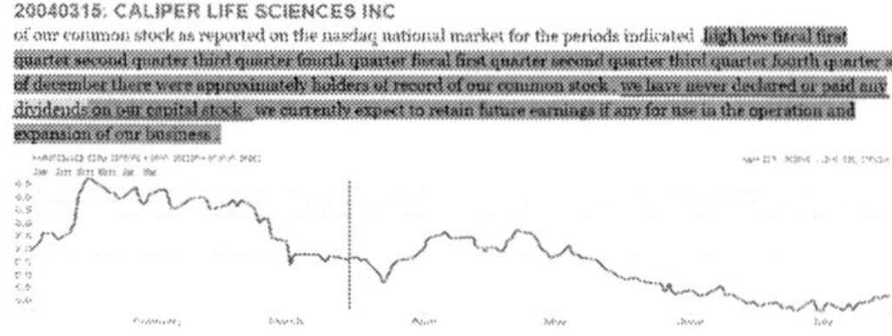

Figure 2: A positive word in a high-risk sentence

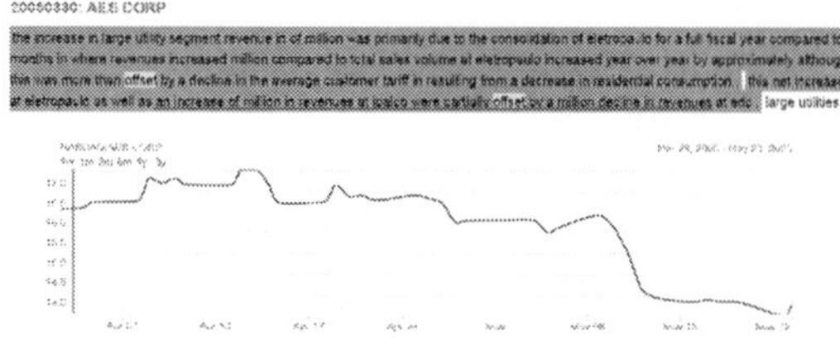

Figure 3: The tone transition word

of each financial report. Therefore, in addition to highlight the high-risk sentences, our system also displays time-aligned quantitative information for comparison purposes, such as historical prices and trading volumes of the selected company's stock, as shown in the chart (5) of Figure 1. In particular, the release date of the report is highlighted through a red vertical line in the chart; users can adjust the window (6) to show the corresponding quantitative information for a certain period. Note that two types of historical stock prices are provided in the proposed system: the original stock prices and those adjusted due to stock splits and dividend payouts; the mode can be altered through (7).

3 Case Study

Framing negative or high-risk information through negations of positive financial sentiment words is prevalent among the drafters of financial corpora. Such type of expression could alleviate the adverse effect on market participants' sentiment, but that makes the identification of high-risk statements far more complicated than the discussions in extant finance and accounting literature. From word-level to sentence-level analysis, our proposed RiskFinder system can effectively recognize high-risk information padded with positive words. The positive word "dividend" in stock markets is a notable example; Figure 2 shows that Caliper Life Science Inc.'s stock prices trend downward after the announcement of its year 2004 financial report stating that "we have never declared or paid any dividends on our capital stock ...." In a more complex form of the expressions with the positive words "favor-

able," the system identifies the information "we cannot assure you that these markets will continue to grow or remain favorable to the life science industry ..." as a high-risk sentence. Moreover, our system also detects the tendency that the drafters of 10-K financial reports use the word "offset" to hide high-risk information behind the low-risk one. For instance, Figure 3 shows that AES CORP.'s stock prices trend downward within 2 months after the announcement of its year 2005 financial report stating that "... an increase of million in revenues at ipalco were partially offset by a million decline in revenues ...." These examples show that our system can greatly facilitate case studies and be of great help for practitioners in capturing meaningful insight within large amounts of textual information in finance from the sentence-level point of view.

4 Conclusions

In this paper, we introduce RiskFinder to broaden the textual analysis of financial reports from the word level to sentence level. This extension is essential for the analytics of financial reports because the sentences are usually long and complicated, and high-risk information is sometimes hided with positive sentiment words. Built on financial reports in the 10-K Corpus with a set of risk-labeled sentences, this proposed system applies FastText to automatically identify high-risk sentences in those reports. For comparison purposes, the system even displays the time-aligned relevant quantitative information to visualize the financial risk associated with the announcement of each report.

This work is a preliminary study, the purpose of which is to demonstrate the importance of sentence-level analysis and the integration of soft and hard information in finance. Therefore, in the future, we will continue to extend the system, with an emphasis on incorporating more state-of-the-art learning algorithms or developing new algorithms to better detect risk-related sentences. In addition, one of our future work is to obtain more labeled sentences with respect to financial risk or even different financial aspects, which should further enhance the performance and usability of the proposed system.

Acknowledgments

This research was partially supported by the Ministry of Science and Technology of Taiwan under the grants MOST 106-3114-E-009-011 and 107-2634-F-002-011.

References

Piotr Bojanowski, Edouard Grave, Armand Joulin, and Tomas Mikolov. 2017. Enriching word vectors with subword information. *Transactions of the Association of Computational Linguistics*, 5(1):135–146.

Narasimhan Jegadeesh and Di Wu. 2013. Word power: A new approach for content analysis. *Journal of Financial Economics*, 110(3):712–729.

Tom Kenter, Alexey Borisov, and Maarten de Rijke. 2016. Siamese cbow: Optimizing word embeddings for sentence representations. In *Proceedings of the 54th Annual Meeting of the Association for Computational Linguistics (Volume 1: Long Papers)*, ACL '16, pages 941–951.

Shimon Kogan, Dimitry Levin, Bryan R Routledge, Jacob S Sagi, and Noah A Smith. 2009. Predicting risk from financial reports with regression. In *Proceedings of the 2009 Annual Conference of the North American Chapter of the Association for Computational Linguistics*, NAACL '09, pages 272–280.

Yu-Wen Liu, Liang-Chih Liu, Chuan-Ju Wang, and Ming-Feng Tsai. 2016. Fin10k: A web-based information system for financial report analysis and visualization. In *Proceedings of the 25th ACM International on Conference on Information and Knowledge Management*, CIKM '16, pages 2441–2444.

Tim Loughran and Bill McDonald. 2011. When is a liability not a liability? textual analysis, dictionaries, and 10-ks. *Journal of Finance*, 66(1):35–65.

Tim Loughran and Bill McDonald. 2016. Textual analysis in accounting and finance: A survey. *Journal of Accounting Research*, 54(4):1187–1230.

Tomas Mikolov, Ilya Sutskever, Kai Chen, Greg Corrado, and Jeffrey Dean. 2013. Distributed representations of words and phrases and their compositionality. In *Proceedings of the 26th International Conference on Neural Information Processing Systems*, NIPS '13, pages 3111–3119.

Navid Rekabsaz, Mihai Lupu, Artem Baklanov, Allan Hanbury, Alexander Dür, and Linda Anderson. 2017. Volatility prediction using financial disclosures sentiments with word embedding-based IR models. In *Proceedings of the 55th Annual Meeting of the Association for Computational Linguistics (Volume 1: Long Papers)*, ACL '17, pages 1712–1721.

Ming-Feng Tsai and Chuan-Ju Wang. 2017. On the risk prediction and analysis of soft information in finance reports. *European Journal of Operational Research*, 257(1):243–250.

Ming-Feng Tsai, Chuan-Ju Wang, and Po-Chuan Chien. 2016. Discovering finance keywords via continuous-space language models. *ACM Transactions on Management Information Systems*, 7(3):7:1–7:17.

SMILEE: Symmetric Multi-modal Interactions with Language-gesture Enabled (AI) Embodiment

Sujeong Kim, David Salter, Luke DeLuccia, Kilho Son, Mohamed R. Amer and Amir Tamrakar*

SRI International, 201 Washington Rd, Princeton, NJ08540

https://sites.google.com/view/smilee

Abstract

We demonstrate an intelligent conversational agent system designed for advancing human-machine collaborative tasks. The agent is able to interpret a user's communicative intent from both their verbal utterances and non-verbal behaviors, such as gestures. The agent is also itself able to communicate both with natural language and gestures, through its embodiment as an avatar thus facilitating natural symmetric multi-modal interactions. We demonstrate two intelligent agents with specialized skills in the Blocks World as use-cases of our system.

1 Introduction

Recent advances in speech recognition and natural language processing techniques have resulted in increasing use of intelligent assistants, such as Google Assistant, Siri, and Alexa, in our daily lives, replacing keyboard or touch interfaces. However, the interactions with these assistants are still limited to just the verbal modality.

In this paper, we present an intelligent conversational agent system (SMILEE) designed to advance the state of the art in human-machine interaction. The main idea underlying this system is the observation that **non-verbal behavior** (primarily gestures) encodes information that both complements and supplements speech in human-to-human communication. Our studies in the Blocks-World (BW) have shown that gestures are frequently used with speech taking on both complementary roles (reinforcing the meaning) and supplementary roles (adding information to what was verbalized), and contribute towards facilitating communication (Kim et al., 2018). Thus we assert that gestures need to be taken into account when deducing the meaning of complex ideas exchanged during communication and this has to be

---

ảmir.tamrakar@sri.com

done in a joint-inferencing process along with the natural language understanding process.

In the same vein, we also assert that communication between humans and computers should be symmetric and multi-modal in both directions for it to be truly natural. Thus, in order to facilitate the communication of a machines complex ideas to the human, the machine's utterances also need to be embellished with appropriate non-verbal behaviors. This argues for using a computer-generated avatar for embodying the machine. Only then will humans be able to naturally communicate with machines, as they do with other humans. Not only will this ease the communication but it also allow the communication to be more accurate.

In the following sections, we summarize various components of SMILEE and demonstrate two preliminary use-cases we have built.

2 Related Work

(Foster et al., 2009) explores different strategies for generating instructions given to the users by the robot for collaborative toy assembly type of tasks. (Perera et al., 2017) propose a system to learn new concepts (e.g., unseen structure) in BW environments from the descriptions of its properties. (She et al., 2014) propose a method to teach a robotic arm new actions for placing blocks using dialogues. There have also been efforts to understand language in the BW domain. Human-generated instructions in virtual blocks world are collected by (Bisk et al., 2016). Using this dataset, a neural-network model for 3D spatial operations has proposed (Krishnaswamy et al., 2018). In terms of non-verbal behaviors, (Salter et al., 2015) present a dataset containing two people building structures with basic shapes while only communicating with non-verbal queues.The key difference

Proceedings of NAACL-HLT 2018: Demonstrations, pages 86–90

New Orleans, Louisiana, June 2 - 4, 2018. ©2018 Association for Computational Linguistics

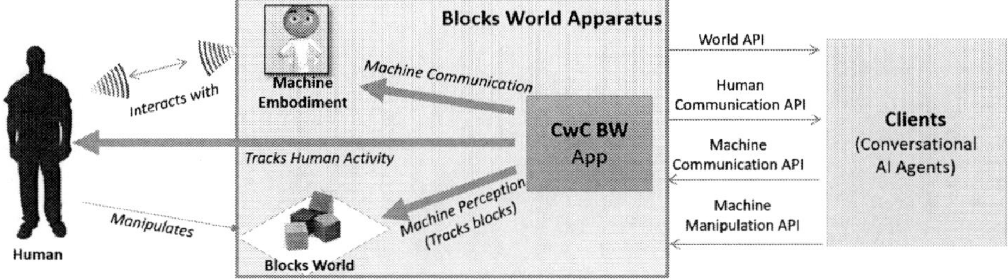

Figure 1: The Functional Architecture of the BW Apparatus. See text for details.

of our work from these work is that we use speech and gestures together for understanding human intents.

3 The Blocks World (BW) Apparatus

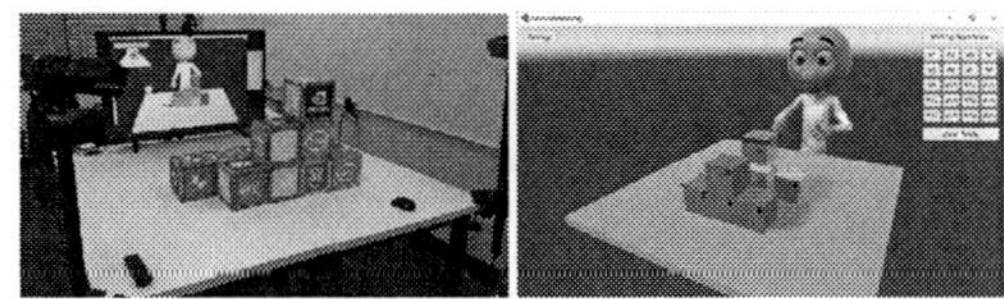

Figure 2: **Blocks World Apparatus** Physical setup (left) and a virtual setup (right).

The Blocks World Apparatus (Figs.1 & 2) is a computer vision based platform to provide I/O abilities for AI agents (Son et al., 2015). It was designed for the purpose of having intelligent conversations about blocks on a table, i.e., the Blocks World. The platform acts as the eyes and ears for the AI agent, tracking not only the blocks on the table (Son et al., 2016) but also multi-modal behaviors of the human interacting with it, both verbal and non-verbal (Siddique et al., 2015). It also provides an embodiment of the machine in the form of a simple humanoid avatar for the users to interact with. The Apparatus provides a number of APIs for the conversational AI agents to interface with the system.

The apparatus is also available as a virtual system (Fig. 2). The virtual version was developed using Unity (Unity, 2017) as an option for users who are not able to setup the full physical system. It allows the users to use the same exact APIs to interact with the apparatus. The virtual system is also deployed as a web app for remote users. This system is publicly available for use by the research community (Salter et al., 2017)[1].

[1] https://sites.google.com/view/playwithsmilee/home

4 SMILEE

SMILEE is the realization of our goal to allow natural verbal and non-verbal communication between a human and a conversational AI agent. Although the current system has been built for having conversations in the Blocks World, it is not restricted to this use case. We have used The Rochester Interactive Planning System (TRIPS) architecture (Ferguson and Allen, 1998) for realizing our system. The TRIPS framework approaches conversations as collaborative problem solving tasks. It provides a parser and an interpretation manager to normalize many forms of utterances into logical forms (LF) which is then formed into problem solving acts represented in AKRL. The TRIPS agent architecture utilizes a loose coupling of a number of independent agents communicating with each other via standardized KQML messages. In this section, we describe various agents that compose the SMILEE system (Fig. 3).

4.1 Scene Perception Agent

The scene perception agent processes the block tracking information from the BW apparatus to generate perceptual interpretations of the overall structure defined by the collection of positions and orientations of the tracked blocks. The perceptual interpretations include geometric relations between blocks, physical constraints, and perceptual grouping of blocks into larger substructures (such as row, stack, columns, etc). This grouping can also be done based on an attribute of the blocks, such as color, to generate other sub-grouping proposals to aid in the communication. The set of these relations are used to describe the scene.

4.2 Deictic Gesture Interpretation Agent

The gesture interpretation agent interprets the raw human communication signals from the BW apparatus. Current implementation of our gesture inter-

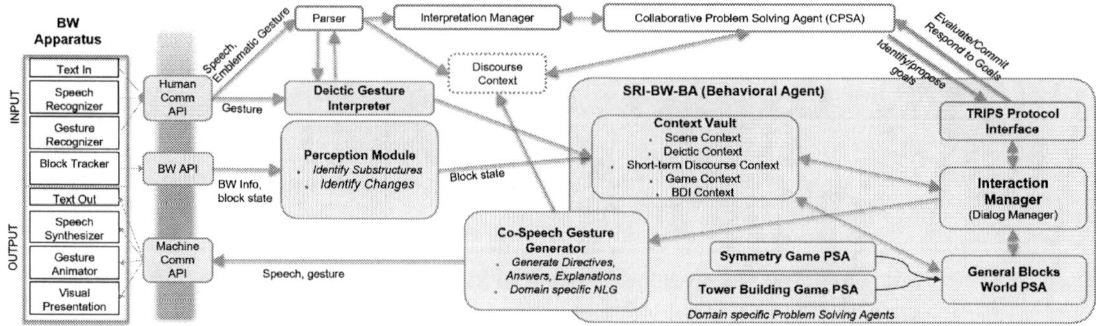

Figure 3: The SMILEE conversational AI Agent and its interactions with BW Apparatus and TRIPS modules. The modules highlighted with green are our own agents while the modules in blue are preexisting modules in the TRIPS system.

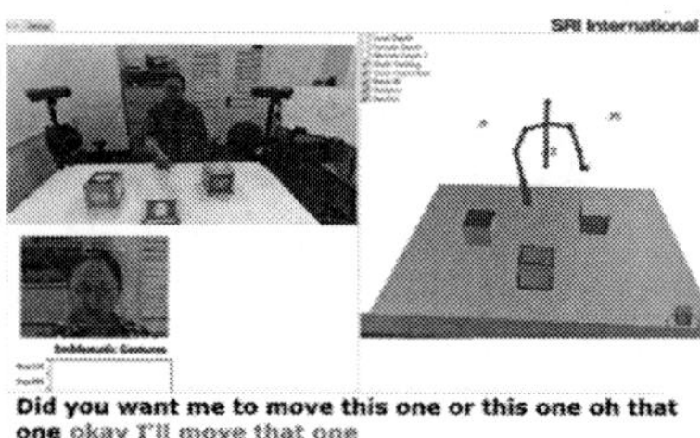

Figure 4: Real-time deictic gesture recognition. (Right) The block pointed by the user is highlighted with bold edges. (Bottom) The words from the live speech recognition. (Left-Top) Raw video input (Left-middle) facial behavior recognition.

pretation module converts the tokenized emblematic gestures directly into verbal utterances and allows them to be parsed in the normal manner. For deictic gesture interpretation, we use a real-time ASR engine for the verbal input and temporally align it with the information from the deictic gesture recognition stream to perform reference resolution (Fig.4). The pronoun-resolved utterance string goes through the parser to the rest of the interpretation modules. Our system is capable of tracking both the pointing and touching types of deictic gestures.

4.3 Co-speech Gesture Generation Agent

This agent is responsible for generating communication behaviors for the AI embodiment, in terms of deciding 'what to say' and 'what to do'. We approach this problem in two separate steps (Kim and Tamrakar, 2017). First, we convert the targeted instruction (machine computed plan step) into a fully verbal utterance and optimize it using appropriate contexts. Next, we explore the possibility of replacing parts of this utterance with gestures or simply supplementing them for better communication.

Below, we show various utterances generated by the agent for the same instruction "put a block at a position (x, y, z)", along with the cost (complexity) of the instruction. The spatial and task-related contexts significantly lowers the complexity.

$cost = 0$, Please put a block on top of it
$cost = 0.5$, Please put a new block on top of the block you just placed
$cost = 0.5$, Please put a new block behind the stack you just made
$cost = 1$, Please put a new block on top of the block on the top
$cost = 2$, Please put a new block on top of the block that is at the back and on the left

Deictic gestures also increase the chance of correct and efficient communication, by simplifying the dialogue or by confining the region of interest. Note that even when a gesture increases the length of the utterance, the communication can still be more effective. For example, "put a block on top of the stack there" can make it easier for the user to locate the stack than just saying "put a block on top of the stack".

4.4 SRI-BW Behavioral Agent (BA)

This behavioral agent (BA) is the main agent that enables the continuous interactions between the user and the machine. When the agent understands the user's intent without ambiguity, it performs an appropriate action. Otherwise, the agent asks clarifying questions to resolve missing or ambiguous information. For example:

USR: Put a block on the table.
SYS: Where on the table?

USR: Right there. [points to a location].
SYS: OK. I am putting a block at $(0, 0, 0)$
USR: Put another block next to it.
SYS: Can you be more specific? in front of/behind it? or to the right or left of it? or on top of it?
USR: Put it to the left of it.
SYS: But there is already a block there. Do you mean to the right of it?
USR: Yes.
SYS: Ok. I am putting a block at $(1, 0, 0)$.

The behavior agent consists of the following modules:

TRIPS protocol Interface handles the TRIPS choreography. It routes messages to the appropriate Problem Solving Agents.

Interaction Manager manages the state machines for dialogs/interactions.

Context Vault keeps track of all the states and contexts for the Problem Solving Agents (PSAs).

The BW PSAs are the domain specific problem solving agents for the Blocks World in the TRIPS architecture. They contain problem-specific general knowledge including appropriate representations and specific capabilities needed to carry out the actions requested by the user. They also keep track of the state of the problem.

We demonstrate use-cases in Section 5.

5 Use cases

We demonstrate two use-cases of specialized PSAs, namely, the general blocks-world PSA and the symmetry game PSA. Please see the videos on the website for more details.

5.1 The General Blocks-World PSA

The general blocks-world agent has knowledge about general tasks and properties of the BW environment. The properties of the world consist of physical properties like measurements, counts of the blocks with particular attributes and/or in particular locations, and spatial relationships between the sub-structures, etc. The tasks are related to manipulating blocks to build a structure, such as putting or moving blocks to certain positions. Either the user or the machine can take initiative to ask the other to perform a task-related actions.

5.2 The Symmetry Game PSA

The symmetry game is a collaborative turn-based game in the Blocks World. The user and the computer collaborates to create a symmetric structure out of the blocks. Both the user and the agent have total creative control on the building process but they can also choose to collaborate towards a common goal. The structure should be symmetric at the end of each turn.

The symmetry game agent understands the concept of symmetry within the blocks world and performs tasks like evaluating symmetry of an arbitrary structure. The agent utilizes a planner to formulate moves (plans) to construct symmetric structures, predicting potential solutions several steps ahead of the current step. The symmetry game agent also utilizes a state machine to keep track of the game state based on the rules of the game.

One of the highlights of the symmetry game agent is that it is capable of explaining itself – explaining its plans and the reasonings for its actions.

6 Conclusion and Future Work

We have demonstrated a system for symmetric natural communication with a computer which can interact with its users with verbal and non-verbal communication allowing it to have more robust conversation. We demonstrated two use cases in the BW domain. These use cases are like skills that can be rapidly expanded upon.

We are working on expanding our capabilities for interpreting additional non-verbal cues such as iconic and pantomimed gestures. We are also working on generating natural behaviors for the avatar such as dynamically reacting to the user's actions.

We are also working on performing studies to evaluate the system in terms of the task performance and user experience based on the criteria described in (Kozierok et al., 2018). The SMILEE web page (see Section 3 for detail) is open to public and collects feedback from the users.

Acknowledgments

This work was funded by the Defense Advanced Research Projects Agency (DARPA) under agreement number W911NF-15-C-9244. The views, opinions, and/or conclusions contained in this paper are those of the author and should not be interpreted as representing the official views or policies, either expressed or implied of the DARPA or the DoD. We would like to thank Lucian Galescu of IHMC for his help with TRIPS system. We also thank MITRE for providing the feedback about the system and evaluations.

References

Y. Bisk, D. Marcu, and W. Wong. 2016. Towards a dataset for human computer communication via grounded language acquisition. In *Proc. AAAI Workshop on Symbolic Cognitive Systems*.

George Ferguson and James F. Allen. 1998. Trips: An integrated intelligent problem-solving assistant. In *Proceedings of the Fifteenth National/Tenth Conference on Artificial Intelligence/Innovative Applications of Artificial Intelligence*, AAAI '98/IAAI '98, pages 567–572, Menlo Park, CA, USA. American Association for Artificial Intelligence.

Mary Ellen Foster, Manuel Giuliani, Amy Isard, Colin Matheson, Jon Oberlander, and Alois Knoll. 2009. Evaluating description and reference strategies in a cooperative human-robot dialogue system. IJCAI.

Sujeong Kim, David Salter, Timur Almaev, Tim Meo, and Amir Tamrakar. 2018. Dataset of human-human interactions while engaging in a tower-building task in the blocks world. Technical report, SRI International.

Sujeong Kim and Amir Tamrakar. 2017. Co-speech gesture generation for communication in the blocks world. Technical report, SRI International.

Robyn Kozierok, Lynette Hirschman, John Aberdeen, Cheryl Clar, Christopher Garay, Bradley Goodman, Tonia Korves, and Matthew Peterson. 2018. Darpa communicating with computers: Program goals and hallmarks.

Nikhil Krishnaswamy, Pradyumna Narayana, Isaac Wang, Kyeongmin Rim, Rahul Bangar, Dhruva Patil, Gururaj Mulay, J. Ross Beveridge, Jaime Ruiz, Bruce A. Draper, and James Pustejovsky. 2018. Learning interpretable spatial operations in a rich 3d blocks world. Association for the Advancement of Artificial Intelligence (AAAI).

Ian E. Perera, James F. Allen, Lucian Galescu, Choh Man Teng, Mark H. Burstein, Scott E. Friedman, David D. McDonald, and Jeffrey M. Rye. 2017. Natural language dialogue for building and learning models and structures. In *AAAI*.

D. A. Salter, A. Tamrakar, B. Siddiquie, M. R. Amer, A. Divakaran, B. Lande, and D. Mehri. 2015. The tower game dataset: A multimodal dataset for analyzing social interaction predicates. In *2015 International Conference on Affective Computing and Intelligent Interaction (ACII)*, pages 656–662.

David Salter, Sujeong Kim, and Amir Tamrakar. 2017. A virtual blocks world apparatus for the darpa cwc program. Technical report, SRI International.

Lanbo She, Shaohua Yang, Yu Cheng, Yunyi Jia, Joyce Yue Chai, and Ning Xi. 2014. Back to the blocks world: Learning new actions through situated human-robot dialogue. In *SIGDIAL Conference*.

Behjat Siddique, David Salter, Gregory Ho, Amir Tamrakar, and Ajay Divakaran. 2015. A blocks world apparatus for the darpa cwc program. Technical report, SRI International.

Kilho Son, David Salter, Tim Sheilds, Tim Meo, Jihua Huang, Sujeong Kim, and Amir Tamrakar. 2015. A blocks world apparatus for the darpa cwc program. Technical report, SRI International.

Kilho Son, David Salter, and Amir Tamrakar. 2016. Accurate block structure understanding in real-time with time-of-flight cameras. Technical report, SRI International.

Unity. 2017. Unity engine (5.6.3).

Decision Conversations Decoded

Léa A. Deleris, Debasis Ganguly, Killian Levacher, Martin Stephenson, Francesca Bonin
IBM Research - Ireland
Dublin, Ireland
`lea.deleris, debasis.ganguly1, killian.levacher,`
`martin_stephenson, fbonin@ie.ibm.com`

Abstract

We describe the vision and current version of a Natural Language Processing system aimed at group decision making facilitation. Borrowing from the scientific field of Decision Analysis, its essential role is to identify alternatives and criteria associated with a given decision, to keep track of who proposed them and of the expressed sentiment towards them. Based on this information, the system can help identify agreement and dissent or recommend an alternative. Overall, it seeks to help a group reach a decision in a natural yet auditable fashion.

1 Our Vision

Decision Analysis is the scientific discipline that formally studies decisions: procedures, methods, and tools for identifying, representing, and assessing important aspects of a decision, ultimately to recommend actions to the decision maker (Matheson and Howard, 1977). One of the focus of decision analysis is on practical aspects of formulating the decision problem (rather than focusing solely on its mathematical resolution). This includes (i) defining the utility function of the decision maker including criteria, risk attitudes and trade-offs, (ii) identifying the relevant uncertainties and (iii) investigating the benefits of gathering additional information. In order to achieve this, the decision analysis process needs certain inputs, specifically **alternatives** (options available to the decision maker), **criteria** (values, risk preferences, and time preferences of the decision maker), **frame** including the constraints associated with the decision (Howard and Abbas, 2015).

Many decisions are taken collaboratively, whether truly collaboratively (where everyone has a voice) or rather when a decision maker consults with a group of trusted advisers. For instance, for complex cases in medicine, it is common to have multiple experts meet to discuss the patient's situation and come up with a recommended course of action. When recruiting, different perspectives are typically taken into account to help inform a final manager of her decision to make an offer to a candidate. In large projects, multiple stakeholders can take part of important architectural decisions. However, collaborative decision discussions are typically unstructured, inefficient and can be frustrating for all participants, as illustrated by the Abilene Paradox [1].

With the proliferation of recording devices in our professional and personal lives (e.g., teleconferencing, intelligent personal assistant or group chat exchanges such as Slack), it would be helpful to develop NLP-based engines to automatically extract decisions related concepts such as alternatives and criteria from decision conversations and make use of that information to facilitate the decision discussions. As a starting point, such a technology could provide the input to generate a visualisation of the decision discussion so that a group can consult it to identify underdeveloped ideas or options, and to recall points of consensus and dissent. It would serve as a summary, enabling people who have missed a decision discussion to catch up or more simply reminding a decision maker of the arguments that were raised so she can make her decision at a later time.

The system output can also be used to document the decision making process in a structured way. This information in turn is key to better understanding power plays and negotiation in group decision making. More practically, it can be essential to prove compliance with processes, e.g., a financial advisor proving she has presented reasonable investment alternatives to her customers.

Note that our objective is to follow how a de-

---

[1] `https://en.wikipedia.org/wiki/`
`Abilene_paradox` retrieved on February 15th 2018

91

Proceedings of NAACL-HLT 2018: Demonstrations, pages 91–95
New Orleans, Louisiana, June 2 - 4, 2018. ©2018 Association for Computational Linguistics

cision is made, rather than focusing solely on its outcome i.e., the final choice (though this is a by-product).

2   Related works

Decisions are often presented as one of the most important outcomes of business meetings (Whittaker et al., 2006). Banerjee et al. (2005) show that updates about the decisions of a meeting are beneficial for persons who had missed the meeting to prepare for the next one. Interest on meeting developments is shown also by the large amount of corpus collections on the topic, e.g., ICSI (Janin et al., 2004) , AMI (Carletta et al., 2005), CHIL (Mostefa et al., 2007) or VACE (Chen et al., 2006). While some annotations in these corpora consider decisions from meetings, the annotated labels (text spans) are either too specific (dialogue acts) or too general (meeting summaries) to study the decision making process.

Some studies have investigated automatic detection of decisions. Hsueh and Moore (2007) attempted to identify patterns of the decision gists, relying on the relevant annotated Dialogue Acts (DAs) in meeting transcripts. Fernández et al. (2008) extended the annotations with new decision-related DAs, and formulated the problem as a classification problem for each class of DAs. They designed an annotation scheme that takes into account the different roles that DAs play in the decision-making process, for instance to initiate a discussion by raising a topic, to propose a resolution, or to express agreement. However, in all this work, the objective was to detect the span of the conversation where the decision is taken. We intend to go further and identify the elements that belong to the *content* of decision-making processes, whether or not a final decision is taken. Cadilhac et al. (2012), while focusing more specifically on the representation of preferences, have proposed an approach to extract what we refer to as alternatives and which in their framework is described as outcomes. They do not pursue the extraction of criteria.

3   System Architecture

3.1   Overall

The various components, that together enable to decode decision conversations, are presented in Figure 1. In this diagram, we present both components that are currently implemented along with others that are in development (italics).

Input Processing Module. Input to the system is in the form of text. This text can originally come from a recording or live dialog, which is converted to text using Speech-To-Text technology. Speaker attribution is also performed as part of this step. Alternatively, input can come from text entered via the UI or from a set of pre-existing transcripts. The text is then pre-processed so as to provide a clean transcript with speakers identified to the Extraction and Summarization module.

Resources. The main part of the resources consists in a set of Machine Learning (ML) algorithms, which are described in Section 3.2. Annotated data used for training models can be enriched via user feedback of already identified criteria and alternatives, i.e the user can verify or refute an identified criteria or alternative. This annotated data can then be used to re-train the models. External resources, such as DBpedia and WordNet are also leveraged in the pipeline.

Extraction and Summarization Module. This module constitutes the core of the NLP pipeline and is composed of multiple sub-components. A) **Decision Segmentation** - As more than one decision may be discussed in a conversation, this component segments the conversation into the corresponding multiple discussion threads. B) **Decision Topic Analysis** - This component determines the topic of the decision. C) **Decision Element Extraction** - Using ML models, this component identifies the location of the decision alternatives and criteria in the text. D) **Semantic Grouping** - This component clusters semantically similar alternatives and criteria. E) **Mapping Alternative to criteria** - This component associates identified alternatives to criteria. F) **Wikification** - This component further enriches the transcript by linking words and phrases to external resources (e.g., Wikipedia). G) **Identification of Expressed Sentiment** - This component determines the expressed sentiment of speakers towards extracted alternatives and criteria.

Finally, the output of this text processing is recorded in a JSON data structure called Structured Decision Summary Output.

Summary Analysis Module. This module analyses the Structured Decision Summary Output based on the following two components. First the recommendation module can make use of the information to identify which alternative seems the

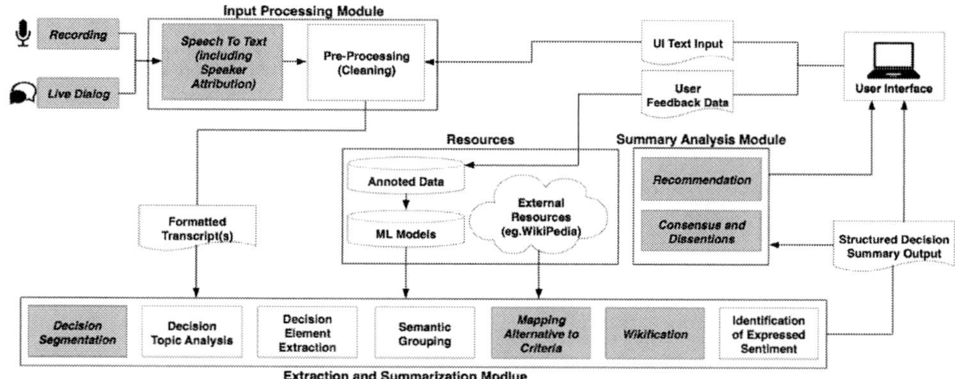

Figure 1: Architecture of our System

most supported by the group. Similarly, it can search for dominated alternatives and suggest they be discarded. Second the consensus and dissent module analyzes where and when in the discussion people agree and disagree on the proposed alternatives.

User Interface. Its main functions are to allow the user to input text directly for analysis and to subsequently present him/her with the alternative and criteria extraction output, in addition to the option to cluster and/or summarise this output as described in Section 4. Finally, it enables the user to accept or refute identified alternatives and/or criteria identified by the system.

3.2 Machine Learning Module

Corpus. We leverage the AMI (Augmented Multi-party Interaction) (Carletta et al., 2005) corpus, which we annotated with alternative and criteria. Description of our annotation process along with access to the corpus is summarised in (Deleris et al., 2018). We use supervised classification settings, where 80% sentences from the AMI corpus are used for training the models and the rest for testing. **Sequence Prediction**. Our automatic identification of alternative and criteria is based on standard sequence prediction approaches. We experimented with many common models namely naive Bayes, MaxEnt, SVM, CRF and LSTM based RNN. As expected the bag-of-words based models (with fixed length context features), i.e. naive Bayes, MaxEnt and SVM were outperformed by the sequence models, namely CRF and RNN. The linear CRF is currently our model with the highest performance as outlined in Table 1 (due to space constraints the results of other models are not shown).

Label	Precision	Recall	F-score
Alternative	0.6311	0.4667	0.5366
Criteria	0.7368	0.3394	0.4647

Table 1: Performance of the CRF model (based on token level evaluation on the AMI corpus).

4 Demonstration Flow

4.1 Describing Interface

Our demo interface starts from a text box where a user can enter the transcript to be analyzed as presented on Fig. 2. Clicking on the button *Analyze Text* located underneath the text box will run the topic analysis and extraction algorithms whose results will then be shown to the user underneath the text box.

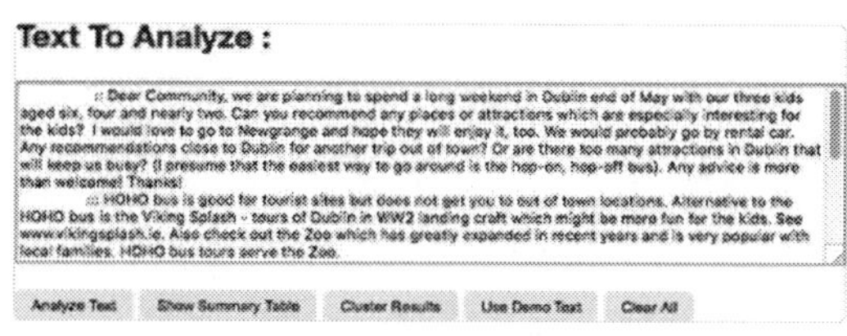

Figure 2: Initial Screen into the System

Specifically the topic analysis provides background information about the main themes of the decision discussion and more importantly describes the frame for the decision that is being discussed, specifically the decision topic e.g. *Can you recommend any places or attractions which are especially interesting for the kids?*, and the context of this decision, e.g., *Dear Community, we are planning to spend a long weekend in Dublin end of May with our three kids*. The results of the extraction algorithm results are then displayed. The input text is presented with sections highlighted to indicate detected alternatives and detected criteria, as shown on Fig. 3.

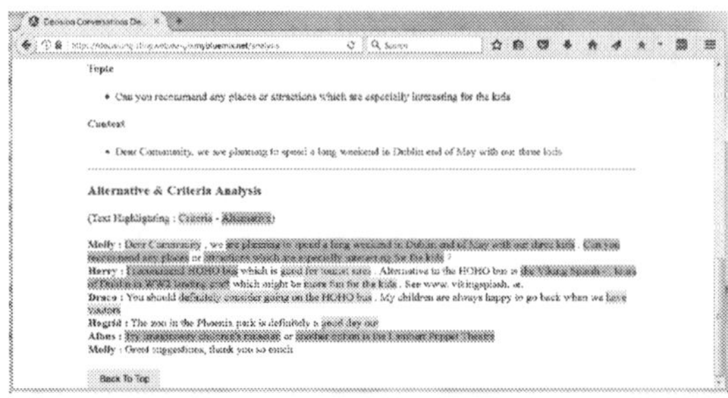

Figure 3: Alternatives and Criteria Extraction

While this representation of the output of the NLP algorithms is instructive to understand how the system operates, we feel a more useful summary to effectively guide decision discussions should be based on grouping alternatives and criteria by person as in Fig 4 and also grouping alternatives and criteria by semantic topic. Those two subsequent analyses are obtained by clicking on *Show Summary Table* and *Cluster Results* shown in Fig. 2. Note that the summary table format also allows to indicate the expressed sentiment of the person towards the alternative or criteria (as represented by the smiley faces). Finally when a user hovers over a detected fragment, we show in an overlay window the part of the transcripts from where it was extracted, so as to provide context for its interpretation if needed.

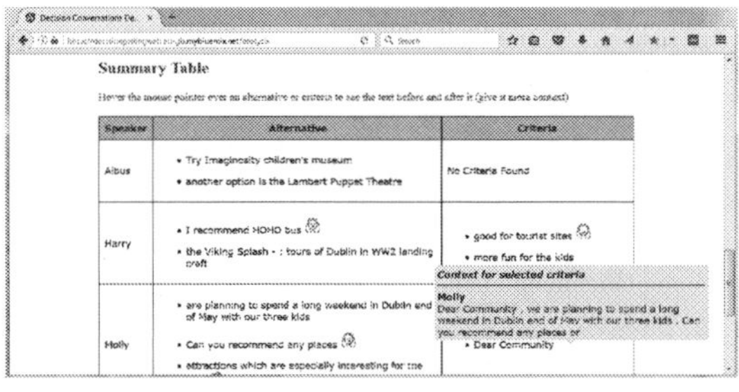

Figure 4: Summarization in a Table with Sentiment and Context Overlay

4.2 Examples of Analyses

In this section, we provide some illustrative results of the use of our technologies on diverse kinds of discussions. Note that we have slightly edited the text, mainly changing the names of the speakers and cutting some long utterances.

Figure 5 top shows an excerpt from the AMI Corpus (Carletta et al., 2005) which corresponds to face-to-face discussions about remote control design (specifically ES 2012). Figure 5 middle relates to a discussion about a visit to Machu Pichu on a travel website where a user has requested advice from other users. Finally, the text in Figure 5 bottom is extracted from the discussions of the European Parliament, using the Europarl Corpus (Koehn, 2005).

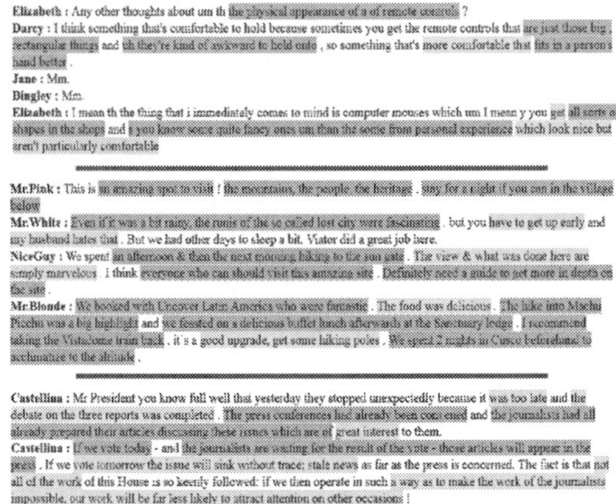

Figure 5: Examples (top: AMI Corpus - ES 2012; middle: Travel Forum Discussion; bottom: European Parliament - September 18th 1996)

5 Conclusion

We make countless decisions every day, some of which are bound to be collaborative, making the decision process all the more challenging. Our system proposes to automatically follow the decision process. It tracks the options being considered, why they are proposed (i.e., which criteria are brought up), by whom and with whose support. It then organizes all collective thoughts into a summary in order to facilitate further discussions, guide the final decision, explain how a decision was made or make recommendations.

As a virtual facilitator, the system objective is to augment collaborative decision making, empowering all stakeholders involved to contribute their perspective and making the decision making process effective and transparent.

References

Satanjeev Banerjee, Carolyn Penstein Rosé, and Alexander I. Rudnicky. 2005. The necessity of a meeting recording and playback system, and the benefit of topic-level annotations to meeting browsing. In *INTERACT*.

Anaïs Cadilhac, Nicholas Asher, Farah Benamara, Vladimir Popescu, and Mohamadou Seck. 2012. Preference extraction from negotiation dialogues. In *Proceedings of the 20th European Conference on Artificial Intelligence*, pages 211–216. IOS Press.

Jean Carletta, Simone Ashby, Sebastien Bourban, Mike Flynn, Mael Guillemot, Thomas Hain, Jaroslav Kadlec, Vasilis Karaiskos, Wessel Kraaij, Melissa Kronenthal, et al. 2005. The ami meeting corpus: A pre-announcement. In *International Workshop on Machine Learning for Multimodal Interaction*, pages 28–39. Springer.

Lei Chen, R. Travis Rose, Ying Qiao, Irene Kimbara, Fey Parrill, Haleema Welji, Tony Xu Han, Jilin Tu, Zhongqiang Huang, Mary Harper, Francis Quek, Yingen Xiong, David McNeill, Ronald Tuttle, and Thomas Huang. 2006. Vace multimodal meeting corpus. In *Proceedings of the Second International Conference on Machine Learning for Multimodal Interaction*, MLMI'05, pages 40–51, Berlin, Heidelberg. Springer-Verlag.

Lea A Deleris, Tuan Tran, Francesca Bonin, Debasis Ganguly, and Killian Levacher. 2018. Preparing a dataset for extracting decision elements from a meeting transcript corpus. Technical report, IBM Research.

Raquel Fernández, Matthew Frampton, Patrick Ehlen, Matthew Purver, and Stanley Peters. 2008. Modelling and detecting decisions in multi-party dialogue. In *Proceedings of the 9th SIGdial Workshop on Discourse and Dialogue*, pages 156–163. ACL.

Ronald A Howard and Ali E Abbas. 2015. *Foundations of decision analysis*. Pearson.

Pei-Yun Hsueh and Johanna D Moore. 2007. Automatic decision detection in meeting speech. In *International Workshop on Machine Learning for Multimodal Interaction*, pages 168–179. Springer.

Adam Janin, Jeremy Ang, Sonali Bhagat, Rajdip Dhillon, Jane Edwards, Javier Macas-guarasa, Nelson Morgan, Barbara Peskin, Elizabeth Shriberg, Andreas Stolcke, Chuck Wooters, and Britta Wrede. 2004. The icsi meeting project: Resources and research. In *in Proc. of ICASSP 2004 Meeting Recognition Workshop*. Prentice Hall.

Philipp Koehn. 2005. Europarl: A parallel corpus for statistical machine translation. In *MT summit*, volume 5, pages 79–86.

James E Matheson and Ronald A Howard. 1977. An introduction to decision analysis. In Miller Howards, Matheson, editor, *Readings in Decision Analysis*, chapter 1, pages 9–43. Stanford Research Institute, California.

D. Mostefa, N. Moreau, K. Choukri, G. Potamianos, S. Chu, A. Tyagi, J. Casas, J. Turmo, L. Cristoforetti, F. Tobia, A. Pnevmatikakis, V. Mylonakis, F. Talantzis, S. Burger, R. Stiefelhagen, K. Bernardin, and C. Rochet. 2007. The chil audiovisual corpus for lecture and meeting analysis inside smart rooms. *Language resources and evaluation*, 41(3):389–407.

Steve Whittaker, Rachel Laban, and Simon Tucker. 2006. *Analysing Meeting Records: An Ethnographic Study and Technological Implications*. Springer Berlin Heidelberg, Berlin, Heidelberg.

Sounding Board: A User-Centric and Content-Driven Social Chatbot

Hao Fang[*]   Hao Cheng[*]   Maarten Sap[†]   Elizabeth Clark[†]   Ari Holtzman[†]
Yejin Choi[†]   Noah A. Smith[†]   Mari Ostendorf[*]
University of Washington
[*]{hfang,chenghao,ostendor}@uw.edu
[†]{msap,eaclark7,ahai,yejin,nasmith}@cs.washington.edu

Abstract

We present Sounding Board, a social chatbot that won the 2017 Amazon Alexa Prize. The system architecture consists of several components including spoken language processing, dialogue management, language generation, and content management, with emphasis on *user-centric* and *content-driven* design. We also share insights gained from large-scale online logs based on 160,000 conversations with real-world users.

1 Introduction

Researchers in artificial intelligence (AI) have long been interested in the challenge of developing a system that can have a coherent conversation with humans: early systems include Parry (Colby et al., 1971), Eliza (Weizenbaum, 1966), and Alice (Wallace, 2009). The Loebner Prize[1] is a Turing test for conversational AI that has challenged researchers since 1990. Recent work has addressed tasks where passing the Turing test is not a concern. Goal-oriented conversational systems facilitate natural user interaction with devices via text and spoken language. These AI assistants typically focus on short interactions, as in commercial products such as Amazon Alexa, Microsoft Cortana, Google Assistant, and Apple Siri. General conversational systems, called chatbots, have constrained social interaction capabilities but have difficulty generating conversations with long-term coherence (Serban et al., 2017; Sato et al., 2017; Shao et al., 2017; Tian et al., 2017; Ghazvininejad et al., 2018).

The Alexa Prize sets forth a new challenge: creating a system that can hold a coherent and engaging conversation on current events and popular topics such as sports, politics, entertainment, fashion and technology (Ram et al., 2017). Our system, Sound-

Turn	User	Sounding Board
1	Let's chat	Hi! This is an Alexa Prize socialbot. How's your day?
2	I'm <u>five</u>.	Glad to hear it! We could talk about robots, Batman, or Superman. Say "next", to chat about other things.
3	Superman.	It looks like you wanna chat about Superman. I was high up in the cloud when I realized: If people don't recognize Clark Kent as Superman because of his glasses, does his eye doctor know his true identity?
4	I guess so.	Did you know that Henry Cavill almost missed the call for the role of Superman cause he was playing "World of Warcraft"
5	Really, I didn't know that.	Weird, right? Speaking of Superman, Did you see: Superman? It was released in 1997. It's a comedy.
6	Yes, it was hilarious.	I'm glad you feel this is hilarious. Which part do you like best about this movie?
7	The part when he met <u>Lewis Leah</u>.	Interesting. Meccartin and Raffi co-directed this film. The movie has a 6.3 out of 10 on IMDB. which seems pretty good! do you like the movie's director?

Figure 1: A sample dialog. Suspected speech recognition errors in the user utterances are underlined.

ing Board,[2] demonstrates that it is feasible to build an agent that can engage in long-term conversation when backed by rich content and knowledge of the user obtained through interaction. Sounding Board won the inaugural Amazon Alexa Prize with an average score of 3.17 on a 5-point scale and an average conversation duration of 10:22, evaluated by a panel of independent judges.[3]

There are two key design objectives of Sounding Board: to be *user-centric* and *content-driven*. Our system is *user-centric* in that users can control the topic of conversation, while the system adapts responses to the user's likely interests by gauging the user's personality. Sounding Board is also *content-driven*, as it continually supplies interesting and relevant information to continue the conversation,

---

[1] http://aisb.org.uk/events/loebner-prize

[2] https://sounding-board.github.io

[3] https://developer.amazon.com/alexaprize/2017-alexa-prize

Proceedings of NAACL-HLT 2018: Demonstrations, pages 96–100
New Orleans, Louisiana, June 2 - 4, 2018. ©2018 Association for Computational Linguistics

enabled by a rich content collection that it updates daily. It is this content that can engage users for a long period of time and drive the conversation forward. A sample conversation is shown in Fig. 1.

We describe the system architecture in §2, share our insights based on large scale conversation logs in §3, and conclude in §4.

2 System Architecture

Sounding Board uses a modular framework as shown in Fig. 2. When a user speaks, the system produces a response using three modules: natural language understanding (NLU), dialog manager (DM), and natural language generation (NLG). The NLU produces a representation of the current event by analyzing the user's speech given the current dialog state (§2.1). Then, based on this representation, the DM executes the dialog policy and decides the next dialog state (§2.2). Finally, the NLG uses the content selected by the DM to build the response (§2.3), which is returned to the user and stored as context in the DM. During the conversation, the DM also communicates with a knowledge graph that is stored in the back-end and updated daily by the content management module (§2.4).

2.1 Natural Language Understanding

Given a user's utterance, the NLU module extracts the speaker's intent or goals, the desired topic or potential subtopics of conversation, and the stance or sentiment of a user's reaction to a system comment. We store this information in a multidimensional frame which defines the NLU output.

To populate the attributes of the frame, the NLU module uses ASR hypotheses and the voice user interface output (Kumar et al., 2017), as well as the dialog state. The dialog state is useful for cases where the system has asked a question with constraints on the expected response. A second stage of processing uses parsing results and dialog state in a set of text classifiers to refine the attributes.

2.2 Dialog Management

We designed the DM according to three high-level objectives: engagement, coherence, and user experience. The DM takes into account user **engagement** based on components of the NLU output and tries to maintain user interest by promoting diversity of interaction strategies (conversation modes). Each conversation mode is managed by a miniskill that handles a specific type of conversation seg-

ment. The DM tries to maintain dialog **coherence** by choosing content on the same or a related topic within a conversation segment, and it does not present topics or content that were already shared with the user. To enhance the **user experience**, the DM uses conversation grounding acts to explain (either explicitly or implicitly) the system's action and to instruct the user with available options.

The DM uses a hierarchically-structured, state-based dialog model operating at two levels: a master that manages the overall conversation, and a collection of miniskills that handle different types of conversation segments. This hierarchy enables variety within specific topic segments. In the Fig. 1 dialog, Turn 3 was produced using the *Thoughts* miniskill, Turn 4 using the *Facts* miniskill, and Turns 5–7 using the *Movies* miniskill. The hierarchical architecture simplifies updating and adding new capabilities. It is also useful for handling high-level conversation mode changes that are frequent in user interactions with socialbots.

At each conversation turn, a sequence of processing steps are executed to identify a response strategy that addresses the user's intent and meets the constraints on the conversation topic, if any. First, a state-independent processing step checks if the speaker is initiating a new conversation segment (e.g., requesting a new topic). If not, a second processing stage executes state-dependent dialog policies. Both of these processing stages poll miniskills to identify which ones are able to satisfy constraints of user intent and/or topic. Ultimately, the DM produces a list of speech acts and corresponding content to be used for NLG, and then updates the dialog state.

2.3 Natural Language Generation

The NLG module takes as input the speech acts and content provided by the DM and constructs a response by generating and combining the response components.

Phrase Generation: The response consists of speech acts from four broad categories: grounding, inform, request, and instruction. For instance, the system response at Turn 7 contains three speech acts: grounding (*"Interesting."*), inform (the IMDB rating), and request (*"do you like the movie's director?"*). As required by the hosting platform, the response is split into a message and a reprompt. The device always reads the message; the reprompt is optionally used if the device does not detect a

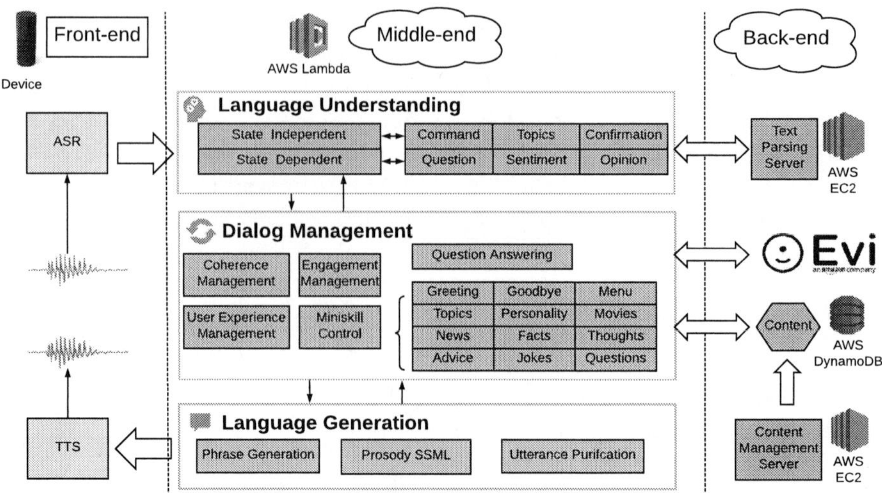

Figure 2: System architecture. **Front-end**: Amazon's Automatic Speech Recognition (ASR) and Text-to-Speech (TTS) APIs. **Middle-end**: NLU, DM and NLG modules implemented using the AWS Lambda service. **Back-end**: External services and AWS DynamoDB tables for storing the knowledge graph.

response from the user. The instruction speech acts are usually placed in the reprompt.

Prosody: We make extensive use of speech synthesis markup language (SSML) for prosody and pronunciation to convey information more clearly. to communicate. We use it to improve the naturalness of concatenated speech acts, to emphasize suggested topics, to deliver jokes more effectively, to apologize or backchannel in a more natural-sounding way, and to more appropriately pronounce unusual words.

Utterance Purification: The constructed response (which may repeat a user statement) goes through an utterance purifier that replaces profanity with a non-offensive word chosen randomly from a list of innocuous nouns, often to a humorous effect.

2.4 Content Management

Content is stored in a knowledge graph at the back-end, which is updated daily. The knowledge graph is organized based on miniskills so that query and recommendation can be carried out efficiently by the DM. The DM drives the conversation forward and generates responses by either traversing links between content nodes associated with the same topic or through relation edges to content nodes on a relevant new topic. The relation edges are compiled based on existing knowledge bases (e.g., Wikipedia and IMDB) and entity co-occurrence between content nodes.

Because Sounding Board is accessible to a wide range of users, the system needs to provide content and topics that are appropriate for a general audience. This requires filtering out inappropriate and controversial material. Much of this content is removed using regular expressions to catch profanity. However, we also filtered content containing phrases related to sensitive topics or phrases that were not inherently inappropriate but were often found in potentially offensive statements (e.g., "your mother"). Content that is not well suited in style to casual conversation (e.g., URLs and lengthy content) is either removed or simplified.

3 Evaluation and Analysis

To analyze system performance, we study conversation data collected from Sounding Board over a one month period (Nov. 24–Dec. 24, 2017). In this period, Sounding Board had 160,210 conversations with users that lasted 3 or more turns. (We omit the shorter sessions, since many involve cases where the user did not intend to invoke the system.) At the end of each conversation, the Alexa Prize platform collects a rating from the user by asking *"on a scale of 1 to 5, how do you feel about speaking with this socialbot again?"* (Ram et al., 2017). In this data, 43% were rated by the user, with a mean score of 3.65 ($\sigma = 1.40$). Of the rated conversations, 23% received a score of 1 or 2, 37% received a score of 3 or 4, and 40% received a score of 5.[4] The data are used to analyze how different personality types interact with the system (§3.1) and length, depth, and

---

[4]Some users give a fractional number score. These scores are rounded down to the next smallest integer.

	ope	con	ext	agr	neu
% users	80.02%	51.70%	61.59%	79.50%	42.50%
# turns	0.048**	*not sig.*	0.075**	0.085**	*not sig.*
rating	0.108**	*not sig.*	0.199**	0.198**	*not sig.*

Table 1: Association statistics between personality traits (**ope**nness, **con**scientiousness, **ext**raversion, **agr**eeableness, **neu**roticism) and z-scored conversation metrics. "% users" shows the proportion of users scoring positively on a trait. "# turns" shows correlation between the trait and the number of turns, and "rating" the correlation between the trait and the conversation rating, controlled for number of turns. Significance level (Holm corrected for multiple comparisons): $^{**}p < 0.001$.

breadth characteristics of the conversations (§3.2).

3.1 Personality Analysis

The *Personality* miniskill in Sounding Board calibrates user personality based on the Five Factor model (McCrae and John, 1992) through exchanging answers on a set of personality probing questions adapted from the mini-IPIP questionnaire (Donnellan et al., 2006).

We present an analysis of how different personality traits interact with Sounding Board, as seen in Table 1. We find that personality only very slightly correlates with length of conversation (# turns). However, when accounting for the number of turns, personality correlates moderately with the conversation rating. Specifically, we find users who are more extraverted, agreeable, or open to experience tend to rate our socialbot higher. This falls in line with psychology findings (McCrae and John, 1992), which associate extraversion with talkativeness, agreeableness with cooperativeness, and openness with intellectual curiosity.[5]

3.2 Content Analysis

Most Sounding Board conversations were short (43% consist of fewer than 10 turns), but the length distribution has a long tail. The longest conversation consisted of 772 turns, and the average conversation length was 19.4 turns. As seen in Fig. 3, longer conversations tended to get higher ratings.

While conversation length is an important factor, it alone is not enough to assess the conversation quality, as evidenced by the low correlation with

---

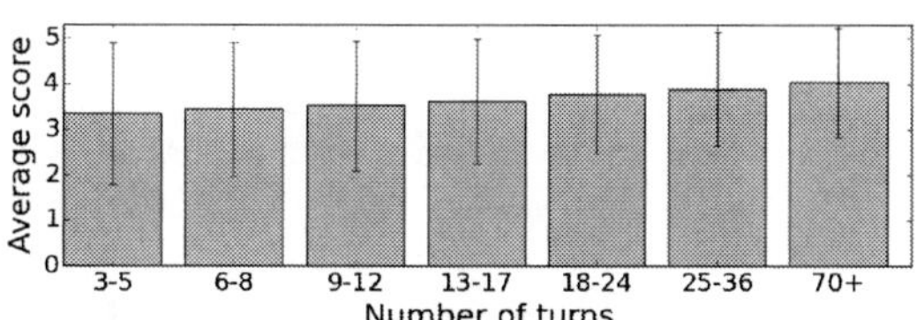

Figure 3: Average conversation score by conversation length. Each bar represents conversations that contain the number of turns in the range listed beneath them and is marked with the standard deviation.

user ratings ($r = 0.14$) and because some turns (e.g., repairs) may have a negative impact. Therefore, we also study the breadth and depth of the sub-dialogs within conversations of roughly equal length (36–50) with high (5) vs. low (1–2) ratings. We automatically segment the conversations into sub-dialogs based on the system-identified topic, and annotate each sub-dialog as engaged or not depending on the number of turns where the system detects that the user is engaged. The breadth of the conversation can be roughly characterized by the number and percentage of engaged sub-dialogs; depth is characterized by the average number of turns in a sub-dialog. We found that the average topic engagement percentages differ significantly (62.5% for high scoring vs. 28.6% for low), but the number of engaged sub-dialogs were similar (4.2 for high vs. 4.1 for low). Consistent with this, the average depth of the sub-dialog was higher for the high conversations (4.0 vs. 3.8 turns).

4 Conclusion

We presented Sounding Board, a social chatbot that has won the inaugural Alexa Prize Challenge. As key design principles, our system focuses on providing conversation experience that is both user-centric and content-driven. Potential avenues for future research include increasing the success rate of the topic suggestion and improving the engagements via better analysis of user personality and topic-engagement patterns across users.

Acknowledgements

In addition to the Alexa Prize financial and cloud computing support, this work was supported in part by NSF Graduate Research Fellowship (awarded to E. Clark), NSF (IIS 1524371), and DARPA CwC program through ARO (W911NF-15-1-0543). The conclusions and findings are those of the authors and do not necessarily reflect the views of sponsors.

---

[5] These insights should be taken with a grain of salt, both because the mini-IPIP personality scale has imperfect reliability (Donnellan et al., 2006) and user responses in such a casual scenario can be noisy.

References

Kenneth Mark Colby, Sylvia Weber, and Franklin Dennis Hilf. 1971. Artificial paranoia. *Artificial Intelligence*, 2(1):1–25.

M Brent Donnellan, Frederick L Oswald, Brendan M Baird, and Richard E Lucas. 2006. The mini-IPIP scales: tiny-yet-effective measures of the Big Five factors of personality. *Psychological assessment*, 18(2):192.

Marjan Ghazvininejad, Chris Brockett, Ming-Wei Chang, Bill Dolan, Jianfeng Gao, Wen-tau Yih, and Michel Galley. 2018. A knowledge-grounded neural conversation model. In *Proc. AAAI*.

Anjishnu Kumar, Arpit Gupta, Julian Chan, Sam Tucker, Bjorn Hoffmeister, and Markus Dreyer. 2017. Just ASK: Building an architecture for extensible self-service spoken language understanding. In *Proc. NIPS Workshop Conversational AI*.

Robert R McCrae and Oliver P John. 1992. An introduction to the five-factor model and its applications. *Journal of personality*, 60(2):175–215.

Ashwin Ram, Rohit Prasad, Chandra Khatri, Anu Venkatesh, Raefer Gabriel, Qing Liu, Jeff Nunn, Behnam Hedayatnia, Ming Cheng, Ashish Nagar, Eric King, Kate Bland, Amanda Wartick, Yi Pan, Han Song, Sk Jayadevan, Gene Hwang, and Art Pettigrue. 2017. Conversational AI: The science behind the Alexa Prize. In *Proc. Alexa Prize 2017*.

Shoetsu Sato, Naoki Yoshinaga, Masashi Toyoda, and Masaru Kitsuregawa. 2017. Modeling situations in neural chat bots. In *Proc. ACL Student Research Workshop*, pages 120–127.

Iulian Vlad Serban, Alessandro Sordoni, Ryan Lowe, Laurent Charlin, Joelle Pineau, Aaron C Courville, and Yoshua Bengio. 2017. A hierarchical latent variable encoder-decoder model for generating dialogues. In *AAAI*, pages 3295–3301.

Yuanlong Shao, Stephan Gouws, Denny Britz, Anna Goldie, Brian Strope, and Ray Kurzweil. 2017. Generating high-quality and informative conversation responses with sequence-to-sequence models. In *Proc. EMNLP*, pages 2210–2219.

Zhiliang Tian, Rui Yan, Lili Mou, Yiping Song, Yansong Feng, and Dongyan Zhao. 2017. How to make context more useful? An empirical study on context-aware neural conversational models. In *Proc. ACL*, pages 231–236.

Richard S. Wallace. 2009. *The Anatomy of A.L.I.C.E.*, chapter Parsing the Turing Test. Springer, Dordrecht.

Joseph Weizenbaum. 1966. ELIZA – a computer program for the study of natural language communication between man and machine. *Commun. ACM*, 9(1):36–45.

Index